Praise for *America's Cheapest Family Gets You Right on the Money*

"Everybody, even a queen, likes to save money. And the practical tips and tricks in this book by Annette and Steve Economides represent a royal treasury of great ideas. They're practical and effective, and anyone can benefit from the down-to-earth advice inside this wonderful book."

—Linda Cobb, The Queen of Clean®, *New York Times* bestselling author of *Talking Dirty with the Queen of Clean*®

"*America's Cheapest Family Gets You Right on the Money* is a wonderfully practical and helpful book. The best part: authors Steve and Annette Economides have been living these principles you will learn in this easy-to-read book. I heartily recommend it to all those who want to be faithful in handling money God's way."

—Howard Dayton, radio talk show host and author of *Your Money Counts* and cofounder of Crown Financial Ministries

"As an attorney, I've represented thousands of hardworking families who are trying to make it in modern America on a single income. This book breaks down any financial barriers that would prevent a family from home schooling or living on one income."

—Scott W. Somerville, Esq., Home School Legal Defense Association

"Having known this couple since 1988, I can tell you everything they say works and is true. Steve and Annette have a heart for God and helping others. I've seen them at their best and at their lowest, when true character is revealed. Anyone wanting a handle on their finances can learn and profit from their principles. In America, 80 percent of us are slaves to our possessions. What the book doesn't say directly is that living as an economizer builds character, marriages, and families, and frees people to focus on what is important in life."

—Wilson J. (Jody) Humber, Ph.D., C.FP., investment counselor and author of *Dollars and Sense* and *The Financially Challenged*

"Steve and Annette Economides' last name just happens to match what they do joyously and well: economize. The word 'cheap' attracts attention, but it's misleading. With five children, this family eats well, dresses well, and has wonderful times together, all for amazingly little money. A pleasure to read, this book gives superb practical advice—lots of it—about money. It also teaches how to save time, cut stress, and enhance relationships. This wise and sensible couple are models for a life of joy and fulfillment, not to mention good parenting. It's the best how-to-live book I've ever read, by far."

—Archie M. Richards, Jr., syndicated columnist and author of *Understanding Exchange-Traded Funds*

AMERICA'S
CHEAPEST
GETS YOU RIGHT

THREE RIVERS PRESS · NEW YORK

STEVE AND ANNETTE ECONOMIDES

FAMILY

ON THE MONEY

Your Guide to Living Better,
Spending Less, and Cashing In
on Your Dreams

Three Rivers Press and the Tugboat design are registered trademarks of
Random House, Inc.

Library of Congress Cataloging-in-Publication Data
Economides, Steve.
    America's cheapest family gets you right on the money : your guide
to living better, spending less, and cashing in on your dreams / Steve and
Annette Economides.— 1st ed.
        p.   cm.
    1. Finance, Personal—United States.   2. Home economics—United States.
3. Family—Economic aspects—United States.   I. Economides, Annette.
II. Title.
HG179.E27 2007
332.02400973—dc22
2006018326

ISBN 978-0-307-33945-4

Printed in the United States of America

DESIGN BY ELINA D. NUDELMAN

10   9   8   7   6   5   4   3   2   1

First Edition

To the memory of Larry Burkett (1939–2003) cofounder of Crown Financial Ministries. He was an incredible author who had great compassion for others and a deep sense of discernment for the financial predicaments of the people he helped. His materials helped us create a financial foundation that has allowed us to accomplish so much more than we could have ever dreamed.

And to our parents, Athan and Frieda Economides and Sylvester and Carol Meola. They taught us both that frugality was a good thing and that embracing it would benefit our lives.

CONTENTS

ONE

AMERICA'S CHEAPEST FAMILY

We've been called "America's Cheapest Family," "the First Family of Frugal," "cheapskates," "thriftaholics," "tightwads," or one of many other less flattering terms. Even calling us by our real last name, Economides, relates to saving cash. Yes, that's our real name—it's pronounced "econo-*mee*-dis." It's Greek and means "son of the steward."

As the nicknames make clear, we don't like to spend a lot of money. But we don't economize just for the sake of skimping. We have big dreams—goals that together we are working toward. We are living proof that even in tough economic times, it's possible to:

· Raise responsible kids
· Purchase a home and pay it off in nine years
· Buy cars for cash
· Enjoy fabulous debt-free vacations
· Feed a growing family on a grocery budget of just $350 each month
· Put savings in the bank

What's more, all this was done during the first twelve years of our marriage on an average income of less than $35,000.

A WISH FULFILLED

This is a book we wish had existed when we were starting out on our financial journey. We're not going to bog you down with pages of hard-to-follow economic theory and calculations. Instead, we focus on practical advice that even the most financially challenged can easily implement. *America's Cheapest Family Gets You Right on the Money* will show you how to buy groceries smarter and less expensively, create a household budget that really works, buy affordable cars and homes, find alternative sources for dressing fabulously, deal with medical care and expenses, discover fun recreational activities that are free, plan and take great vacations that don't break the bank, teach kids to earn and manage money, build a great savings plan for the future, get out of debt and emerge from the vicious cycle of living paycheck to paycheck, and so much more.

Neither of us has a finance or accounting background. Neither of our parents taught us to manage money—they were frugal, but by no means financial wizards. We are just an average couple who have discovered the secrets to living well on way less than most people can imagine.

Many people believe that thrifty living can be more easily accomplished in a rural setting. We are here to tell you that it just isn't so! Living in the suburbs all of our lives, we can strongly say that there are great bargains to be had at every turn. With a dense population comes greater opportunities to scoop up steep discounts and free items.

Writing from the perspective of a family, we hope to bring our message to every age group. The younger generation needs to hear that there is an alternative to today's credit-charged lifestyle—frugal living can be fun and very rewarding, something our children know well. Those in the throes of the middle years, whether raising kids, building careers, or both, need to hear that work doesn't need to own them. We can vouch for the fact that they can live on less and still reach incredible goals. And as we edge our way toward retirement, we can offer guidance to seniors, many of whom live on Social Security or are learning to stretch their savings. As economizers, we proclaim that no matter what your financial state, and regardless of what the economy is doing, you can not only survive but thrive.

THREE PRINCIPLES FOR GETTING YOU RIGHT ON THE MONEY

There will be three themes that you'll see recur throughout this book: avoid debt like the plague, live below your means, and embrace the thrifty lifestyle.

Avoid Debt Like the Plague

Why avoid debt, especially when many financial experts advocate credit card usage to establish a good credit score? Because the overuse of credit actually lowers your standard of living. After spending freely, eventually you'll have to pay back what you've borrowed. This will have to be done with money that could better be spent on today's needs rather than yesterday's desires. The restriction of your cash flow after experiencing credit-enabled "freedom" is always a bitter pill to swallow. The average American family has a credit card balance of over $7,000. We have seen the dark side of credit abuse in which relationships and families crumble under the heavy weight of unpaid debts. The good news is that most people can be debt-free (with the exception of their home) in about eighteen months if they develop a plan and stick with it. We'll show you exactly how it can be done!

While some call us naive to live without the "benefits" of credit (that's right, we don't have any credit cards), we're here to say that it can be done—and life can be good! We have more things than we need, experience more good living than we deserve, and thoroughly enjoy all that we can afford. Can life be any better than this?

Live Below Your Means

This important principle is best accomplished by using a written budget. This is really much easier than you think—and in Chapter 3:

Budgeting, we'll show you how you can use a budget to set aside money in advance of all your expenses. In today's fast-paced lifestyle, spending can easily get out of control. A budget is a great tool to manage spending and makes living below your means achievable. How do you know when you are living below your means? Is it when all the bills are paid and you've still got money left over? We think it's much more than that. Budgeting is the cornerstone of family finances. In every chapter we'll build upon that foundation with loads of ideas to free up money that you didn't even know you had.

Embrace the Thrifty Lifestyle

Being thrifty means that we should always strive to be efficient and resourceful with what we have. (Uggh! That sounds about as exciting as oatmeal.) But in reality, we look at this lifestyle as a game and the savings in time and money as the prize. Every chapter will contain tips, secrets, and new skills you can learn to help you win every time.

Many people say that avoiding credit, living below your means, and being thrifty are a waste of time. Ha! We say that as you experience success in reaching your financial dreams (and you will), you'll be so convinced these practical principles work that you'll never go back to the way you were living before. And you'll leave the scoffers behind you, eating your financial dust!

HOW "AMERICA'S CHEAPEST FAMILY" GOT STARTED

When we dreamed up the idea for the *HomeEconomiser* newsletter in March 2003, we had no idea that our thrifty advice would be so warmly embraced. There was tremendous interest from the media, and within one month several newspaper stories appeared, as did TV spots and radio interviews. In the next eighteen months the story spread from Phoenix across the United States and even to London, Hong Kong, Turkey, Australia, and New Zealand.

We were first hailed as "America's Cheapest Family" when we appeared on *Good Morning America* in 2004. Initially we flinched at the use of the word *cheap*. *Uggh!* We have never thought of ourselves as cheapskates. We think of ourselves as deal makers and bargain hunters. But in a language that has no positive adjectives to describe people who live within their means, are careful to evaluate every purchase, and always have money in the bank, we can understand the dilemma. To a world that loves to spend, those of us who love to save just aren't looked upon in a positive light. What options are available to reporters trying to describe a family they believe to be the ultimate in our line of work? Are we the Frugalest? The Most Miserly? The Tightwaddiest, the Thriftiest, the Most Parsimonious? The Economical Economideses? Or the Super Skimpers? If they called us Smart Shoppers, then what would that make everyone who didn't shop as we do? After a long evaluation and numerous discussions, we decided that if being "America's Cheapest Family" provided us with a platform to help many thousands of families break away from financial enslavement, then we would be willing. (Besides, it's much easier for most people to pronounce than Economides.)

Necessity Is the Mother of Economizing

Annette was raised in a large Italian family on Long Island, New York, and Steve grew up in a large Greek family on the South Side of Chicago. We met in 1979, married in 1982, and began our frugal journey together. As a newly married couple, we received lots of advice. Some family members recommended that Steve should work two jobs and Annette ought to work as well—all this so that we could save our money and purchase a house in three years' time. But Annette wanted to learn to make our home and we wanted to be able to spend time together as a newly married couple, so we chose to do things differently. Steve worked just one job, while Annette stayed home and stretched our money until it begged for mercy.

By our first wedding anniversary, our family had grown to three. Steve was earning a whopping $7 an hour as a graphic designer. Annette worked diligently following our spending plan—pinching pennies really paid off as our savings grew. In his best-seller *Life's Little*

Instruction Book, H. Jackson Brown Jr. wrote the following to his son: "When starting out, don't worry about not having enough money. Limited funds are a blessing, not a curse. Nothing encourages creative thinking in quite the same way." This quote describes our early years to a T, and we certainly did feel blessed.

Almost exactly three years later, with baby number two on the way, we purchased our first home—a four-bedroom repo-fixer-upper. We put 15 percent down and then began aggressively paying down the principal and fine-tuning our spending plan. Nine years later, we made the last payment on that house. Our average annual income at that time was less than $35,000. Making the last payment was a monumental occasion for many reasons, not the least of which was that we were now totally convinced that thrifty living really did pay off. Our kids were happy, and we had many of the things that you would associate with a suburban family—except that we had absolutely no debt.

We'd been married twelve years by 1995, and our family had grown to include five children. Our wonderful 1,450-square-foot home, however, seemed to have shrunk. We were literally tripping over each other. After months of searching, we bought and moved into a much larger house, our dream home. It was comparatively huge—3,500 square feet with five bedrooms. The house was set on three-quarters of an acre with a citrus orchard—and lots of room for the kids to learn, grow, and do plenty of chores. Applying the same principles we used in our first home, we've continued to pay down our mortgage, establish an emergency fund, build some retirement savings, and buy a couple of new (used) cars with cash. Our income has increased in the intervening ten years, but we kept our expenses low and concentrated on making our money stretch as far as we could.

While financial goals are important, our greatest success has been raising five well-adjusted, happy children: John, twenty-three; Becky, twenty-one; Roy, seventeen; Joseph, fourteen; and Abbey, twelve. Economizing as a family has taught our kids important lessons about managing money, grounded them in nonmaterialistic values, and, most significantly, brought us together as a family. We've chosen to involve our children in managing our household finances and in turn, they have helped *us* economize better. Our daughter Becky discovered the thrill of consignment store shopping when she needed a dress for the prom—she uncovered a stunning lavender gown for less than $20. Our youngest son, Joseph, absolutely glowed when he encountered a virtually new baseball bat that retailed for $150 on sale at a thrift store for $10. Our youngest daughter, Abbey, was thrilled to find a long-desired Barbie horse at a silent auction fund-raiser. Not only did she use her own money for a wonderful toy, but the money went to a great cause. We know that our tightwad ways can teach the next generation skills that will last a lifetime.

We've been asked many times if financial success would alter our lifestyle. It hasn't and won't. While our economizing started out of necessity, it has now become a creative and enjoyable lifestyle that we would never abandon. We have discovered an equilibrium in our lives and a contentment in what we possess. Our greatest desire is to help others discover the same peace and contentment.

Reaching Out

In October 1983, Steve stood up in front of a group of 150 men from our church. As a young man just starting out on his financial journey, he asked if there were any older men who would be willing to help us and other young families learn to manage their finances and make sound plans for the future. Not one of them offered to help. Steve was flabbergasted. As we refined our saving and money management skills over the years, people started asking *us* for advice. Since then we have coached scores of individuals and families, helping them straighten out some pretty sticky financial situations. In dealing with creditors, past-due bills, and bloated budgets, we've helped these families cut a path through the money jungle to the pastures of financial stability. In many cases, we've had to disentangle them from a credit-induced paralysis and help them see the value of using a little bit of planning and a lot of creativity instead of their credit cards. The results have been heartwarming.

For five years we managed a volunteer financial coaching ministry at our church. At that time our kids were relatively young (ages one through twelve)—a full-time job in itself. Add to that Steve's ever-increasing work responsibilities, and we came to realize that this growing ministry was just too overwhelming a task for us to maintain. When we turned over the reins of the ministry, it consisted of seventeen volunteer counselors whom we had trained, with more than seventy people then being helped by the ministry.

In 2003, after twenty-one years in the workforce, first as a graphic designer and later as an advertising account executive, Steve quit his job. We felt led to help more people, but at a less frenetic pace, so we decided to pursue teaching about economizing full time.

We took our personal lifestyle and our many coaching experiences and put them in written form—and the *HomeEconomiser* newsletter was born. The response from readers has been amazing: families are taking control of their finances and seeing fantastic results. In three years' time we expanded from local distribution to having subscribers in numerous countries around the world. Many readers have said that through reading our newsletter they have come to feel like our family is part of their family. We hope you'll feel the same way too. Writing this book is an extension of the *HomeEconomiser* newsletter, years of "economizer" living, and thousands of hours spent helping others reach their financial goals.

We also know that there are some of you out there who could run circles around us with your thrifty knowledge and habits. We applaud you and urge you to keep setting the standard for careful living. We realize that we're still a work in progress, always looking for new ways to improve. We hope that those of you who are black-belt economizers will catch the vision and join with us in helping so many others who are looking for ways to make their money go further.

HOW TO MAXIMIZE YOUR USE OF THIS BOOK

The concept for this book has been developed from our own family budgeting habits, years of personal budget coaching, and family budgeting seminars that we have presented since 1989. The process of going through every area of a family's budget as we do in this book and sharing how we manage expenses is similar to what we did in the past, sitting around our kitchen table while we coached a family on their finances. You can think of the following pages as your own private coaching session!

While we've included hundreds of ways to help you make your money go further, we couldn't possibly cover every area of household finances. It would make this book an enormous reference manual instead of an easy-to-read guide with some humor mixed in to help the medicine go down.

This book can be used any number of ways: you can read through it from start to finish, you can refer to it as a reference manual, or you can just jump from chapter to chapter to deal with needs as they arise. For instance, if you discover that the amount you're spending on kids' clothes has gotten out of hand, read Chapter 9: Clothing. If your utility expenses are crippling your budget, read Chapter 6: Utilities.

We've put much thought into the order of the chapters in this book. We start with the grocery chapter because for most families this is one of the fastest ways to achieve significant savings quickly. We follow that with budgeting, because it is the foundation to building a sound financial future. It has been the single most valuable tool in helping us reach our financial goals. The chapters that follow are organized from the necessities down to the more optional expenses in the family budget. We put the debt chapter near the middle of the book because we didn't want to hit you with a lot of heavy stuff right away. But if you are struggling with a mountain of debt, you may want to start with Chapter 7: Debt and then read the rest of the book in order. We know that our chapters may not be in the same order as most financial books (like our attitudes chapter, near the end of the book), but then again, we've always done things differently—that's what makes life with us so much fun!

We won't lie to you—there aren't many quick fixes to household finance problems. Sometimes things we propose might seem radical. But please allow the ideas to sink in and take time to germinate. When a real need crops up in our lives, sometimes it's those crazy ideas that provide the answer we're looking for. We can promise that if you focus on one issue at a time, you will eventually find a solution that works for your family. And with each victory will come a renewed conviction that you can and will be able to clear the next hurdle to come your way.

We've included lots of stories from our lives and from the lives of people we've helped. The stories we tell are all true, but to protect the privacy of the people involved, we have changed the names and any other identifying details. Thrifty subscribers to the *HomeEconomiser* newsletter have also added lots of their great tips throughout the book.

THE SIGNIFICANCE OF THE MOUSE, THE OWL, AND THE ANT

We realize that everyone reading this book will be at a different place on their journey toward saving money. Some will be considering the frugal life for the first time, while others will be seasoned veterans. In each chapter, we present three levels of practical steps that can be taken right now: the Timid Mouse, the Wise Owl, and the Amazing Ant.

What do a mammal, a bird, and an insect have to do with America's Cheapest Family? Well, nature plays a big role in our family. We home-school our kids and encourage them to observe and investigate animal and insect behavior. We pay attention to what these animals do, and often we become aware of how some of our own behaviors—good and bad—parallel theirs.

The habits and characteristics of three particular creatures can be an encouragement to you as a seeker of deals and discounts. Each chapter concludes with a page titled "What You Can Do Now About . . . ," in which we present three levels of application of the principles and stories that we have related in the chapter. We know that not everyone reading this book will be at the same degree of thriftiness, so we've broken down our advice for beginners (Timid Mouse), intermediates (Wise Owl), and—for those hard-core tightwads—the advanced (Amazing Ant).

These titles may seem a bit juvenile, but once you understand some of the characteristics of these creatures, we think you'll agree with our reasons for relating them to the different stages of frugal living.

Timid Mouse

Mice are shy creatures. They rarely come out during the day. At night, when they do go on the prowl, they tend to do so secretively. They stay close to the walls or other objects that will conceal them. They don't want to be detected. They find what they need or want, then scamper back to their hiding place and enjoy their loot.

Fledgling economizers are much the same. It may be embarrassing to think that someone might catch them at a garage sale or thrift store. They don't want anyone to know that they are hunting for "cheap" stuff. So they go out in neighborhoods where they won't be detected or shop late at night, when they're less likely to be noticed. They would be mortified if anyone knew that the clothes that they are wearing were purchased at a thrift store. Although they enjoy the bargains they find, they won't be quick to tell anyone else about their great finds.

It's okay to be timid at the outset—we all were a little uncertain about how and where to start. Our encouragement to the timid mouse is to keep looking for new ways to save. Keep going out and searching. Soon you'll be so confident in your thrifty ways that you won't have to be so secretive about it and your pile of loot will really start to accumulate.

Wise Owl

A family of great horned owls inhabits the area around our home. We often see them fly to the top of our tallest pine trees and peer out over the neighborhood, watching and waiting for something to consume (contrary to common belief, they don't hunt only at night). They are patient—very patient. Waiting quietly and hidden, they watch. When the time is right and their quarry is in sight, they silently swoop down from the treetops and strike. They carry their prey to a hideaway and share it with their family. They'll stay in one area for a time, but once the food supply is diminished, they move on to greener pastures. Although they are wise in their hunting habits, they only gather enough food for a few days at a time—there is no reserve, so life is a constant pursuit of food.

Intermediate thrifty people are much like owls. They know that there are bargains to be found in abundance—they'll just have to watch and wait. They know that patience pays, and pays big-time. They still aren't too keen about others knowing what they are up to and how they find their deals—especially if someone gets to a bargain before they do. But they are confident enough about their hunting skills to do it day or night—it really doesn't matter. Hunting for treasure is a great way to provide for their needs, and they enjoy it. But it takes constant vigilance and consumes much of their time and mental energy.

Amazing Ant

Ants are truly unbelievable creatures. They are organized, diligent, and tireless. They use their nests to store food for their seasonal needs. In areas where winter is harsher and longer, ant nests are larger and deeper in the ground, providing room to store more food for the long winter and more protection from the cold. Ants look at the weather and plan for the future needs of their colony. When scouts go out and find food, they lay a scent trail for other workers to follow. You'll often see columns of ants marching ceaselessly to and from a food source. Ants are strong. They can carry material equivalent to many times their body weight. If they encounter an obstruction to their work, they either go over or around it or call in the reserves to move it out of the way. Teamwork and diligence are some of their most admirable attributes.

Advanced economizers are very much like ants. Organization is their key to success. Their pantries are arranged so they can track what supplies they have and what they need, and their clothes are organized as well. They are always looking for bargains, and when they find them they let others know. The network of other frugal-minded friends they have established provides them with greater savings and the encouragement to press on with diligence in the face of a culture that wants to squish them. Planning in advance for events that they see coming in the future is their strength. They know that their kids will need larger clothes, so they develop a storage system and a network of friends with whom they can trade outgrown clothes. They store bargain-priced food to feed their family quality products at a lower cost.

HOW WE WRITE

This book is truly a family effort. The kids are the laboratory for many of our great ideas, and unfortunately some of our more unpopular ones too. We've given them space in each chapter to express their opinions about various topics.

We—Annette and Steve—have written this book together. For the most part, we have written in the first person plural, except when we speak of ourselves individually. There we've decided to refer to ourselves in the third person—"Annette says" or "Steve thinks." It makes our writing less cumbersome and easier to understand. Although it may be atypical, we write as one voice.

Too often, books on the frugal lifestyle are written by one spouse, and it leaves us wondering what the other spouse is feeling about the decisions being made. We have agreed to agree before making any major decisions. This policy may result in delays, but what's more important is that it builds unity and protects us from mistakes. This book was written the same way—together. That isn't to say that we agree on everything in life, but regarding the essential points of living within our means, saving in advance of every purchase, and teaching our kids to do the same, we are of one mind and on the same page.

REFERENCE MATERIALS

One of the most important things we'll teach you in this book is the power of knowledge and the value of research. In pre-Internet days, research was much more time-consuming and daunting. With the proliferation of information available through free Web sites, becoming powerfully informed is much easier. While all of our research is not done on the Internet, having access is most helpful. Throughout the book we have included recommendations for Web sites and helpful books. Our Web site, AmericasCheapestFamily.com, also contains a wealth of information and many more links to aid you on your quest. If this is something new to you, just remember that most public libraries offer online access and assistance in navigating the Internet.

TAKING NOTES

We've intentionally left wide margins in this book so you can make notes, scribble down ideas, set goals, or just doodle.

But even if you don't write anything in here, try to document your progress somewhere. Many people say they set goals, but only a small percentage actually take the time to write them down. You are much more likely to reach your goals if you've taken the time to think them through, write them down, and review them often. You should see some of our old lists of goals—whew, a few of the things we jotted down seem silly now. But the list of the things we have accomplished is staggering—it contains so many things that originally seemed insurmountable when we wrote them down years ago.

PLEASE BE CAREFUL

Much of the material contained in this book chronicles our experiences. There are also some ideas that have been sent in by readers of our newsletter. We make every effort to do things by the book, safely and legally. There are so many ways to save money that cheating or fudging the truth just isn't necessary. But economizers are typically rebels at heart and trailblazers, people who don't follow the beaten path. While that is a good thing, there are risks involved with veering outside the lines. It is up to you to exercise your best judgment and care when you employ the concepts we discuss. Use what we write as a point of departure for your own research. Making sound financial decisions must be based on your personal values, time, research, and in many cases the advice of a financial professional.

Through our newsletter and its coverage in the media, America's Cheapest Family has touched millions of lives. We hope that this book will reach and help millions more.

TWO

GROCERIES:

Savings by the Bagful

When it comes to reducing household expenses, one of the fastest and easiest ways is to look at your grocery spending habits. How much can you save? That all depends on how much effort and time you have to spend.

According to the U.S. Department of Labor, the average American family of four spends $8,513 per year on groceries. That's $709 each month—$177 per person! By comparison, we spend just $350 per month to feed a family of seven, including three growing boys! That's $50 per person—66 percent less than the national average. Implementing just a couple of Annette's many strategies in your grocery-buying habits can have a huge impact on your food budget. If the average family could reduce their food bill just 20 percent, they'd have an extra $1,702 in the bank each year.

Remember that what we share are just a few of the strategies that we use. There is so much to say that we could fill a whole volume on groceries alone. But we *are* going to present plenty of ideas for you to be able to save hundreds of dollars on your groceries this year. Not all may apply to your lifestyle or family, but stick with us. We're writing from over twenty-four years' experience practicing and perfecting these habits. Try a few, and you may be pleasantly surprised not only with the benefit to your household but with the savings you'll gain.

THE COST OF IMPULSIVENESS

When Steve was working as an advertising account executive, he had a client who marketed cheese products on military bases worldwide. We were shocked to read in a food industry publication that grocers expect six of ten items consumers pick up in the store to be unplanned purchases. Sixty percent!

Later, Steve and this client created an in-store promotion where they set up a display showcasing regularly priced spaghetti, pasta sauce, Parmesan cheese, and Italian salad dressing. Above it was hung a banner announcing "Pasta Tonite." They also handed out a very confusing coupon sheet that required the consumer to purchase three different items from the display in order to redeem any one coupon. Sales of the regularly priced items from the display increased 38 percent, just because it was easy for shoppers to pick up an entire meal. Coupon redemptions were less than 1 percent. The manufacturer saw a huge sales increase without having to "pay" for it through coupon redemptions. This promotion was repeated for five years, and the sales results were consistent.

J. Jeffrey Inman at the University of Wisconsin, Madison, and Russell S. Winer at the University of California, Berkeley, researched the effects that in-store activity such as promotions, displays, and signage had on consumer purchases. In their study "Where the Rubber Meets the Road: A Model of In-Store Consumer Decision Making," they present an analysis of the decisions of over 4,200 customers who made 30,000 purchases in fourteen different cities. In a nutshell, they discovered the following habits:

- Shoppers making a "quick trip" to the store to pick up a few specific items usually purchase 54 percent more than they planned.

- Forty-seven percent of shoppers go to the store three or four times each week.

· Consumers graze at the grocery store, with impulse buys making up between 50.8 and 67.7 percent of total purchases.

(In the following three statistics, the number represents the percentage of times unplanned items are purchased from these displays.)

· End-of-aisle displays encourage higher impulse buys—61 percent.

· In-aisle displays encourage moderate impulsive purchases—58 percent.

· Checkout displays—candy and magazines—generate the highest impulsivity, a 64 percent rate.

(Even though this study was conducted in 1998, our observations and discussions with store managers tell us that if anything has changed, we as a society are more impulsive now than before.)

The more often you go to the store, the more often you will walk past displays, endcaps of special items, and the ever-enticing goodies in the checkout lane. The more often you pass these locations, the more likely you'll be to spend more than you intended. This is exactly what retailers are banking on. They study the numbers, watch our habits, and record our purchases.

If you're not careful, a trip to the store to pick up ten items will easily grow to sixteen. Curb the impulse and save!

CHOPPING SHOPPING:
REDUCING TRIPS TO THE STORE

"I'm running to the store to pick up a couple things for dinner—be back in two minutes." This is the mantra of the harried shopper, hurrying home from work or rushed at the end of a day of running errands or transporting kids to various activities. For some families a trip to the grocery store has become a daily necessity.

We think otherwise. We shop once a month and spend an average of $350, which includes all food items, paper goods, personal care items, and cleaning supplies. Limiting our food shopping saves not only loads of money but time too.

It wasn't always this way. When we were first married and living in an apartment with a very small refrigerator/freezer, Annette went food shopping once a week. A year later, she met a neighbor who had an upright freezer in her apartment. This neighbor offered to share a shelf in her freezer, an offer we took her up on. With this, we stretched our shopping interval to two weeks. It took about the same amount of time to shop for two weeks' groceries as it did for one, so with this single change we cut our shopping time in half.

In 1984, we purchased a used 9-cubic-foot chest freezer, with the thought that we would try to trim our food shopping to once a month for our family of three. It worked so well that we've been doing it together ever since. Twelve times a year we go on a hunt for a month's worth of food. The whole process from leaving the house to putting the groceries away takes about five hours. While this may sound like a lot of time, just consider that a two-hour shopping trip once a week will consume eight hours in a month's time—and don't forget all those quick trips in between!

We've learned a few things over the years about how this works best. With a large family, shopping for a whole month is a sizeable task that shouldn't be attempted single-handedly. Honestly, there are times when neither of us feels like starting this five-hour marathon, but we figure it only happens once a month and we can get through it together! If you have a smaller family, planning and shopping will take much less time.

When Steve first started shopping with Annette, the extent of his involvement was limited to picking up specific sale items. As time went on, he learned to match coupons with sale items and even graduated to his own coupon envelope—*Shazam!* Now we divide the store into two sections: the inner aisles, which are Annette's domain, and the outer loop of meat, dairy, deli, and produce, which is Steve's area. But even those on their own can do this—single parents can shop with an older child, or ask a relative, neighbor, or someone else to help. And you could even accomplish this type of shopping trip alone, with one shopping cart, if you have a smaller household.

The week we go shopping, we purchase or borrow the Wednesday newspaper; that's the day grocery ads are published in our area. We plan our menus and shopping list based on what is on sale. No brand loyalty here; this is war—we go for the best price in most cases.

The first time Annette did a monthlong menu plan (more on how to do this later in the chapter), it took almost a whole day to map out just the dinners. Now she can crank it out in about thirty minutes because she has developed a huge repertoire of meals in her menu book, enough to go about three months without repeating a meal. (But ask the kids and they'll tell you that they have a few favorites that Mom cooks each month.)

We review our coupons (we each have our own coupon containers, with coupons that correspond to our area of the store), weeding out expired ones and seeing which can be combined with sale items to make a real killing. In our area most grocers offer to double manufacturer's coupons up to 50 cents off. With a little planning, we can often get needed items—and sometimes frivolous ones—for pennies or for free. Reviewing the coupons this way also provides us with a reminder of which coupons we have, so we can take double advantage of those unexpected sales that we may stumble across.

When the kids were younger, we would hire a babysitter while we went to the store. It is well worth the money to be able to concentrate and calculate the best values. We love our children dearly, but trying to make them behave for hours of intense grocery shopping is an unrealistic expectation. As they've grown up, they occasionally accompany us to the store and are a great help with the hunt.

Often Steve has questions about specials or manager's closeouts he has come across and whether to buy them. He used to walk the outer loop looking up and down each aisle to find Annette, but this was time-consuming, so one day he decided to bring a pair of walkie-talkies, and now he rings her with questions or phenomenal deals he has discovered. We sometimes feel like spies—"Hey, Annette, you won't believe the deal that I just found. . . ."

By working together and using the aisle and loop system, we can visit two stores in one night—one store for sale items and the other for the balance of the month's worth of shopping. You'll see later on how we occasionally purchase some other specific items elsewhere.

Once we get home, we put away only the perishable items. We're usually too exhausted to put everything away, and the kids love to forage through the bags looking for "surprises." The next morning, all of us work together to put away the dry goods. We have to store them carefully so as not to lose track—for example, we label the cereal boxes with the month and year so we don't end up with two-year-old Raisin Bran sitting on our shelves.

Limiting our trips to the store means that certain fruits and vegetables must be eaten earlier in the month because they are more perishable. Grapes and bananas usually last a week. Once they're gone, we move on to other fruits. Pears, lettuce, cucumbers, and peppers can last two weeks. Apples, cabbage, radishes, oranges, and celery can last a month.

We are often asked about storing bread, cheese, and milk. How could we possibly make those last a month? Well, we carefully freeze all three.

- Bread needs to be carefully set in the freezer to avoid crushing and creating grotesquely misshapen loaves.

- Cheese is easier if you buy shredded, as we do; be aware that if you do freeze chunks of cheese, you will have difficulty slicing it. Once thawed, it will crumble if you attempt to slice it.

- Milk should be poured off a little to allow for expansion.

We know that we've shared some pretty radical strategies for food shopping and storage. Many of you might think that once-a-month shopping is crazy, but before you give up on this idea, please remember that we've been doing this since 1984. Don't expect to do what we do. Simply use our concept as a catalyst to question if what you are doing is really efficient. Can you make some changes and implement a couple of these ideas? Sure you can! If you're going to the store several times each week, try to reduce it to only once. If you don't have a freezer, you can still limit your shopping trips by planning a weekly menu. If you currently go once a week, try to make your purchases stretch for two weeks. Even if you can reduce your trips to the store to two or three per month, you will see a significant decline in your food budget. Remember the big picture: finding ways to make our money go further and reduce the stress in our lives. Minimizing the number of shopping trips can accomplish both. The less you shop, the more you save.

MENU MANIA: BASIC MENU PLANNING SAVES MORE THAN JUST TIME

"I don't need to do it, I don't want to do it, my mother didn't do it, and none of my friends do it!" That was Annette's response in 1983 when Steve suggested she develop a weekly menu plan. As a teenager Annette shunned anything having to do with cooking or housework. The full extent of her domestic aptitude was the ability to boil water and scramble eggs. But we decided early on in our marriage that Annette wanted to stay home and learn as many homemaking skills as possible. Even so, she didn't think that coming up with a weekly menu plan was part of the job description! A few days later, however, she gave it a try. Since then, she has streamlined the process, turned it into a monthly plan, and embraced the freedom it provides. Initially, Annette planned only dinner meals, but over time she included a rotation of breakfast and lunch meals also. Having a menu takes the stress out of end-of-day meal preparation: she's no longer a victim of the money-sucking "It's 5:00 P.M., what should I make for dinner? Nothing sounds good—let's go pick up a pizza" problem.

Creating a monthly menu can seem like a monumental task, but if you start with one week at a time, it will eventually get easier and easier. We realize that our system may not work for everyone, but we hope you will glean some helpful ideas that will direct you toward a solution that works.

This is how we do it. Early in the week in which we're going to do our once-a-month grocery shopping, Annette takes stock of what we have in our pantry, refrigerator, and freezer. She records items in the following categories, noting what we'll need to buy in order to make it through the month. We check our stock of the following items:

- *Breakfast foods:* eggs, hot cereal, bagels, cold cereal, and ingredients for pancakes, waffles, and French toast. Annette also makes sure the pantry is stocked with flour, baking soda, baking powder, cinnamon, vanilla, and other spices.

- *Lunch foods:* peanut butter and jelly, lunch meat, tuna, bread, eggs for egg salad, tortillas and shredded cheese for cheese crisps (our Spanish-speaking friends call them quesadillas—we call them yummy), yogurt, hot dogs, cottage cheese, salad fixings, and plenty of fruit.

- *Dinner foods:* Annette looks at general categories, counting the number of items in each before preparing her menu: pork/ham, chicken/turkey, beef, pasta, lamb, beans, and other items for meatless meals.

Once she knows what we have, Annette checks the grocery store ads for sale items.

Stocking Up

We have a certain dollar amount set aside for groceries each month (see Chapter 3: Budgeting for more details). Some months, with careful shopping, we won't spend the entire allotment, and then we accumulate an excess of dollars earmarked for groceries. Some of this money is used to stock up on special items that have rock-bottom pricing once a year. For example, we know we can purchase several turkeys at Thanksgiving, hams at Christmas, and corned beef the week of St. Patrick's Day. Stocking up saves us loads of money in the long run (and our full pantry enables us to lend others a hand occasionally).

Having determined what sale items she will buy, Annette starts to create the month's menu. In reality, some of the sale items purchased this month will not be incorporated into the menu but will instead be saved for future months. This stockpiling concept allows us to always be eating food purchased at the lowest prices.

It's easy to do now, after more than twenty years, but you may not have that kind of kitchen background. What do you do if you are menu-challenged?

Early in our marriage, Annette grew tired of the limited number of meals in our diet. She invited some friends over, hoping she could get some new ideas from a recipe swap. It worked wonderfully: they were like kids playing Go Fish. ("Got any really fun cake recipes?" "Hey, I need a chicken recipe.") She came away with fresh enthusiasm for cooking and a wide variety of recipes, including some that are now family classics, including her famous Christmas Pumpkin Bread. After years of planning, researching, and experimenting—some with successful results and some . . . well, don't ask about Tapioca Soup—Annette now has more than ninety different meals to choose from when she creates our monthly menu.

But there are other ways to find new ideas. Don't forget your public library. Ours has an entire section of cookbooks—thirteen feet long and eight feet high—with every kind of ethnic and specialized food category represented. You can make it a game to try to find one new recipe each month.

Bad Ad Day

Even having lots of recipes, though, doesn't mean that you won't encounter some pitfalls. For instance, about a year into Annette's menu-planning journey she ran into a brick wall. The food ads offered no great sales, and we didn't have much variety in the freezer. The best meat deal she could find was a sale on Italian sausage at $1.50 per pound. Previously she had used this type of sausage only in her Italian pasta dishes, and she wanted more of a meat-based main course, so she pulled out her cookbooks to research other options. As a result of that bad ad day, she discovered one of our all-time favorite meals—Cheese Sausage Spinach Pie. Sometimes commitment to an economical approach to menu planning takes research and extra effort. But the payoff can be phenomenal—you save money, and you can broaden your culinary horizons.

With her meal list, a calendar, and a menu planning sheet in hand, Annette is ready for the final phase of menu mania. Why the calendar?

Simple. She plans the menu based on our family's schedule for the month. She doesn't want to cook a roast on a night when Joseph has baseball practice and Becky has a night class and needs to rush out the door. We like to sit down and eat as a family as often as possible.

Dinner. These are a few of the dinner combinations in our monthly menu plan:

  · Chicken enchiladas, rice, and cauliflower
  · Salisbury steaks, baked potatoes, and broccoli
  · Ham with scalloped potatoes and carrots
  · Marinated lamb shoulder chops, yams, and green beans
  · Vegetable lentil soup with dinner rolls or cheese muffins

Annette usually plans fifteen to eighteen dinner meals to be cooked on our once-a-month cooking day. (We look at it like our once-a-month food shopping trek—it is efficient and helps make the household run more smoothly.) These meals are stored in the freezer for use throughout the month. Once she has the freezer meals planned, she fills in the remaining days with leftovers or roast chicken, pasta (sauce made earlier in the month), chops, or steaks on the grill—meals prepared on the day they are eaten.

Breakfast. We have a rotation of various meals for breakfast. This is an example of one weekly menu:

  · *Monday:* cold cereal with bananas
  · *Tuesday:* hot cereal with grapefruit
  · *Wednesday:* pancakes, waffles, or French toast (from the freezer) and ham
  · *Thursday:* eggs with toast
  · *Friday:* bagels with fruit
  · *Saturday:* pancakes (made from scratch) and sausages
  · *Sunday:* scrambled eggs with cheese, ham, and potatoes

When we cook French toast, pancakes, or waffles, we usually prepare a quadruple batch. The leftovers are neatly packed into freezer storage bags and frozen. Then they are put into the rotation of meals for the weeks that follow.

Lunch. This rotation varies greatly depending on what we have purchased on sale and what leftovers we have in the refrigerator. Here's a sample:

- *Monday:* mac and cheese and bananas (as a fruit, not mixed in!)
- *Tuesday:* yogurt with fruit and crackers
- *Wednesday:* PB&J with orange slices
- *Thursday:* tuna fish sandwiches and apples
- *Friday:* leftovers
- *Saturday:* lunch meat sandwiches and pickles
- *Sunday:* BLTs

If the prospect of planning thirty days' worth of meals is overwhelming, don't panic! Start with a seven-day dinner menu. Just completing a week's worth should lessen your mental panic time at night and also decrease trips to the store as you check and use the foods you have in the house. Regular menu planning and checking what you have in stock will minimize wasted grocery dollars and rotting food that needs to be tossed because you forgot it was there.

A practice that Annette originally viewed as a burden has actually become a real burden lifter. It's rewarding to see how each bit of planning you do will provide multiplied minutes of freedom and peace. With a little practice, you too can alleviate stress, save money, and enjoy some really great meals!

A Real Cut-up

If you have small children (under four years old), you'll love this idea. How often has this scenario played out at your house? Dinner is finally on the table, the kids are seated, you drop into your chair exhausted and famished. Then you spend the next fifteen minutes cutting up the meal for the younger kids. This process was especially daunting for Annette on evenings when Steve worked late and wasn't home at the start of dinner. As a result, Annette started using many recipes she developed that included diced or cubed chicken, ham, turkey, or ground beef. Because the meat was already in bite-sized pieces, Annette was able to enjoy her meal along with the kids.

LEFTOVERS

Some families view leftovers as revolting. But we view leftovers as another way to save time and money. And in our home, when we announce that leftovers are on the menu, there is usually a race to the kitchen to be first in line and first to choose. When Steve packed lunches to take to the office, they were the envy of all who saw or smelled them.

Do you realize what it costs to purchase a $6 lunch every workday? Do the math: fifty weeks times five days times $6—are you sitting down? Fifteen hundred dollars per year! Even if you take leftovers two or three days each week, your savings will be significant.

COUPON CRAZY? NOT! A MODERATE APPROACH TO COUPONING

Couponing isn't for everyone. If you're a single mom raising young kids, you may not have time for extensive couponing. That's okay, do what you can without losing your sanity. If you're a grandma with some extra time who can clip coupons for your kids, you can be a real blessing in their lives by helping them stretch their pennies. We don't advocate the "coupon queen" approach to couponing, where you spend entire days each month clipping and going to the store to get hundreds of dollars' worth of groceries for nothing. We try to take a more balanced approach to life.

The Coupon Network: Gathering

Where do we get all our coupons? Mainly from the Sunday newspaper. We have developed a sharing network of relatives, friends, and neighbors (you could add co-workers if you find some thrift-minded colleagues). Clip the coupons you want to keep, then pass the leftovers to someone else, who takes what she wants and passes them along again. We all have different tastes, so some pretty valuable coupons may remain, even at the end of the loop. And in using this method you could end up with multiple copies of some great coupons.

Many people who get the newspaper don't even care to mess with the coupons. Ask around and you may find people willing to throw them into a plastic grocery bag and give them to you every couple of weeks.

Clipping Coupons

How and when do we clip and organize coupons? Clipping new coupons and/or purging expired ones occurs a few evenings each month at the dinner table, while Steve reads a chapter book to the kids. At other times, Annette will do clipping and/or weeding of expired coupons while watching a family movie, at a Little League game, or while waiting for a doctor's appointment. Sometimes we give each of the kids an envelope or two to weed out expired coupons—this really saves time. (Abbey became very proficient at weeding when she turned eight.) Once clipped, the coupons are piled into categories and then filed into corresponding envelopes.

Sorting by Categories

Annette likes to work with as few categories (and envelopes) as possible, while Steve likes to microsort his coupons into multiple subcategories. Of course, he can do this because his area of the store, the outer loop, has fewer coupons for its products than the inner shelf areas. Annette's original categories included frozen foods, personal care, cleaning products, dairy, and shelf items. As time went on and her coupon collection increased, she created other divisions to keep individual envelopes from becoming unwieldy. In addition to the five groupings previously listed, her categories now include pet supplies, cereal, snack foods (granola bars, crackers, chips, cookies, and candy), and paper products (this is kind of a catchall and includes film, batteries, books, and games).

Within each envelope, she groups similar items together to make finding them easier. For example, the paper products envelope contains groupings for facial tissue, toilet tissue, paper towels, foil, plastic zip bags, and disposable tableware. The arrangement of the shelf items envelope—a real monster—is based on the aisles of the store at which Annette first shopped: peanut butter, jelly, ketchup, mustard and mayo, pickles, olives, vinegar, salad dressings, canned fruits and veggies, canned meals, canned meats, soups, rice, pasta and Italian products, Mexican products, chocolate drink mixes and syrups, baking supplies (oil, sugar, evaporated milk, chocolate chips, cake mixes), coffee, tea, juice, and soda. Creating the groupings made filing and finding coupons a snap—unless Annette asked Steve to find some coupons. It seems that one person's filing system is always a mystery to another person! You'll have to come up with a sorting hierarchy that fits your time and lifestyle. The important thing is to create a system of organizing that works for you, and stick with it.

The Coupon Container

Years ago, Annette's first coupon container was a little nylon zippered pouch about the size of a business envelope. She soon came to realize that it was woefully inadequate. She graduated to a shoe box and filled it with recycled envelopes labeled with various coupon categories. Later, Steve built her a custom rectangular box made from quarter-inch black plastic material that he got from a photo lab (they were throwing away scrap pieces, and he asked if he could have them—a great strategy for saving money). The box fits perfectly in the seat area of a shopping cart, holds thousands of coupons, and won't fall out. But don't give up on this concept if you don't have a handy spouse to build a custom box for you! Just start looking around for a container that might come in handy, like a plastic storage box or a cardboard box. Be creative and frugal; you'll find something that works.

Planning for Maximum Coupon Value

When Annette first tried to save money at the grocery store, she didn't know about the loss leader shopping strategy. Loss leaders are products that a grocery store advertises to sell at or below their cost, in hopes that consumers will be enticed to shop at their store. They count on customers picking up other full-price items while they shop. She also didn't know about the cherry-picker tactic—shopping at various grocery stories only to pick up the loss leader items—so she shopped at the store nearest home. Not for long!

We live in a suburban area where six to ten chains—including health-food grocers—compete for market share through their weekly ads. This makes for some great deals as they duke it out for customers. Some stores regularly offer double and sometimes even triple coupons. When the deal is right, Annette checks her coupons and stocks up on things like shampoo, salad dressing, cooking oil, ketchup, mustard, deodorant, salsa, cold cereal, and other staple items.

How do you know when the deal is right? Amy Dacyczyn, retired publisher of the *Tightwad Gazette,* advocated creating a price book to track pricing on items that you regularly purchase. We did this for a while and eventually were able to remember what the best prices were. If you live in an area where there is less competition, the deals may not be as great, but the same principles still apply.

The Redeeming Strategy

Now, this is the really important part of using coupons, so pay close attention. *Annette doesn't just buy something because she has a coupon.* Coupons are strategically used—unless we are having an ice cream craving—to allow as little money as possible to seep from our checking account. Coupons combined with sale-priced items are good, but the best deals occur when you use those same coupons for the smallest-size items possible and get them for free or just a couple of pennies. Even though a smaller item may start out with a higher price per ounce, after we apply the coupon, it ends up much less expensive. The only exception to this rule is for items that we use in large quantities and that seldom go on sale. For instance, we use a coupon to buy the large bottle of teriyaki sauce for marinating chuck steaks.

Let's take another example. Salsa recently went on sale for 99 cents (regularly $2.89–$3.29 per bottle). Annette had a coupon for $1 off the purchase of two jars, so each bottle ended up costing 50 cents. She used every coupon she had and stocked our pantry for the next six months. For her, the real value of couponing is playing the game to get the highest percentage off the retail price and, ultimately, the least amount out of her wallet. (Obviously, you'll have to temper your stocking up with your available storage space and your ability to consume the food in a reasonable amount of time.)

While planning the menu and shopping list from the grocery store ads, Annette will often pull out coupons that she can combine with store specials. These are put into an envelope for use at that store. Once inside the store, as we walk the aisles and come across closeouts or manager's unadvertised specials, we grab our coupon envelopes, find the coupon we need, and evaluate the discounted price. If it's a killer deal, we whip out the walkie-talkies, give a whoop of success, and toss the item into the cart. Ah, the sweet taste of victory!

Is it crazy to use coupons? We don't think so, but we also try to balance the time it takes with the rest of our daily priorities. There are times when we are extremely busy with kids' activities, and so coupons are sometimes clipped but may not get filed or used at the store. Keeping life simple and sane is more important than making a killing at the store.

Just remember that the best thing about being a smart couponer is not necessarily saving money or getting things for free. When the entire family participates in stretching your cash, it builds unity, develops an understanding of consumer habits, and can teach valuable math skills to your kids. And of course, there is the humorous side of couponing: seeing the faces on the people in line behind you with their six retail-priced items. They stand, arms akimbo and slack-jawed, just gawking at you, as you purchase the same items they have in their cart for next to nothing. Now, that's really crazy!

TEN SIMPLE WAYS TO INSTANTLY SLASH YOUR GROCERY BILL: DOS AND DON'TS

We've covered our basic principles for conserving grocery dollars: strategic shopping, less frequent trips to the store, menu planning, and couponing. Here are a few tips we use to achieve extra savings at the store. We look at these dos and don'ts not as restrictions but as boundaries that make life more interesting.

1. Lunch Meat

DON'T buy prepackaged lunch meat. We also don't buy lunch meat from the deli counter. With prices ranging from $3.99 to $7.99 per pound, it's just not in our budget.

DO look for "chubs" of lunch meat. (A chub is a large chunk of processed and cooked ham, turkey ham, or other meat products.) We mainly limit our choices to turkey ham or cooked ham. In the meat section of most grocery stores we've found chubs of both of these products. The turkey ham is usually in one- or two-pound packs and the ham is usually in a five-pound pack. We watch for a price of $1.29 per pound or less, then we pick up the meat and take it to the butcher or deli counter to be sliced thin. (By the way, always ask the deli person to include the ends when he slices your meat. Some clerks routinely toss the ends and think nothing of it. We chop up the end pieces and add them to scrambled eggs.) Once, while standing at the deli counter, a retired couple observed Steve handing the deli person a chub of ham to be sliced. They asked how much our sliced ham cost. When he told them it was $1.12 per pound, the wife looked at the husband and said, "Why didn't you think of that? We're living on Social Security and don't have money to burn!"

At home, we divide the meat into smaller portions, place it in zippered plastic bags, and freeze for future use. When we're ready to use it, we place it in a plastic container with a paper towel under the meat to absorb moisture and store it in the refrigerator. We change the paper towel when wet. This little system keeps bacteria from building up and keeps the meat fresh longer. It can usually last at least a week stored this way.

2. Warehouse Stores

DON'T think of your local warehouse store as a grocery store. You've got to know your prices. Often, grocery store sale prices combined with coupons beat the pants off warehouse stores. Additionally, impulse buys at grocery stores may cost you $1 to $3, whereas at the warehouse store impulse buys are much more expensive—$5 to $10 or more!

DO your homework and comparison-shop. Know your prices. We have specific items our family likes that we purchase about six times each year at the warehouse stores because we know the prices can't be beat.

3. Bread

DON'T buy bread at the grocery store.

DO try to buy bread at a bread outlet. We like to purchase whole-grain breads. These typically sell for $2 to $4 per loaf at grocery stores in our area. There are several bread outlets within fifteen miles of our home, and we visit one about every six weeks combined with another errand. At the outlets, prices vary, but often we'll run into special sales, such as three loaves for $2.09; sometimes even four for $1! We usually load about fifteen loaves into our cart. The bread in these stores is great quality and indistinguishable from the loaves in the grocery store. Once home, we double-bag the bread, two or three loaves together in a plastic grocery bag, and tie the top closed. This prevents condensation and icy buildup in the bag. Then we carefully load it into the freezer, being sure to avoid crushing and permanently misshaping the loaves. With deals this good, grocery store prices just aren't worth it.

4. Play the Market

DON'T just shop in one store. Store loyalty is nice for the grocer but death to your budget.

DO look over every food ad in your area. Don't forget to look at alternatives to food stores—Walgreens, Smart and Final (a restaurant supply grocer open to the public), 99-cent stores, Big Lots, and dented can/grocery outlet stores. While these won't be your regularly visited venues, you'll occasionally find great deals and be able to stock up on several months' worth of great-priced items.

5. Use Coupons

DON'T buy something just because you have a coupon—unless it's super-delicious ice cream or chocolate (our weaknesses). We once met a woman who was so compulsive that her whole garage was dedicated to storing all the stuff she bought with coupons. She'd buy five Sunday newspapers and go to the store five or six times each week, and it came to the point where she was trying to sell off the excess at a garage sale. We don't advocate such compulsive couponing.

DO clip coupons for categories or items that you normally purchase. Buy luxury items only if they are on sale and combining the sale with a coupon means they cost only a few cents. But there are some months when our schedule is so full that we don't have time to do coupons. You've got to weigh the value of the savings against valuing your family.

6. Buy a Freezer

DON'T buy a freezer through one of those home-delivery food services. You'll pay three times the going price for the freezer and oftentimes more for the food.

DO put the word out to friends and family and ask around. You may just find someone with an unplugged, not-in-use freezer they're willing to give away. We started small with a 9-cubic-foot freezer when there were just three in our family. We've since graduated to a 27-cubic-foot monster. The advantage of a freezer is that you can stock up and, if you're a careful shopper, can always be eating food that was purchased at the lowest possible price.

7. Stock Up on Sale items

DON'T go to the store several times each week. And don't just buy items you'll use this week.

DO learn to watch prices. We've changed our attitude from that of a consumer to that of a commodities buyer. When we find an item at our "buy" price, we stock up. So when the price for tomato sauce is eight for $1, we buy a case or two. If toilet paper is less than $.20 per roll, we stock up. This means we seldom run out of an item and have to make an "emergency" purchase at full retail price. It takes time to fully stock your pantry so you can always buy the least expensive items available, but eventually you'll be able to stay within your food budget and still stock up. Be careful, though, not to stock up on items that don't store well. Otherwise, your savings will end up in the trash—and that's not saving.

8. Eat Leftovers

DON'T turn your nose up at this suggestion. Unfortunately, some people think leftovers are good only for the trash. We disagree.

DO view leftovers as a time and money saver. When Annette prepares a meal, she usually makes several extra portions. A few days later, it's offered for a leftover lunch. Steve took these kinds of lunches to work for fifteen years and was the envy of the office lunchroom. Since we homeschool, our kids are always home for lunch, so consuming leftovers is easily accomplished. Just beware of the fights and hurt feelings that may occur when a hotly desired leftover has only one serving left! It's an excellent opportunity to teach the finer points of negotiating and trading.

9. **Picky Eaters**

DON'T allow them! Period!

DO encourage kids—and spouses, for that matter—to try everything that is served. We have a three-bite rule at our house. Steve has learned to "enjoy" beets, even though he used to think they tasted like "dirt." Now he thinks they taste like "sweet dirt." As parents, we have to set the example. Realize that some experts say it takes at least fifteen exposures to a new food to acquire a taste for it. Start this habit when your kids are young and you'll never regret it.

> ## WHAT THE KIDS SAY
>
> Joseph, fourteen, says, "Sometimes my parents' money-saving ideas get a little crazy. Like the time I woke up the morning after they had gone grocery shopping and I found a tower of cereal boxes stacked in the kitchen—it reached almost to the ceiling! I guess they found a great deal because they bought about thirty of them. When I asked why they bought so many, my parents told me that they got a smokin' deal—only one dollar per box after coupons. Mmm . . . it was really good stuff and lasted about five months!"

10. **Seasonal Produce**

DON'T just buy what looks good in the produce section regardless of the price.

DO learn which fruits and veggies are in season, and only purchase when they are at their lowest prices. With the availability of produce imported from other countries, you can buy apples or oranges all year long, but you'll find the best prices when local or domestic produce providers are selling their in-season fruit to local grocers. In our area, we watch carefully for the one week in the summer when blueberries are at their lowest price. When they are—you guessed it—we purchase several pounds and freeze them in plastic storage bags to be used throughout the next year. Seasonal prices usually follow this pattern:

Summer: melons, peaches, nectarines, apricots, plums
Fall: apples
Winter: citrus
Spring: strawberries, artichokes, asparagus

Better yet, plant fruit and nut trees, and put in a garden if you have space. You'll love being able to go out and pick your own fresh produce.

You can save money on food: all you need is the desire to save money and the willingness to try new ideas. Walk into the store with eyes wide open, armed with the knowledge of what retailers are expecting you to do. Then . . . do what's best for you and your family. Make a list, check it twice. Bring your coupons. Evaluate your purchases. Know your prices. Minimize your trips to the store. If you do happen to come across a manager's special or unadvertised deal, stock up prudently. And enjoy the meal!

WHAT YOU CAN DO NOW ABOUT GROCERIES

TIMID MOUSE:

Reduce your trips to the store from several to one each week. Plan a simple menu for one week's worth of dinners.

WISE OWL:

Try to extend your grocery shopping to once every two weeks. Start planning a list of meals for breakfast, lunch, and dinner. Try your hand at matching coupons with sale items for maximized savings.

AMAZING ANT:

Do all of the above plus research, and buy a freezer so you can start stocking up on sale items. Start cooking from scratch—you'll be amazed at how inexpensive, healthy, and rewarding it can be. When you do cook, make extra to be served as leftovers or taken to work for lunch.

THREE

BUDGETING:

The Cornerstone of Family Finances

How can you pay off a house in nine years on a limited income? How can you pay cash for all of your cars? How can you completely remodel a kitchen without a home equity loan? The budget system we have used and fine-tuned since 1982 has been *the* tool that has helped us reach all of these incredible goals and hundreds more.

Businesses realize the importance of having a plan for all the money they earn and spend. Have you ever heard of a corporation that didn't have a budget for every department within the company? If you have, it probably wasn't a profitable one. Why should our families be any different?

This chapter is one of the most important in the entire book. We're going to redefine the word *budget* and show you how using a living and active budgeting system will help you keep thousands of dollars each year in your pocket, dollars that might otherwise just be frittered away. After all, we can show you hundreds of ways to save money, but if you have no way of managing the money you've saved, chances are all of your gains will evaporate.

But in order to do so, we aren't going to profile any one family's budget or give you recommended dollar amounts for spending in various areas. While you might think this would be helpful, there are a couple of reasons why we won't do it. First, if we give you a specific number for a spending category, such as recreation expenses, one group of people may think that the recommended number is way too much money and that any person spending that much just isn't frugal in the least. Then there would be a second group of people who would choke on that number and say, "There's no way that we could spend that little and still enjoy ourselves. We just aren't willing to live a life of deprivation." We've experienced these reactions as we've presented our seminars, and we don't want to prevent anyone from embracing the principles we are going to present. The bottom line is that you need to spend less than 100 percent of your take-home pay.

NO, NO, NOT A BUDGET! IT'S TOO RESTRICTIVE!

Very few people have been instructed in how to manage household finances. Most of us were just thrown into the pool and told to swim. No instruction, no training—no hope. But there is no mystery to household financial management, and you don't need to be a trained financial professional to find success. We certainly don't have that kind of background; we're just everyday people who found a better way to manage money on a day-to-day basis. The way we handle our accounts may not work for everyone, but we hope you can take a few of the principles we share here and use them to develop your own way of tracking income and controlling spending. Every little bit helps—any effort you make to manage your money will start producing immediate dividends.

We understand that there are many misconceptions about budgeting, and several mental roadblocks to overcome. Here are four of the more common myths we've heard:

Myth 1: *"We just don't make enough money to budget!"*

We say: Even the little you have can be stretched so much further than you ever thought.

Myth 2: *"Our income is so erratic that budgeting is impossible!"*

We say: Budgeting is the perfect tool to smooth out the peaks and valleys of your income.

Myth 3: *"I don't need to write it down, I've got it all in my head."*

We say: A written plan takes spending out of the ethereal ("Well, I think I can afford this") and puts it down right there in front of your eyes, in black and white ("I know I've got the money saved for this"). Numbers don't lie.

Myth 4: *"Oh, we gave budgeting a try. It was too restrictive and just didn't work for us."*

We say: Rather than being restrictive, a written and regularly maintained budget will provide you with financial relief, security, and freedom.

If you can overcome these hurdles, you will start to see that it is possible to live—and live well—on a budget. But it does take dedication. In numerous interviews, reporters have asked how we've accomplished so much while spending so little. They're looking for some sort of magic formula. Well, unfortunately there is no magic. What we've done is a result of committing to a system. Because we've employed a budgeting system since day one of our marriage, we've had years to practice and fine-tune the management of our living expenses. And even though our income has fluctuated greatly over the years (over twenty-four years it averages around $45,000), we have limited our monthly expenses to establish a lean yet comfortable lifestyle. During the plentiful earning years, rather than raise our standard of living, we were able to pay off mortgage debt, invest in retirement savings, and put aside emergency funds (see Chapter 13: Savings and Investments for more details). Our budgeting system has allowed us to survive wild swings in income, reach our goals, and still have lots of fun.

Most people can benefit from a budget or spending plan. It has been said that 5 percent of the people are so frugal they'll never spend all the money they earn. Another 5 percent earn so much, they couldn't possibly spend it all—Bill Gates and Oprah Winfrey fit this category. Then there's the 90 percent of us who are left, and we need a system that helps us save, stretch, and spend wisely.

MONEY AND EMOTIONS

Without a budget, your bank account is constantly bombarded by unexpected expenses: kids' school clothes, escrow account deficits, auto repairs, doctor or dentist visits, Christmas and birthday presents, credit card bills, and vacations. It's really discouraging, and it often leads to fear, stress, arguments, and strained relationships. Having a written spending plan allows you to prepare for almost all of these expenses and more, in advance. This will eliminate most of the conflicts and negative emotions that are tied to money.

An added bonus to having a budget is that it produces unity. We've seen many marriages where spending money has become a kind of power struggle: "Well, if he's going to buy a boat, then I'm going to buy a new bedroom set!" For others, spending or shopping is a salve for emotional wounds. We aren't qualified to help heal the past emotional hurts, but we can promise you that knowing where you are financially and having control of your spending will bring peace and more security than you can imagine.

HOW AMERICA'S CHEAPEST FAMILY'S BUDGET WORKS

A family budget isn't like a New Year's resolution, written once and then stashed away on some shelf to gather dust. And it's not like some business budgets, based on projections and then reevaluated six months later. An effective family budget is a live, functioning tool, continually updated, consulted, and adjusted

Our Budget Defined

Budgeting, in our world, is taking the money we have and saving it in a number of separate categories in advance of planned and unplanned expenses. This type of plan eliminates 90 percent of the financial emergencies that commonly befall a family.

as needs change. It keeps you on track while controlling your spending. It is tailored to your family's habits and lifestyle. Again, we aren't going to give you specific dollar figures for setting up a budget. We know that because every family's financial priorities are different, there is no one budget that everyone should use. But the principles we'll share with you about setting up a budget will work for everyone.

The basic premise of our budget system is saving predetermined amounts of money from every paycheck (and other sources of income) in advance of upcoming expenses. For example, our auto insurance is due every six months and costs about $900. In anticipation of paying that bill every May and November, we set aside $75 every two weeks into our auto insurance account, which is really just a division of our checking account kept on paper.

Saving for vacation is a more enjoyable illustration. According to the American Automobile Association (AAA), the average daily amount that a family of four will spend on vacation for food and lodging is about $254. Multiply that by seven days and you have a total of $1,778. Of course, there are other expenses that need to be calculated, but for simplicity's sake, let's round this vacation figure up to $2,400. That's a big chunk of change to spend in one week. What choices do we have? Well, the average American puts that amount on his or her handy-dandy credit card and pays for that vacation for the following twelve to eighteen months. But who wants to be average? Not us. We set aside about $100 every two weeks into our vacation budget account (again, just a paper division of our checking account, not a separate account in the bank). When it's time to hit the road, the money is already in the bank, and we are ready to have a great time (see Chapter 11: Vacations).

But it wasn't always this way. In 1981, just before Steve proposed to Annette, he decided to take a motorcycle trip to Colorado. Two days before he was scheduled to take off, he received an unexpected bill for his motorcycle insurance. Draining his savings account to pay the bill, he went on his way to Colorado. That's not a very disciplined (or wise) way to live. Steve could have made a financial emergency like this disappear with a system that accumulates money before expenses appear.

THE BUDGET BOOK

We divide our budget into twenty separate categories, or accounts. Early in our marriage, when life was simple, we had eight accounts, but as our lives have grown more complicated our budget has expanded as well. We try to anticipate 98 percent of our annual expenses—it's not as hard as it sounds. Listed below are a number of possible budget categories that you might include in your family's budget. We can't cover every possible spending category, so we'll just present the most common ones that we've seen.

- Allowances (cash for your wallet)
- Auto: gas/maintenance
- Auto: insurance/registration, taxes, and/or license
- Business expenses (reimbursed and unreimbursed)
- Charitable giving
- Clothing
- College tuition and books
- Food
- Gifts
- Haircuts
- Home repair
- Impound or escrow (property taxes and homeowner's insurance)
- Kids' activities/day care
- Life insurance
- Medical expenses
- Medical insurance
- Miscellaneous (magazine subscriptions, dry cleaning, and postage)
- Mortgage
- Paycheck holding (this account is used to help you budget on a fluctuating income; see the Q&A on pages 56-60)
- Pet food/supplies (including licensing and immunizations)
- Recreation (eating out, activities, cable TV, and/or Internet access)

· Savings
· School supplies/curriculum
· Utilities (electricity, gas, home phone, cell phone, and water)
· Vacation

We keep track of it all in a large three-ring binder with pocketed pages. Each pocket contains one or two individual account sheets (see the Money Tracker sheet on page 62) on which we track the spending of money we have already saved for that particular category. Basically, each sheet is an account register for one expense category. If you took the amount in each of our twenty budget categories and added them together, it would equal our checkbook balance.

We've found that it's easier to know if we have enough money for various expenses if we keep track of the individual categories, rather than looking at the larger balance in the checkbook. If we looked at the total in the checkbook, we might be tempted to think we have enough money for a cruise to the Bahamas or some type of large home improvement project! But since we only look at the total amount contained in our vacation or home repair account, we see a more realistic—if not conservative—total. We also know that the rest of the money in the other budget accounts is there for similar purposes—to be spent on those specific needs and goals. We feel secure in knowing what we can and can't spend.

Our home repair account sheet, for example, shows us how much money we have socked away for small projects around the home, and whether we can afford something like a new garage door opener. This actually happened: our garage door stopped moving—about halfway up. This made getting the cars in and out of the garage a bit difficult. Steve did some research and priced new units, which cost between $150 and $200, and the parts to repair the existing one, about $35. We had enough money in the home repair account to buy a new garage door opener, but it would have left the account pretty lean. So he decided to spend $35 and get his hands greasy repairing the existing one.

With this budgeting system, we maintain a checkbook balance that's greater than just a couple of paychecks. Rather, it holds the accumulated total of several months of saved homeowner's insurance, property taxes, auto insurance, unspent clothing money, and so on.

We're also careful to not allow our "overhead" (monthly obligations) to creep up. If we want to purchase an expensive item, such as a car or new kitchen, we don't finance it, which would increase our overhead with a monthly payment. We save for the item in advance, negotiate the best deal possible, and pay cash.

One final key point: we separate fixed and fluctuating expenses. An example would be two auto budget accounts. The first is for fixed auto expenses, such as auto insurance, license fees and taxes, and a car payment (if you have one). We want to protect this money, so it is kept separate. The second auto budget account is for fluctuating expenses, such as auto maintenance and gas (speaking of gas, the skyrocketing price of fuel has caused us to reevaluate our budget and slightly reduce the money we put into some other categories so we have more for this one). When a car needs maintenance, we know exactly how much is available to repair it. If all of the auto money had been combined, we might inadvertently spend insurance money on car repairs. Not a good idea.

How It Works

This system takes some effort, but as with any discipline, after a while it becomes second nature and produces freedom. We sit together twice a month (on the fifteenth and thirtieth) and reconcile, or "do the budget." We've tried to extend the interval—for example, to once a month—but we end up with more discrepancies and the process takes longer. Depending on paycheck cycles, some people might choose to do their budgets every two weeks instead of twice a month.

Record Every Expense. We share one checking account; Annette carries the master register in her purse. This habit started years ago when she did the majority of the shopping and errands while Steve was at work. Steve carried a bank debit card and a single counter check for emergencies—kind of like Barney Fife's single bullet in his shirt pocket. Later, when

Steve moved into sales and was driving all over the city, he would run a few errands between appointments. He then carried a pad of checks and a second checkbook register to record his transactions. When we do the budget, we transfer items from Steve's register into the master register, then we total everything. All of our expenses are paid out of our checking account, so tracking each payment is easy.

Which Account. Next we identify each expense with a two-letter code (in our checkbook register) that indicates which account it will be taken from. Every expense must come from a specific account—we have no miscellaneous or catchall account. So all clothing-related expenses are marked with *CL,* and utility expenses such as electricity and gas are marked with *UT.* When we make a purchase we ask ourselves, "Which account is this coming from?"—assigning categories makes doing the budget quicker. For example, when Steve was fixing the garage door, he recorded the expense in the checkbook as *HR*—which means the expense came out of our home repair account.

Out and Then In. We divide the next process into two steps because it reduces our math errors. Yes, we do make them . . . with regularity.

The first step is called the "out." We take the expenses recorded in the checkbook *out* of the budget sheets. As each expense is recorded on the appropriate individual account sheet, it receives a check mark in the checkbook register, indicating that it has been recorded in the budget. We total each account sheet and then compare the total of all twenty of our accounts to the checkbook register; they must balance.

Once we've balanced the "out," then it's time for the "in"—that is, putting the money from our paycheck(s) *into* the budget. We divide the current paycheck into predetermined amounts—for example, $75 for auto insurance, $100 for vacation, and so on—and record that amount on each account sheet. Then we total all twenty accounts again. When it all balances, we rest and celebrate.

It may sound arduous, but the peace we experience knowing that our current and future expenses are all covered allows us to enjoy what we have—whether it be little or much.

WORKING TOGETHER

We've seen numerous examples of the husband totally abdicating the family finances and the wife picking them up by default. Many men say that their wives are better at handling financial details than they are. We say, tough! It's just not right. Even if the wife is better at handling money, both husband and wife ought to be involved in managing the household budget.

If you need help learning to work together on your finances, visit Crown Financial Ministries' Web site at Crown.org or call (800) 722-1976. They have free volunteer counselors available in every state.

Another reason for both spouses to be involved is in case one spouse dies. If both have handled the finances, the surviving spouse doesn't have the stress of learning to manage the household while dealing with grief.

HOW TO START YOUR OWN BUDGET

Make a copy of the Household Budget Work Sheet on page 63. This is a work sheet that will help you determine your monthly income and how it balances against all of your expenses. It is the first step in implementing a budget that is custom-tailored to your needs. You'll probably need to do a little research to fill in some of the categories, to figure out how much you spend each month on clothing, groceries, and so forth. Old checkbook registers, credit card statements, and receipts can help. Do a little research, and then put down your best estimate.

Over time, as the budget is employed, the amounts will become absolutely and unarguably clear. We've helped some friends who swore that they only spent $150 each month to feed their family of three. As we worked with them over a period of several months, it became painfully obvious that their food budget was seriously in need of additional funding. This is one of the wonderful things about our system: as you realize a need such as this, you can simply adjust the amounts in your budget. Of course, all the individual account allocations must not exceed your monthly income .

Other Methods

Doing a budget on paper isn't the only way. Some people like using computer-based budget programs. These are fine if you update them regularly. The drawbacks are that they require you to have a computer, and usually only one person can do the work. We've used Quicken and did a time test comparing it with our paper budget. It was a little faster, but not much. The advantage we've found in our paper system is that it can be taken to Little League games or brought in the car for road trips—no power required.

Another less complex option is using a cash envelope system for some or all of your expenses. To make it work, you set aside predetermined amounts of cash in envelopes for those areas in which you most often overspend—usually food, recreation, and clothes. Each time you get paid, you take your paycheck to the bank and ask for a predetermined amount of money in cash. That money is put into the individual envelopes and is spent as needed. You'll still leave money in the bank for regularly occurring fixed expenses such as rent or mortgage, auto insurance, utilities, and others.

The value of using cash in envelopes is that it helps people to realize the connection between money and material goods. When cash is used, oftentimes people think twice about whether they should make a purchase or not. When you run out of cash in a particular envelope, it gives you a realistic visual message: "When the money's gone, the spending stops!"

We started our budget this way in 1982, but we soon realized that even on $838 take-home pay each month, we were accumulating what we considered a small fortune in cash that we needed to hide in our apartment. The idea of someone breaking in and stealing our nest egg just wasn't a pretty thought. That's when we started utilizing the individual account sheets and keeping the money in the bank.

Teamwork

Because we work on the budget together, we both see the totals in the accounts, and work as a team to make it balance. It's really a great bonding time. If you're a single parent, you may want to confide in a friend or relative who can encourage you on this journey. If your kids are a little older, involving them can be a great way to build family unity, teach them to manage money, and get rid of the "gimmes."

The Bottom-Line Benefits

Creating a budget really helps you track and reach goals step by step. Checking your accounts every two weeks lets you see how every dollar helps when you're making progress toward paying off debt or accumulating money for a special event or project.

Following a budgeting system can help most of us, no matter what our financial situation. If you're living paycheck to paycheck, this system is an invaluable tool to get out of that vicious cycle. If you have all your expenses covered or have been blessed with an excess, having a tool to manage it will help make the money go further than you dreamed possible.

In the next section we'll detail how to start the budgeting system with minimal cash on hand and introduce you to a couple who actually started their budget with a negative balance in the bank.

THE EMERGENCY ROOM: CREATING A BUDGET WHEN MONEY IS TIGHT

We hope we've persuaded you that a budget will help your financial situation and bring stability to your household. But where do you start? Do you pull money from savings? Do you sell a car? With bills piling up and hardly anything in the checking account, how can you make it happen?

Meet Paul and Sara (not their real names), friends we helped several years ago. When we first met them, their checking account balance was *negative* $393. (They had paid several bills on March 3, anticipating a paycheck on March 9.) Not the best way to start a budget. But their hearts were willing, so we wheeled them into America's Cheapest Family's "emergency room." Sure, it might sound corny, but we use the emergency room analogy because most people can relate to what happens there.

Step 1: Stop the bleeding, get the vital signs, and determine the problem.

Step 2: Stabilize the patient—set broken bones, etc.

Step 3: Recovery and rehabilitation.

One reminder about the emergency room: the doctor can't be concerned about the patient enjoying the procedure! He's got a life to save, and he knows a fully recovered patient always feels much better. The same thing applies to the process we are going to describe. It can be painful, tedious, and at times heart-rending. But if you follow the doctor's instructions, you'll be well on your way to a full recovery.

Vital Signs

Paul and Sara's vital signs weren't good, but they didn't even know it. They suffered from "overspenditis." Today, people can become infected with this condition from watching too much television, reading too many magazines and catalogs, or hanging out with free-spending friends. Unknowingly, Paul and Sara had been lured into believing that they needed to have and do all the things they saw their friends doing—whether or not the money was there. This became clearly evident when they filled out the Household Budget Work Sheet. According to their "conservative figures," they were overspending "just $150 each month." When Steve pulled out the calculator and showed them that their monthly overspending would equal $1,800 each year, and that in ten years they would owe $18,000 more, their jaws dropped.

This wasn't the only problem. In seventeen years of marriage, they'd accumulated $7,500 worth of consumer debt in the form of a consolidation loan and an appliance they purchased with a credit card. They had a small amount of savings—about $300 from some overtime work—that Paul was hoping someday would grow into enough for a European vacation. And they'd saved another $525 from a tax refund and garage sale proceeds, planning to use this money toward a $1,000 vacation with friends just five months away. They also had two teenagers very close to college age—but they had no college savings at all. Their net monthly take-home pay was $2,780. They knew they were in trouble, but they didn't know what to do. The stress was so great that neither Paul nor Sara was sleeping at night.

Once we had their vital signs from their list of debts and the completed Household Budget Work Sheet, we went right to work, pencils scribbling, numbers flying, questioning, planning, and erasing. Paul and Sara stared in stunned silence as we consulted and discussed their case. They hadn't realized that they were so sick. We gave them hope that recovery was very possible and explained how our budgeting system worked.

But before we could set them up with a working budget, we had to stop the situation from getting worse, and get them caught up on their bills. Here's what we recommended to get Paul and Sara stabilized.

Splint and Stabilize

Because their checkbook balance was negative, we needed to put some restrictions on them. A splint prevents freedom of movement but also promotes healing. It is only used until the broken bone is strong enough to handle the weight of everyday life. In Paul and Sara's case, they agreed to stop all unnecessary spending for a while. This spending restriction lasted about six weeks, during which time they paid only the necessary bills that we all determined were most pressing. Examples were their mortgage, gasoline credit card bills, the phone bill, their orthodontist's monthly payment, and their consolidation loan.

The Recovery Starts: Liquidate and Accumulate

When they left our home that first night, they were dazed but hopeful. We had helped them identify other sources of readily available cash (besides Paul's paycheck) that they would try to gather before the next meeting. Over the next week, a penny jar was liquidated, a business expense was collected, and prescription receipts were turned in to Paul's employer for reimbursement. All told, they brought in about $150. It wasn't much, but it was a good exercise in paying attention to the little things, and at this point in their recovery it helped stretch their next paycheck.

This was all that Paul and Sara could do, but you might have other options, including selling large assets such as musical instruments, art, sports equipment, boats, motorcycles, and the like. You can also return unused items to the store from which they were purchased: another friend we helped went through her drawers and found about $150 worth of new clothes, with the price tags still on them (though many stores today will not accept returned merchandise unless you have your receipt).

The Rehab Plan

The next time we met, we reviewed Paul's paycheck stub to see if there were deductions being made that could be stopped temporarily to free up cash. Then we evaluated the amount of taxes that were being withheld. When finances are tight, allowing Uncle Sam to borrow your money until after April 15 just isn't a good idea. If you normally receive a large tax refund, meet with your payroll administrator and ask about reducing the taxes you have withheld from your paycheck so that the extra money can be funneled into your monthly budget.

Next we helped them list all their bills and due dates to determine which would need to be paid with the next paycheck they'd receive. Then we made a paycheck allocation plan. Paul would receive $1,390, but we needed to subtract the checkbook deficit of $393 and add the $150 in cash we had scrounged. We ended up with a total of $1,147 to

PAYCHECK ALLOCATION

BALANCES AND CATEGORIES		INSTRUCTIONS
STARTING BALANCE	$1147.00	
Charitable Giving	-100.00	(Charitable giving was a nonnegotiable item for Paul and Sara)
BALANCE	$1047.00	
½ of House Payment	-450.00	(The second half will come from the next paycheck)
BALANCE	$597.00	
½ of Monthly Utilities	-100.00	(Pay the current phone bill and save for next bill)
BALANCE	$497.00	
Food	-50.00	(Use food in house)
BALANCE	$447.00	
Auto	-120.00	(Gas $40, gas cards $80) (Most auto $ will go to gas cards 1 and 2 for the first two paychecks)
BALANCE	$327.00	
Debt	-168.00	(½ of consolidation and appliance loans)
BALANCE	$159.00	
Orthodontist	-75.00	(½ of balance due)
BALANCE	$84.00	
Department Store, 1	-15.00	(Minimum payment)
BALANCE	$69.00	
Miscellaneous	-25.00	(For unexpected expenses)
ENDING BALANCE	$44.00	(For newspapers or recreation)

work with. We made sure that every dollar was allocated somewhere, and we left them just enough ($44) for recreation so they wouldn't feel totally deprived.

See the table above for how we divided up their first paycheck.

We explained the strategy and helped them set up the Money Tracker account sheets for each category (see page 62). As a result of allocating the paycheck to the individual account sheets, each account now had a positive balance. And the total of their individual account sheets equaled the balance in their checkbook.

After getting Paul and Sara caught up on their bills, our focus changed to funding all of their monthly budget categories. There are several ways to do this. If you've got money in a savings account, you can use it to fund all of your budget categories (within your checking account) to their monthly levels. Once that's done, you can start the cycle of regular paycheck deposits to each category. With every paycheck you allocate one-half of each budget category's monthly amount. But if you don't have a chunk of cash to transplant into your budget, then you'll have to make the transition in several stages, just like Paul and Sara.

Over the next few weeks we repeated this exercise with Paul and Sara, but with less strain and worry. Because we met just prior to each paycheck, they knew exactly what to do with the money when it arrived. We challenged a few of their "sacred cows," those "wants" that they were having a tough time letting go of, such as the daily newspaper and the European vacation. Eventually they realized that sacrificing those things now would help improve their financial picture faster.

As their financial therapy continued, their expressions changed from apprehensive—thinking they'd have to live like paupers forever—to hopeful. They could see that with some careful planning, they could live on less, pay all their bills, and start putting more money into savings.

Drastic Measures

Don't worry if your situation is more dire than Paul and Sara's—we've seen some that are. You just need to be open to solutions. When an abandoned mom with three young kids and virtually no income came to us, we contacted a few local food banks, where she was given several bags of food, and then we helped her get signed up for food stamps. If you're serious about making your budget and debt reduction plan work, using a food bank is a reasonable option. (There may be income restrictions or limits on the number of times you can visit specific food banks each year.) Just remember that with determination, planning, and a little encouragement, this kind of assistance will only be temporary. Before the end of our first meeting with this mom, Annette had raided our pantry and filled a couple of grocery bags with two days' worth of food. (This kind of giving is one of the reasons we believe in stocking up when we shop.)

Rehab Exercises

Each time we met with Paul and Sara, we reviewed their finances, balanced their budget with their checkbook, and discussed assignments for the next pay period. Some of this homework might have included getting new quotes for auto or homeowner's insurance, changing automatic savings deductions to provide more cash for debt repayment, canceling subscriptions, and finding free recreation ideas for a date night.

You too can use your regular budgeting sessions to plan what you can do during the next pay period to improve your financial situation. We still do this for our own finances—in 2004, we finished researching health insurance and home refinancing options. It took many months to make a decision, but it was worth the effort. With each goal you reach you'll feel less like an accident victim in shock and more like an Olympic gold medalist.

A Full Recovery

Paul and Sara's story has a happy ending. After a few months of focusing on their finances and learning to manage their spending, Sara took a part-time job. Her extra income went to eliminating debt and building savings. About eighteen months later, they called us to say that all their debt had been paid off. To celebrate, they were taking the kids on a weekend jaunt to Disneyland—and yes, they had the cash saved. And, believe it or not, a few years later they actually did take that trip to Europe. How's that for a recovery? They went from the emergency room to a room with a view!

HELPFUL RESOURCES

If you're feeling totally overwhelmed and can't work through this on your own, call Crown Financial Ministries at (800) 722-1976 and ask for the name of a trained volunteer budget counselor in your area—there is no charge for their services. If you need help with debt manage-

ment, contact Money Management International at (866) 889-9347—
the initial consultation is free. They charge a small fee if you enter into
an agreement with them; the average monthly fee is about $25.

ANSWERS TO COMMON HOUSEHOLD BUDGETING QUESTIONS

There will always be personal questions about making a household
budget work ("Yes, that makes sense, but what about *my* situation?").
Here are a few that we've received over the years as we've written on the
subject and spoken at seminars.

Q: In your budget system, should I physically put cash aside into a bunch of different envelopes or is it just on paper?

—**Bewildered Budgeter**

A: Dear Bewildered,

It depends on how you have set up your budget. If you use cash envelopes, then you should divide your money and physically put it into
various account envelopes. Then when it's time to pay bills, pull cash
from the relevant accounts. Leave unspent money in its specific envelope. Each pay period, add a predetermined amount of cash to each envelope. Over time you may find that you have a large accumulation of
cash sitting in the envelopes—clothing, for example. Many people buy
clothes a few times each year. So if you are putting $40 each pay period
into your clothing envelope and not spending anything, in three
months' time you should have accumulated about $240. You may want
to consider putting larger accumulations in the bank and using the
Money Tracker sheets.

If you track funds on paper as we do, keep the money in one
checking account. Each pay period, you subtract every expense in your
checkbook from the account sheet of the relevant category, then add
your predetermined paycheck allocation to each category. The total of
all your accounts should equal the checkbook total.

Q: How do you budget on a fluctuating income?

—Ups and Downs in Utica

A: Dear Ups,

We've lived with a fluctuating income for many years. We base our monthly budget on a low average of our income. We've tracked earnings over several years to arrive at this number.

In the months when our income is higher, we put the extra money into a budget category called "paycheck holding." Then we can draw upon it during months when we don't earn enough to fill our budget categories.

We keep several optional budget categories at the back end of our budget. If we have money, we fund them; if not, we don't. These include gifts and money for kids' sports and lessons.

As we mentioned earlier, we're also careful not to allow our overhead to creep up. We avoid financing new purchases, which would increase our overhead with a new monthly payment. If we want to purchase an expensive item, such as a car or new kitchen, we don't finance it. Instead, we save for the item in advance, negotiate the best deal possible, and pay cash.

On a fluctuating income, using a budget allows you to determine if you are free to spend the excess money you earn.

Q: I read about you in the August 2004 *Good Housekeeping* magazine. I am a stay-at-home mom and want to save money. I read that you paid off your first house in nine years. How on earth did you pay off your house mortgage so quickly? Did you simply pay as much as you could each month?

—Principled Payer

A: Dear Principled,

You ask a very good question. Paying off a mortgage early isn't easy, but it is good. Because we have a very detailed budget and we review it every two weeks, it helps keep us on track to reach big goals like this.

First of all, we keep our overhead low and don't spend all that we earn. Living within our means has become a lifestyle and we enjoy the freedom it brings.

Second, we pay extra when we can. We started years ago by paying just an extra $2 toward principal each month, and as our income increased and as we received unexpected bonuses or other money, the extra payments soon grew to be $200. But you have to be careful about "paying as much as you can," because it's crucial that you have all of your budget categories funded and are putting money regularly in savings. A budget is critically important in helping you decide how much extra you can afford to pay each month.

As you close in on the final few thousand dollars, you'll reach a point where most other goals pale in the light of finally hitting the milestone of being mortgage-free.

Q: Many financial experts advocate spouses keeping money in separate checking accounts to help them manage their household income and spending. My husband and I tried that; however, because I work at a seasonal job, before long I was thousands of dollars in debt while trying to cover my portion of the expenses. What do you say?

—Vexed in Virginia

A: Dear Vexed,

A husband and wife working as a team will always fare better than if they go it alone. In addition, you'll build a stronger marriage when you work on your financial goals together. Not only does short- and long-term goal setting bond you, but as you reach goals, the enthusiasm is contagious. You'll accomplish more than you ever dreamed possible.

Unfortunately, there are a couple of exceptions to our "working together" rule. We hate to write about this, because so much good comes from managing finances as a team, but it must be said.

Boys' toys. Some men just can't resist buying toys. And some of the worst overspending we've seen occurs when a man who is the sole breadwinner has an insatiable desire to possess more "things" without regard to his family's income. If there is no hope of restraining Mr. Super-Spender, then we recommend putting a limited amount of money into a separate checking account each month for his whims, with no overdraft protection (this will, we hope, serve as a reminder to spend within his limits). This isn't ideal, but if it helps you cover the household essentials, then it must be done.

The Lucy syndrome. In several episodes of the *I Love Lucy* television show, Lucy constantly overspent what Ricky earned. In one of the most memorable scenes, she put all of the bills on a lazy Susan in the middle of her kitchen table and then gave the lazy Susan a spin. Any bills that stayed on would be paid; all the rest would have to wait. If, like Lucy, a wife has a hard time staying within the boundaries of a spending plan and is constantly overspending the limits, we see two solutions.

One is a separate checking account at a different bank used to cover the expenses she is responsible for (again, with no overdraft protection). It's a drastic step and will usually fail because anyone who won't stay within personal limits will most likely do the same with the limits of a checking account.

Another, better option is to use cash envelopes. Set aside specific, reasonable amounts of money each week for groceries, clothes, and recreation. If any money is left at the end of the pay period, simply add it to your next allotment in the envelope. Having tangible cash is often a cure for overspending. We've seen this method turn on the light for many a wayward spendthrift.

If you're having trouble working together on your finances, we recommend getting a knowledgeable third party involved (see the "Helpful Resources" section on page 55).

WHAT THE KIDS SAY ABOUT BUDGETING

Becky, twenty-one, recounts an interesting story about her budget system. "Just this last year, we had a producer and camera crew from a television station at our house shooting a documentary about our frugal family. At one point I was showing the producer my budget book—it's similar to my parents', only smaller. He started thumbing through the pages, looking at the various accounts I have and noting the balances: savings, $3,000; gifts, $200; and on and on. Now you've got to remember that this is a working professional, a guy almost thirty years old, wearing a $200 designer shirt, and probably earning at least ten times more than I earn working part-time. Finally he looked at me and said, 'I'm so embarrassed and financially irresponsible, you have more money than I do.' He continued, 'This is such a great system, everybody needs to know about it.' I was amazed at his curiosity, honesty, and enthusiasm."

Q: We really want to set up a budget that works, but I get paid on the fifteenth and the thirtieth of each month and my husband gets paid every other week. How can we make this work with your system?

—Get Us on the Same Page

A: Dear Page,

This isn't as hard as it seems. You may need to tighten your belt for about a month to build up some excess to fund your budget. But after that, simply putting both of your paychecks into a budget category called "paycheck holding" will probably solve this problem. This is what we do with our fluctuating income. All money—even bonuses, overtime, and unexpected gifts—is deposited into our checking account and later recorded into the paycheck holding category when we do the budget (the fifteenth and thirtieth of each month). On budget day, we simply take the amount we need out of paycheck holding—half of our total monthly budget allocation—and distribute it into the various accounts in our budget.

Once you master these techniques, you'll wonder how you ever survived living paycheck to paycheck. Budgeting is truly the cornerstone of family financial stability.

WHAT YOU CAN DO NOW ABOUT BUDGETING

TIMID MOUSE:

Fill out the Household Budget Work Sheet. Starting today, write down all of the money you spend each day. After one month, see how closely your actual expenses match up with the work sheet.

WISE OWL:

Set up cash envelopes for the three categories where you most commonly overspend. The most commonly overspent categories we've seen are food, clothing, and recreation. Make a game of it to see how much of your cash remains in the envelope at the start of the next pay period.

AMAZING ANT:

Develop and regularly use a paper or computerized budgeting system. Practice saving your money in advance of expenses. As you start reaching some of your incredible goals, be sure you tell others about the freedom and joy you've found in budgeting.

MONEY TRACKER

ACCOUNT NAME	MONTHLY AMOUNT	PAYCHECK AMOUNT	YEAR

DATE	NAME OF STORE/DESCRIPTION OF EXPENSE	WITHDRAW	CREDIT	TOTAL	MONTHS AVERAGE

HOUSEHOLD BUDGET WORK SHEET

DATE _____

INCOME	Pay 1 (after tax)	Pay 2 (after tax)	Other	Other	**NET INCOME**
PER MONTH	_____	_____	_____	_____	
PER PAYCHECK	_____	_____	_____	_____	

Put totals for each section in gray boxes

EXPENSES	PER PAYCHECK	PER MONTH
Charitable Giving		
Home-Fixed		
Mortgage/Rent	_____	_____
Insur/Taxes	_____	_____
Home-Variable		
Maint/Repair	_____	_____
Home Utilities		
Gas/Oil	_____	_____
Water/Trash	_____	_____
Electric	_____	_____
All Phone(s)	_____	_____
Groceries		
Car-Fixed		
Payments	_____	_____
License/Tax	_____	_____
Insurance	_____	_____
Car-Variable		
Maint/Repair	_____	_____
Gas/Oil	_____	_____
Debt Repayment		
Credit Cards	_____	_____
Other Loans	_____	_____
Other	_____	_____
Clothes		
Insurance		
Life	_____	_____
Medical/Dental	_____	_____
Presents		
Birthdays	_____	_____
Holidays	_____	_____
Wedding/Baby	_____	_____

EXPENSES	PER PAYCHECK	PER MONTH
Entertainment & Recreation		
Eating Out/Lunch	_____	_____
Sitters	_____	_____
Activities	_____	_____
Cable TV/Internet	_____	_____
Vacation/Trips		
Medical Care		
Doctor Visits	_____	_____
Dental Visits	_____	_____
Prescriptions	_____	_____
Kids' Expenses		
Day Care	_____	_____
Tuition	_____	_____
Club Fees	_____	_____
Lessons	_____	_____
Camp	_____	_____
Misc. Expenses		
Haircuts/Beauty	_____	_____
Allowances	_____	_____
Dry Cleaner	_____	_____
Subscriptions	_____	_____
Bank Charges	_____	_____
Postage	_____	_____
Savings		
Investment		

Income v. Expenses	PER PAYCHECK	PER MONTH
Net Income		
Expenses		
Surplus/Deficit		

FOUR

CARS:

Cutting Car Costs

Americans are in love with automobiles. They are cool, fast, and sleek, or perhaps comfortable and elegant, or maybe large enough to transport every kid in the neighborhood plus a dog or two. They meet our needs, they take us from point A to point B, and for some of us they enhance or become our identity.

In 1960, there were about 61 million cars and trucks in America. Today there are over 222 million. While it's true that cars today are built better and last longer, they also cost more than ever before. Cars are the second most expensive purchase most of us will ever make. According to the U.S. Bureau of Transportation Statistics, the average yearly cost for car ownership is about $6,500—this includes financing and sales tax, registration and license fees, and insurance. The Bureau calculates that it will cost you another $2,000 for gas and maintenance each year. Based on their annual statistics, since 2004 the total cost for automobile ownership is increasing about 8 percent each year. It adds up over time—some sources estimate that forty years of car ownership will cost you more than $500,000. Whew, that's a lot of money!

For many of us, car ownership is a necessity. But are we purchasing our vehicles based on transportation needs or for some other reason? We think cars are a great tool for convenient living, but if not carefully monitored, these money guzzlers can easily put a choke hold on your finances. Is there a way out of this? How can you save on car purchases? Can you buy a used car and not get burned? What do you do when your car dies and you have no money to fix it and no backup vehicle? As we share how we've purchased and maintained our cars since 1982, we hope we'll persuade you to pay less attention to the new car ads and more attention to finding ways to slash your transportation costs.

HOW AMERICA'S CHEAPEST FAMILY BUYS CARS

We purchase our autos "previously owned." That's right, we've always bought used cars—four of them from 1989 to 2001—and most of that time we've been a two-car family. (In the insurance section of this chapter you'll read about the fifth car we purchased as a result of an accident.) We've spent a total of $37,300, or $148.02 per month, for those four cars. Not only did we spend way less than the monthly U.S. national average, but because we drive older cars, we've spent less for insurance also.

And we've always paid cash. As newlyweds we were told, "You'll always have a car payment." We responded, "We'll see." Now, with more than twenty-four years of frugal living under our belts, and not one of them with a car payment, we can proclaim with confidence, "No way!"

But buying that first cash-only car required a bit of help. At the time, we owned an old Chevy Nova, and we used another car provided by the small design studio where Steve worked. When the company became financially unstable, he was laid off, and we lost our second car. We were earning so little at that time that we hadn't saved for a replacement. Fortunately, Annette's parents had a spare car, an old station wagon, and they loaned it to us for several months while we saved the additional money we needed to purchase another car. We kept the car maintained and gave it back to them in better condition than when we borrowed it. Having a supportive network of sharing family and friends was crucial to survival. When Steve got a new job, it came with a large increase in salary, but we kept our monthly expenses the same—except for adding a car replacement account to our budget. We made car payments to ourselves and received interest on them to boot, preparing ourselves for our next purchase. This is still a practice we continue to this day.

OUR SEVEN STEPS FOR BUYING A USED CAR

Step 1: Save First

Saving for car replacement is a regular part of our budgeting system. We've learned not to start looking at cars until almost all of the money is in the bank. The thinking behind this is that we might find a great deal and be tempted to buy on credit and accrue debt, rather than sticking with our cash-only policy.

Step 2: Research, Research, Research

Once we've got a good pile stashed away, we start the next step. Based on the amount of money we have saved in our replacement account, we do a quick review of the classified newspaper ads for vehicles in that price range. This will help us determine if we have saved enough money to purchase the year and make of a vehicle that we're interested in.

A few years back, we wanted to replace our 1986 Ford conversion van that seated seven. We'd saved a good amount of money over an eight-year period and started our research for a larger van that would seat twelve. Another thing we did was to check out the *Consumer Reports* used car reliability information for the year and model in which we were interested (most libraries have *Consumer Reports* available as reference materials). Next we called our faithful mechanic—who has serviced our van for ten years—to get his opinion on the types of vans that he'd serviced and those he thought were most reliable.

Step 3: **Comparison Shopping**

Because buying a car is a major expense requiring extensive research, we created a folder to contain all of the information we would collect. We scoured the newspaper classified ads, searched online classified ads, and purchased a few issues of the weekly publication *Auto Trader* (also available online at www.AutoTrader.com). Next we created a comparison sheet of several vehicles in our price range, which included the price, mileage, year, special features, and contact information of the seller.

Step 4: **Initial Phone Questions to Ask as You Research**

We called about the cars that interested us and asked several questions.

- Is it still available? (If the car has already sold, ask for the selling price and any other details the owner will share.)

- Are you the original owner?

- Why are you selling this vehicle?

- Does it have a clean title? (Avoid a salvage title, which indicates that the car has been considered a total loss by an insurance company, as a result of either theft or damage. Many people or repair shops purchase salvaged vehicles at auction and fix them up to resell.)

These questions gave us insight into the owner and the car and helped us determine if we wanted to move to the next step and actually see the vehicle in person. Learning about the integrity of the owner also may determine what may be true about the car. Ideally we like to purchase our used cars from the first or second owner, not someone who is buying and reselling cars as a hobby or side job.

While the classified ads showed us what cars are selling for in our area, the Kelley Blue Book (www.kbb.com) and National Automobile Dealers Association (NADA) (www.nada.com) Web sites show us what experts think the used car value should be. By inputting information about the year, make, model, and features of each car you are researching, the Web sites will calculate a price you should expect to pay either from a dealer or from a private party. Knowing these values can give you the upper hand in negotiations. For example, if someone wants to sell a car for $12,000 when the Kelley Blue Book says it's only worth $9,000, you might be able to get the owner to drop his price. It's also possible that if the asking price is significantly lower than the book price, you are missing some features or upgrades, or the mileage is relatively high.

After a few weeks of data gathering, we determined that we could afford a four- or five-year-old half-ton or three-quarter-ton full-size window van. Armed with this information and our classified research, we were ready to negotiate when we found a vehicle that we wanted to buy.

Step 5: **Inspecting the Car Before You Buy**

Once we found a van that fit our specifications, we made an appointment with the owner. Here is a short checklist of things that we take with us and look for when inspecting a potential purchase.

1. Bring any previous research and some blank paper to write notes on.

2. Always inspect the car in daylight. Scan down the sides of the car to look for paint irregularities or surface unevenness.

3. Check all engine fluids. Transmission fluid should be reddish in color but transparent. If it smells burnt, that's not a good sign. Oil should be golden in color; if it's black, that's not a good sign.

4. Bring a mirror to check the underside of the vehicle—look for oil or transmission fluid leaks on engine parts, and dents or scrape marks indicating that it has been driven over rough roads and may have sustained other damage.

5. Bring a strong magnet and a piece of cloth. Cover your magnet with the cloth and check out different areas on the car to

see if the magnet sticks to the metal. If it sticks in some areas and not in others, chances are that the car has sustained body damage and has been repaired with Bondo or some other filler material. If there are extensive repairs of this type, we usually pass on the car.

6. Bring a dollar bill. Open each door and hang your dollar bill over the top of the door and close it. As you pull on it, it should be snug. Check a couple of places on each door. If it slips out of some areas, then the car has probably been damaged.

7. Look at the tires for uneven wear. If the outside or inside edges are worn, it is an indication of alignment problems.

For more in-depth information on what to look for when checking out a used car, visit www.samarins.com/check.

When you're face-to-face with the owner, you'll want to ask him some probing questions as well, such as:

· How has the car been maintained? Can we see the maintenance records?

· What repairs have been done?

· Where has this car been driven—on the highway, off-road, or around town? (On the highway is best.)

· What accidents or damage has this car had? (The fewer, the better.)

· Can we see the title? (When we were helping our son John buy his first car—yes, he paid cash—we asked the owner about the title but didn't see it until we had agreed on a price. We knew from the inspection we performed that the car had been damaged, but we didn't know that it had a salvage title. Even though the car was in great shape, when we discovered the title status, we negotiated for a greater price reduction.)

If you're satisfied by the visual inspection and by the owner's answers, take the car on a ride. Listen for any unusual noises, such as clunking over bumps or squealing when turning the steering wheel. If the car pulls to the left or right on a flat surface, new tires could have recently been installed to cover up an alignment problem. If the test spin goes well, arrange for your mechanic to look at the car. It's worth spending $50 to $100 to have a thorough inspection and a non-emotional opinion.

Step 6: **Make an Offer They Can't Refuse**

If your mechanic gives the car a clean bill of health, it's time to talk about money. Don't be the first one to state a price. Go over any draw-backs your mechanic discovered or that you uncovered during your inspection and then ask the seller what his best price is. You can counter that offer based on your research and knowledge of the marketplace.

Step 7: **Drive Home**

How to pay for the car and transfer the title varies from state to state. We always get a cashier's check and have the title signed over to us.

THAT NEW-CAR SMELL

Some people just love that new-car smell (which is nothing more than a combination of toxic fumes emitted from new carpeting, upholstery, glues, and paints). If you are irresistibly drawn to purchase a new car, at the very least save for a big down payment and finance as little as possible. When the salesperson starts talking about what kind of monthly payment you want, change the subject and focus on the total price of the car. Don't be afraid to walk away if the dealership won't bargain with you.

Leasing

A word about leasing . . . *don't!* In our experience working with families and their finances, we haven't seen a single situation in which someone leased a car and came out of it ahead financially. Yes, it's easy to get into a leased car. Yes, the payments can be less than a purchase. But at the end of the lease, after you've spent thousands of dollars in payments, what will you have? Zero, nada, zilch. Actually, you will have something: more charges, such as for additional mileage, repairs, and any other fine-print items that you forgot about when you leased the car.

If you don't have cash for a car, consider taking that as a sign that you should search for other options—bicycles, public transportation, carpooling, or working closer to home. In our lives, we view the lack of money as a sign that the answer is No, or at least not right now.

HOW AMERICA'S CHEAPEST FAMILY SELLS CARS

Because we've never purchased a car from a dealer, we've also never traded in our well-used and well-loved cars. Here are seven things we've done on our own to sell our old cars quickly and for a fair price.

1. **Research Kelley Blue Book and NADA for a realistic price.** Also look in the newspaper classified ads and see what similar cars are being advertised for.

2. **Clean the car.** This may seem basic, but we can't tell you the number of dirty used cars we've looked at. A shiny, clean car just has more appeal.

3. **Run an ad.** Check out your smaller local newspapers. Often they have reduced-price or free classified ads.

4. **Park the car on a busy street corner.** Steve did this with our 1976 Chevy Nova. Unfortunately, he parked in a no-parking zone and received a $20 ticket. The car sold in one day, though, and we chalked the ticket price up as our advertising expense. Just make sure if you do this that you are *not* in a tow-away zone—that could get really expensive.

5. **Make a window sticker.** Steve typed up a sticker just like the dealers have, listing all the features for the car.

6. **Be brutally honest.** Each time we sell a car, we also include a list of known problems it has. Our 1984 Honda Accord had 250,000 miles on it when it was sold, and we knew that it was burning oil on one cylinder. We told the prospective owner, and he still bought it. Our price was fair—and our communication was too.

7. **Provide maintenance records.** We always hand over a file folder with all mileage and maintenance records. Buyers love to have the assurance that the car has been well maintained.

DRIVING DOWN YOUR COST OF CAR OWNERSHIP

If your monthly car expenses are so great that you can't pay for other necessities in your life, then you may need to take some drastic measures. Lowering your auto expenses may be a process that requires a couple of steps. Reducing your car payments by trading in your newer car for a used car could be an excellent first step—with the savings on your monthly payment, you can start conserving cash for your next car purchase. Just be careful. Some money experts advocate buying the cheapest car you can stand, to be instantly free of car debt. We disagree with that philosophy. Replacing your existing car with a $2,000 clunker will most likely mean thousands of dollars in repair bills that could eat you alive! A couple of exceptions to purchasing a $2,000 used car would be if someone you know (who took good care of the car) is trying to help you out, or if you find a single-owner car with very low mileage—possibly from someone in a retirement community. If you do decide to go with an older car, please be sure to have a reserve of between $1,000 and $2,000 for repairs. Keep reading and find out why.

Keepin' It Running

Ah, maintenance and repair. We've learned well how important they are. When we were first married in 1982, Annette owned an old Chevy

Nova, and Steve had a 1978 Yamaha 750 motorcycle. We sold the motorcycle to a friend in exchange for a bicycle, some cash, and help building some solid mahogany furniture that we still use. Most days Steve rode the bicycle two miles back and forth to work.

A year later, the Nova started overheating. We replaced the thermostat. What we didn't know was that the water pump was dying; we eventually blew the head gasket, and the car then needed major engine work. This began a long, four-week period in which we had no car at all. We had some money saved for car repair, but not enough to completely repair the engine. So we waited, researched, and worked at saving a bit more money for the repair. Some dear friends let us use their second car on weekends so we could run errands and get to church. It was a true test of living within our means and solving financial predicaments without resorting to using credit.

Based on this experience and information gleaned from *Consumer Reports,* we've determined that the average car requires $1,000–$1,500 per year for maintenance, and that's money above and beyond gasoline. With each paycheck we put aside money specifically earmarked for keeping our vehicles in tip-top shape. Having maintenance money and/or the ability to repair most problems has allowed us to keep our cars until they are fourteen to sixteen years old—and still sell them for at least $1,000.

The bottom line is that cars are expensive, and they aren't going to get any cheaper. Proceed with caution. Research. Then take good care of good ol' "Bessie" so that she can serve you for a long, long time.

GOT INSURANCE?

It was a sunny Saturday afternoon in January. Steve was driving home from baseball practice with Joseph, who was then twelve. As they approached an intersection, the traffic light turned yellow. It was impossible to stop our one-ton van in that short distance. Steve hit the horn as he and a driver on his right proceeded through the intersection on the yellow light. A young driver in a 2005 Chevy Malibu inched forward and proceeded to make his turn directly into the path of the oncoming vehicles. In that split second, tires screeched, metal buckled and crunched, glass flew in a hundred different directions, and our insurance coverage was sorely tested. We were thankful that many witnesses stayed to report to the police, and Steve was the only driver who didn't receive a citation. Fortunately, everyone involved in this accident walked away physically. But fiscally, it's quite a different story. If you're underprotected, a split second can change the course of your emotional and financial life forever.

Of the three vehicles involved in our accident, two were totaled. That's enough to ruin your day right there, but it gets worse. Our van was the only vehicle with any type of auto insurance! Fortunately for us, we carry full coverage on our cars, including collision coverage. But the story for the other drivers wasn't nearly as rosy.

The driver who caused the accident had been covered under his mother's insurance policy until she dropped the coverage a few months prior to the accident. We don't know why—perhaps because her twenty-year-old son had had two prior accidents and the insurance premiums were too high. Unfortunately, that meant she had no coverage for her financed 2005 car. When we spoke to her, she said that her finance company charged her a premium each month for insurance—she thought she was covered. It turns out that most finance companies, especially those that finance high-risk borrowers, always take out a policy to cover the value of their loan with the vehicle as collateral. The borrower, however, is responsible for all damages caused by the vehicle *and* has to repay the outstanding balance on the loan even if the car is totaled.

If you have a car, you've got to have insurance. In our state, auto insurance is mandatory; however, many people purchase insurance when they register their car, then promptly drop the coverage afterward. If you can't even afford the most basic liability insurance, then sell or park your car and find another means of transportation. We know this sounds harsh, but the ramifications of driving uninsured are just too great. Loss of all assets, garnished wages, lawsuits, and bankruptcy are all very real possibilities. In our accident, both of the other drivers were ticketed for not having insurance—and the young man was liable for the accident and all the damages that resulted.

Evaluating the Insurance Companies

When was the last time you reviewed your auto insurance? Yes, we know, the prospect of spending a couple of days making phone calls to review liability, deductibles, and other details is about as much fun as getting a splinter out of your finger. But the protection and cost savings it provides are well worth the investment of time. We encourage readers to requote their auto insurance every three to five years.

There is a Department of Insurance in every state. You should be able to receive, either in printed form or via the Internet, a complete listing of companies that are licensed to sell automobile insurance in your area. (Visit www.ican2000.com/state.html for a complete listing of insurance departments.) Some states go so far as to provide a price comparison guideline and a report on the number of complaints registered against each company.

Consumer Reports publishes an evaluation of the largest automobile insurance companies every three or four years. Picking up a back issue at the library will provide you with some great and unbiased information on the customer service and customer satisfaction provided by some of these companies.

There are two different ways to purchase auto insurance. Your first option is to use a broker who represents several auto insurance companies. The second is to deal directly with the insurance companies and have their agents give you a quote in writing. When you call or apply online for quotes, be prepared to give information on claims and tickets you've had in the last few years. We have always received better rates or quotes by calling companies and speaking to a live representative as opposed to receiving quotes strictly from online sources. Of course, if you have a close relationship with your current insurance agent, you must weigh this against any savings you might achieve by switching companies—having someone who knows your family well is always comforting during a crisis. Calculate your savings, and if you save more than 20 percent every six months, it might be worth switching. *Just make sure you get every detail—coverage and premiums—in writing before you make a change.* Also check the information carefully to be sure that they provided the coverage you requested.

Another source is to ask friends and relatives whom they use for insurance. Just be aware that about 75 percent of people renew their insurance without ever shopping around. That makes for happy agents but expensive bills.

Check Your Bill

When we added Becky (then age nineteen) to our insurance policy, we were quoted a specific rate from our insurance agent. Later when we received the bill, it was about 4 percent higher. Steve called the agent and received a rather lame excuse from a young assistant. When he called the insurance company directly to complain and told them that we had also received a quote from GEICO that was considerably lower, things started changing. Our premium didn't just go down, it plummeted—by about 27 percent. They said the earlier quote was based on Becky being the principal driver on one of our two cars, but that didn't make sense. When we told our agent the story, she was shocked and thought that the price change was a result of the competitive "GEICO factor."

We realize that insurance agents make mistakes. We also realize that because the insurance industry is heavily regulated, pricing isn't supposed to be negotiable. So ask lots of questions, check and double-check, and get it in writing!

Your Driving Record Matters—But It's Not the Only Thing

In recent years, insurance companies have started gathering more data on their clients in addition to driving records. A company called Choice-Point is a clearinghouse of information for the insurance industry.

They track and report on your accidents, tickets, vehicle history, the number of claims you make, and a world of other data that might make you think Big Brother is watching your every move. Most insurance companies subscribe to their services. However, when Steve recently spoke with ChoicePoint representatives, he was told that every insurance company requests different information and weighs it according to their own standards. For instance, some companies look at speeding tickets as a major problem and won't provide coverage if you have a couple of them in recent years. Others weigh more heavily on your claims history and credit report. The key is to shop many different insurance companies, especially if you have some claims in the past three years or a few blemishes on your driving record.

Getting Discounts Helps

Here are a few tips for lowering your insurance payment:

Payment Discounts. Most insurance companies allow you to pay your premiums monthly. But if you can scrape together the cash and pay semiannually, sometimes you can save big bucks. You may be thinking, "How can I come up with $1,000 for a six-month payment?" Go back and read Chapter 3: Budgeting, and start paying yourself the equivalent of your monthly premium until you have six months' worth saved. You'll want to look around—Allstate's discount is about 1 percent if you pay semiannually and GEICO's is even less, but Progressive Insurance gives a discount of approximately 14 percent. Pay attention, though—Progressive's price before the payment discount is usually higher than most competitors', so the savings might not be as steep as it seems. (We have had multiple experiences with this company, and their customer service was so unsatisfactory that we don't recommend them to anyone.) Factor in a little interest you may earn in your checking account and the fact that you don't have to mail or electronically transfer money each month, and your savings are even greater.

Here are a few other discounts to ask about:

- **Multicar discount.** Insuring more than one car often lowers the price per car.

- **Safe driver discount.** If you've got a great driving record—no accidents or tickets—you'll find some great rates.

- **Good student discount.** Studying hard and having good grades can save you bucks.

- **Homeowner discount.** Insure your home with the same company as your car.

- **Safety feature discounts.** A car with antilock brakes, antitheft devices, daytime running lights, or airbags will often be cheaper to insure than one without.

- **Membership discounts.** If you are part of a group such as AARP or AAA, are in a branch of the military, or belong to a union group such as teachers, firefighters, or police officers, you may qualify for a discount.

- **Quote before you buy.** If you're thinking of purchasing a new or used car, call your insurance agent or broker. A few years back, when we were trying to decide between a Honda Accord or a Civic, the insurance price swayed us to go with the larger car. Believe it or not, the Civic cost about 10 percent more to insure.

READING THE INSURANCE BILL: WHAT DO YOU NEED?

Liability Coverage

In our recent accident, the damage to all vehicles combined was about $35,000. This is the amount that the uninsured motorist who caused the accident was responsible for—his liability.

Your most expensive and most important portion of insurance coverage is liability—covering the damage your car could do to another person's property and body. In today's economy, carrying a bare minimum of property damage liability coverage just doesn't make sense, especially if you have other assets that might be confiscated if your insurance doesn't cover all of the damaged property. We recommend carrying at least $100,000 per person/$300,000 per accident bodily injury liability and $100,000 property damage liability. While this is one of the higher coverages available, given the cost of cars and hospital care and the ease with which lawsuits can come your way, this is just prudent thinking and can save you money in the long run.

Comprehensive Coverage

This covers your car in case it is stolen, gets hit in a parking lot, catches fire, is vandalized, or gets into an accident all by itself. In the past twenty years we've experienced three items on the previous list: a fire, cars hit in parking lots when we weren't in them, and a burglarized car. Oh, the wonders of living in a large metropolitan area!

You can keep this rate low by raising your deductible—the amount you are willing to pay if any of these things should happen. If your deductible is $100 and your car is damaged, the insurance company will pay all of the repair costs except $100. If your deductible is $1,000, you are now responsible for $1,000 worth of repair costs. If you raise your deductible, you need to be sure that you have that amount saved to cover your expenses should your car become damaged. If you don't, then go with the deductible you can afford. Numerous finance experts advocate dropping this coverage once your annual premium for the comprehensive portion of your insurance reaches 10 percent of the value of the vehicle. For example, if your car is worth only $3,000 and the comprehensive portion of your insurance is $300 for the year, they recommend canceling the coverage. We don't! You'll have to decide that one based on what you are most comfortable with. We've always carried full comprehensive even when our cars get old. Our thinking is that it doesn't cost that much more each year for the coverage, and if the car is totaled, we still get some money out of the deal.

WHAT THE KIDS SAY ABOUT CARS

John was our first child to purchase his own car. "When I first started saving cash for a car, I thought I'd never get there. But as I consistently put money in my budget system, it was amazing how fast it added up. When I finally had $6,000 saved ($5,000 for the car and $1,000 for possible repairs), Dad and I went out looking. It was really great to know I had the money saved and could buy any car in my price range." That first car, a 1994 Honda Accord, has since been retired, but John still practices the cash method for buying his cars. John continues, "Now I've got a 1999 Honda Civic that I'm modifying. As I save my money, I make the upgrades I want. It looks and runs really great!"

Collision Coverage

Many people advocate keeping your insurance bill lower by raising your collision deductible. The difference in cost between having a collision deductible of $100 or $500 for two cars, however, is about $14 per month—not much, in our opinion. But if money is tight and you need to cut, beef up your savings and raise your deductible. This is the very coverage that provided an almost brand-new van for us after our three-car accident mentioned earlier.

Medical

If you have a decent medical insurance policy that covers your family and don't normally carry other people in your car, then you can drop this coverage.

Towing

If you have an American Automobile Association (AAA) membership, you can drop your towing coverage and save a little. Plus, the maps alone are worth the membership fee—especially if you use them for vacations.

Rental Car

If your car is damaged and needs repair, this coverage provides you with a rental car. If you have an extra car available or can make use of public transportation in a pinch, this coverage can be dropped. But if you've got a family and need to be mobile, this is a must. Car repairs always take longer than expected and never happen at a convenient time.

. . .

Be sure you understand your insurance policy and your needs. We know that reading through an insurance policy is as exciting as having a kidney stone—just ask Annette—but do it some night when you can't sleep. Make a list of questions and call your agent for clarification. You'll be amazed at what you can learn. Be very careful who you ask for insurance coverage advice. Many agents would love to sell you more insurance based on fear or just to increase their commissions. Look at it this way: you only have to become an insurance expert every few years when you are collecting quotes. Other than that, you can sit back in that comfy bucket seat and know that you're covered *for sure!*

WHAT YOU CAN DO NOW ABOUT CARS

TIMID MOUSE:

Accelerate your car payments and get that vehicle paid off as fast as possible. Requote your auto insurance from at least three sources, and get everything in writing.

WISE OWL:

If you have a car that's costing too much for your budget, trade down for a car with no payment. Start an auto maintenance and repair account to eliminate the need for using a credit card for auto repairs. Build that account to have at least $1,000 in it for repairs.

AMAZING ANT:

Start saving money so you have the funds to replace your current car(s) when it's time. Save wear and tear on your car by reducing the amount of driving you do each month by car pooling, combining and carefully routing errands, and using public transportation. If you're really radical and your lifestyle can accommodate it—particularly those who live and work in larger cities—eliminate your car completely.

FIVE

HOUSING:

Home Sweet Home

Buying and owning a home is one of the most important and expensive decisions you'll ever make. Mistakes can be costly, financially and emotionally, while a carefully researched and executed choice can bless your family for generations. Our goal in this chapter is to help you make wise decisions so you can truly create a home sweet home.

This topic is pertinent to almost everybody. According to the 2000 U.S. Census, there are over 115 million places that Americans call home. More than 69 million homes are owner-occupied, with another 35 million being occupied by renters.

Since 1980, the trend has been to build larger and more expensive homes. Census Bureau data shows that the average single-family home size is now 2,349 square feet—up from 1,740 square feet twenty-seven years ago. Today's new houses have more bedrooms, more bathrooms, and more room for more cars than in 1980. Do we really need all of this space? Can we really afford it?

Most people view home ownership as "The American Dream." Is it really? With careful planning, it can be. But if you're careless or impulsive, your dream can quickly become a nightmare. The bottom line to home ownership bliss isn't just getting into a house. You must balance the goals of saving money, building equity, and getting a great deal with the time and ability you have to maintain a property.

OUR DREAM

The first house we bought was small (1,450 square feet). As we patiently paid off our mortgage and accumulated a large down payment for our next house, we also "accumulated" five kids, two dogs, two hamsters, one turtle, and a houseful of toys, clothes, and all the other paraphernalia associated with raising a family. So we dreamed big. We wanted our next home to be a bigger house on a larger property with more room to garden and grow fruit trees. It would be a place where our kids could run and play, and where we could impart to them a strong work ethic. We couldn't maintain a big piece of property without kids who were willing and able to pitch in and help, and we wanted them to learn to do chores and gain the skills necessary to maintain a house. This was our dream, but it took eleven years to achieve it.

You have a dream too. But before you even start looking, you've got to know what you can afford.

DON'T BELIEVE THE BANK

If you're buying your first home or considering purchasing another home, enter into the mortgage world with eyes wide open. Most lending institutions will "allow" you to borrow up to three times your gross annual household income. But we recommend that your house payment, insurance, taxes, maintenance, and utilities consume no more than 40 percent of your monthly net spendable income—less is always better. (Net spendable income is what is left of your paycheck after taxes, the cost of benefits, and anything else your employer deducts. It's your take-home pay.) And this amount assumes that you have little or no other debt payments. Some may think our figures are too conservative, especially when compared to what mortgage lenders will allow, but we like to think of them as being smart—because it will allow you to fund all the other areas of your budget and not be enslaved to your house.

Even if both husband and wife work, we don't recommend qualifying for a mortgage loan based on two incomes. Sickness, disability, and unemployment (not to mention pregnancy and parenting) are all possibilities, and securing your home with two incomes can be a risky proposition. Using one of many mortgage calculators available online and combining your desired payment with the prevailing interest rate, you can figure the maximum house payment you can afford. Remember to include a reasonable amount for property taxes and insurance. Consult with your real estate agent or banker to get a more accurate estimate. You'll also need to add an amount for home maintenance—a good starting point is 10 percent of your house payment (more on this later).

Here's an example (plug in your own numbers to see where you should be):

Net spendable income: $40,000

Maximum house expenses: Net spendable income $\times$ 40 percent = $16,000 per year

Maximum monthly expenses for principal, interest, taxes, insurance, maintenance, and utilities: $1,333

LOOK BEFORE YOU BUY

Once you've figured out approximately what you can spend, you'll want to take a look at the market. According to the 2004 National Association of Realtors Profile of Home Buyers and Sellers, the average house hunter looks at nine homes before deciding to buy. We've found that the more homes you look at, the better you'll understand the real values of the houses in your market. When we were looking for our first home, we looked at over forty houses—our poor agent thought we'd never sign a contract. For our second house, we visited about twenty. In each case, by the time we did buy, we knew that we were getting a great deal. One way to make your search more efficient is to use the Internet. According to the same Profile of Home Buyers and Sellers, nearly 75 percent of buyers are researching homes on the Web; this is up from 41 percent in 2001. In many states you can even access county records and tax information to help you compare housing values. The more information you possess, the better you'll be able to negotiate.

Down Payments

A recent study by the Mortgage Bankers Association reported a rise in the number of foreclosures by people who were required to put little or no money down when purchasing a home. The down payment on our first home was roughly 15 percent. After our first home was paid off and sold, we were able to put 40 percent down on our next home. Our goal is to pay off any debt as quickly as possible. There is nothing wrong with starting out in a modest home so you can pay it off quickly and have a large down payment for your "dream home."

Another benefit of a large down payment is avoiding mortgage insurance protection (MIP) or private mortgage insurance (PMI). MIP and PMI are insurance policies required by the lender when your equity in a home is less than 20 percent. It guarantees their payment in full if you default. Eliminating this insurance can save you $35 to $60 per month on your payment (based on a $100,000 mortgage).

Most mortgage companies include your property tax and homeowner's insurance in your monthly payment. They hold the money in an impound or escrow account and make the payments when they are due. If you have enough equity in your home, you can petition your mortgage company to allow you to form your own impound account, accumulating and paying your own property taxes and homeowner's insurance. We did this because every few years, just before Christmas, we'd receive a friendly little notice that our impound account

BYE-BYE, PMI

If you have a conventional mortgage with private mortgage insurance (PMI), you may be able to save some money. PMI terms fall under regulations passed in the Home Owner Protection Act of 1998.

Under these rules, any private mortgage consummated after 1999 that was required to have PMI may have the insurance canceled when the homeowner's equity reaches 20 percent of the original value of the property at the time the loan was originated.

You may have to make your request in writing, but by law, when your equity reaches 22 percent, the lender is required to notify you and cancel the policy.

So do your math, and if you fit the description, write a letter and start saving.

was deficient. Our lender just couldn't get the knack of dividing our taxes and insurance payments by twelve! We grew tired of receiving their "You owe us $500" holiday greeting card. So we contacted the president of the company and insisted on doing our own impound. To our surprise, they agreed! Just be aware that to do your own impound you must budget and save and protect that money so it's there when you need it. The interest you can gain isn't bad either.

The Benefit of Paying It Off

We purchased our first house, a beat-up repo, in 1985 for the ridiculous price of $53,000. According to our lender disclosure documents, our 30-year mortgage of $46,000 should have cost us about $150,000 in principal and interest over the full course of the loan. We started paying a little extra each month, and as our income increased, so did our extra payments. At the end of nine years we made our final payment. Steve calculated that we had paid a total of $70,000 in principal and interest. We later turned around and sold that house in 1995 for $80,000. We were telling this story to some friends recently and they stood there amazed, asking, "How often do you hear of someone selling their house for more than they paid in principal *and* interest?" Our bottom line is this, no matter how large your mortgage, working toward paying it off will save you tens of thousands of dollars.

HOUSING STRATEGIES

There isn't just one way to deal with home ownership. Check out the other options we have listed below.

Leaving Home?

In some parts of the country, especially the coastal regions, housing costs are astronomical. We hate to advocate moving and leaving extended family. But relocating for a time to a less expensive area may be an attractive option for prudent home ownership. This is especially true if you want to put a large percentage down and have a manageable mortgage payment. With an aggressive extra payment plan, you might be able to readily accumulate enough equity and cash to purchase a house back in your hometown.

Low-Cost Apartment Living

Becoming an apartment manager is a good way to live rent-free and sock away money for a large down payment. This is something to consider if you're just starting out as a younger couple or planning on staying in a particular city for less than two or three years. As long as you can handle the responsibilities of management and maintenance, this could be a good option.

Townhouses/Condos

If the thought of a house and its accompanying maintenance worries you, there are other options that are particularly attractive to singles or those with a harried lifestyle. Consider buying a townhouse or a condo where there is little or no property to maintain (no lawn to mow or snow to shovel either). Just keep in mind that in some areas of the country, townhouses or condos may be difficult to resell. In addition, they usually require a monthly association fee, which may be quite expensive, so be sure you research the details.

Big Home, Little Energy

If you are a senior citizen, having a "paid-for" house can bring a tremendous amount of security. However, if the home is too large or falling apart or the property is too much work to maintain, the burden can be suffocating. If the house is large enough and you can handle sharing your privacy with others, consider renting rooms to other seniors, single parents with one or two children, or older college students (screen them carefully and get letters of reference). Some younger seniors make great foster parents, and teaching these kids the work skills necessary to maintain a property is a wonderfully constructive activity for them.

Or, if you have enough excess room, consider renting to a young family who could help with property maintenance, home repair, cooking, or cleaning. Or perhaps it's time to stop owning a home and move in with your children. If they have existing space for you, great; if not, then perhaps you could use some of the proceeds from the sale of your house to build an addition on their house. We both grew up with our grandparents living in our homes. This experience created many fond memories for both of us. Finally, consider this radical option: selling your larger home to purchase a smaller one of similar value. Even if rising housing costs mean that the best you can accomplish is a lateral move, do it.

MAINTENANCE COSTS AND COSTS AND COSTS SOME MORE

Remember that the cost of owning a home extends far beyond the mortgage and taxes. Maintenance costs can be a painful reality. There are many different calculations for what to save monthly for maintenance. We like the idea of starting with 10 percent of the house payment. If your payment is $800, then save $80 each month. This money is for replacing faucet washers, broken windows, and other minor repairs. This percentage may need to be higher if you aren't handy and need to purchase professional repair services. For major repairs, we recommend keeping at least 1 percent of the value of your house in an emergency fund. (See Chapter 13: Savings and Investments for more details.) If your home is worth $180,000, then save at least $1,800. This money is allocated for major repairs on roofs, water heaters, furnaces, or burst pipes.

ARE YOU DROWNING?

If you're feeling overwhelmed and your home is grabbing more of your paycheck than is recommended, here are some options. Start by evaluating all areas of expenses.

· Work on reducing your food budget by menu planning, cooking from scratch, and stocking up—see Chapter 2: Groceries.

· Minimize your recreation expenses. Save going out to restaurants for special occasions. Cut out expensive recreational activities and look for inexpensive or free events. If you consult your newspaper and other local resources, you'll be amazed at the fun you can have for free—see Chapter 10: Entertainment & Recreation.

· Another radical option is selling a newer car and replacing it with an older reliable vehicle—see Chapter 4: Cars.

· As a last resort, you may need to sell your home and move to something smaller. There may be some tax consequences, so research this carefully. But this drastic step can actually pave the way for your future financial stability.

HOMES BUILD SECURITY

One of the main reasons we advocate paying off a home quickly is the security that it brings. When we purchased our first home with a large down payment, we kept our monthly expenses very low. We figured that if Steve became disabled or unemployed, we could easily pick up enough work to survive, or we could sell the house and live off the proceeds for a while. Trying to carry a gigantic mortgage payment is just not worth the stress and worry that can accompany it. Home owner-ship won't be a nightmare if you pursue your dream with diligent plan-ning and patience. And instead of counting sheep at night, you'll be able to count the number of payments until your home is free and clear!

PROPERTY TAXES: GETTING IT RIGHT!

If you're feeling overwhelmed or if you don't own a home, you can skip this section—it's an epic story of a struggle against city hall. If you do own a home or are getting ready to buy one, you should consider what you will be paying in property taxes, which in some areas can be a significant amount. When you purchase a house, be aware that many municipalities base your property taxes in large part on the sale price. The basis for the valuation may be correct, but the details of your property may be misrepresented, which can result in higher taxes.

No matter how the economy is doing, we've seldom seen property taxes decline significantly. We don't know about your area, but where we live, property values keep increasing, and as a result so does our tax bill. How can you be sure you're paying the proper amount for your property taxes?

Hmmm, This Can't Be Right

For years, we had a sneaking suspicion that our property was being overtaxed—the assessed value seemed way too high. But every time we'd read through the appeal process, we'd either missed the deadline or our eyes would glaze over as we pondered the jumbled mass of bureaucratic red tape. So year after year we did nothing.

A few years ago, through the wondrous miracle of the Internet, we discovered that various state, county, and city agencies were putting recorded documents and other public information online. We logged on to our county assessor's Web site and were able to check out the assessed value of properties all around us. We found the information quite interesting; we felt a bit sneaky looking at our neighbors' property values, but that's the way it goes when you're sleuthing for answers. This free sleuthing confirmed our suspicions that our tax bill was higher than those of several neighbors. After compiling an extensive list of houses with relatively similar lot size and square footage, we sent in the appeal form—also available online—and requested a meeting with the assessor.

Remember, if you don't have Internet access, most public libraries offer it at no charge. A quick call to your county headquarters will let you know if these records are available online.

Having never done this before, we didn't know what to expect. We figured that the assessor would be dazzled with our voluminous research and our reasoning ability and convinced by our compelling arguments. Um, no. He got right to business and matter-of-factly turned us down. We concluded that if day in and day out he heard people complain about being overtaxed, he had probably developed a pretty callous attitude. *Arrgh.*

Well, we didn't give up. Beyond the comparable values of houses in our area, we had two other measurable arguments. The first was that we have a 100-square-foot atrium in the middle of our home, which has an open roof and is surrounded by glass—definitely not "livable square footage" in Arizona. The second was the size of our swimming pool. Steve had measured and diagrammed the pool and determined that the actual square footage of the pool was roughly half of what the assessor's records had listed.

Given those two discrepancies, we requested a remeasure of our home. The assessor agreed and submitted the paperwork for us.

Are You Unpermitted?

One caution before you proceed. Our home was built in 1978 and has undergone no additions or major renovations beyond the installation of plumbing for natural gas, for which we obtained a permit, and the remodeling of our kitchen, for which no permit was required. If you know that you have unpermitted or undocumented improvements on your home, contesting your assessment may result in a little embarrassment, not to mention an increase in taxes instead of a reduction.

The Visitation

We were told that it would take six weeks before the assessor could visit us. About a week later, after our face-to-face meeting, we received a phone call from John, saying he was in the area and wanted to stop by to measure. We turned him down; it wasn't a convenient time for us. We tried to set a firm date, but he declined. We continued to receive phone calls from him, usually giving us a one-hour notice. It seems that surprise is one of the tactics they use to throw people off guard. Finally, we gave in.

The Plans Weren't the Plans

When John showed up to measure, Steve stayed with him the whole time. John came equipped with a diagram and measurements that the county used to assess our home. As they walked, talked, and measured, it became very clear that the information the custom builder had provided to the county back in 1978 was drastically different from what had actually been built. One side of our house was nine feet shorter than on the diagram. The atrium inside our home was nonexistent on paper, and there were several other measurements that were inaccurate. John was puzzled and amazed. "I've never seen measurements off by this much," he said. He left and told us that he'd call in a few days.

He called as promised but said that he wanted to measure once more. The numbers were off so much, he thought that he must have made a mistake. Later he confided that he was hesitant to present such drastically different measurements to his supervisor without being 100 percent sure. So we measured again and came up with the same number. Boy, were we excited! Our taxes were going down . . . waaay down . . . or so we thought.

Call In the Reserves—It's Getting Confusing

Little did we know that the easy part was over. When we appealed the assessor's denial and requested the remeasure, the appeal went to a county review board, one that basically takes the recommendations of the assessor and either allows or denies valuation changes.

After the errors were determined, the assessor's office said *they* could make the change to our valuation, so we didn't need to go to the board. But the board administrator said that the assessor's office didn't have the authority to authorize any changes to our assessed value. Whom should we believe?

We discovered that, as with so many things in government, the right hand didn't know what the left hand was doing. In the end, the second department did need to approve the valuation change for future years, but the assessor's office was responsible for getting us a refund for previous years. That's right—we received a refund for three prior years—the maximum amount allowed by county statute.

Your Taxes Are Going Down/Your Taxes Are Going Up

This convoluted tale has somewhat of a happy ending. We won our property tax battle and received three years' worth of refunds. Our taxes were reduced $270 per year . . . for about three weeks. Then a new tax bill arrived with an updated valuation—one that was only $20 less than our previous bill. So much for big savings, although we should have been grateful that our tax bill didn't go up the $250 it was originally supposed to. In total, we spent thirty hours researching, arguing, questioning, and fighting. Was it worth it? Well, yes and no. We figured that we earned about $36 per hour, when you divide our current-year savings ($270) plus our three years of refunds ($810) by the number of hours spent (30). But beyond that, we have the emotional satisfaction that we stood up to city hall and won.

We may be bruised and battle-worn, but we can now stand before you and attest to the fact that the savings can be had. Keep in mind, though, that the mental and emotional price may be high. If you have the time and the inclination to embark on this epic journey, don't plan on doing much else during that same time!

Freezing Property Values and Getting Help

If you are of retirement age, check with your county assessor to see if there are any special laws regarding your property taxes. In our area, seniors can request that their primary residence property taxes be frozen. There are other stipulations, but it never hurts to ask the question. If you are looking for help, there are companies that will contest your property taxes for you. Do your research, though, and ask many questions. You may find that their services are not targeted for the individual homeowner. They usually focus on apartment complex owners, commercial real estate owners, and other large property owners.

HIRING A CONTRACTOR: HOME IMPROVEMENTS WITHOUT GETTING NAILED

There are some jobs around the house that require expert know-how. We realize that some thrifty publications recommend that when it comes to home improvements or repairs, you should always "do it yourself." We don't. While we try to do most jobs ourselves, we recognize that there are limits to our abilities and there are limits to the time we can allot to specific jobs. Remember, being an economizer isn't just about saving money—it's about saving time and stress and preserving relationships.

Having a basic knowledge and skill level for plumbing, electrical, drywall, painting, and landscaping will save you thousands of dollars over a lifetime. But tackling a big project without expertise spells disaster, extra expense, and total frustration. For these jobs we call in the experts.

How to Save When You Call In the Pros

We've completed numerous projects in our homes. For some jobs, we consulted or hired experienced contractors to do all or part of the work. Below is a partial list of the tasks we've hired out in the last twenty years, and how we saved some money.

Block Wall. With our big dogs, a solid fence around our yard is a necessity. After years of trying to maintain and repair a rotting wooden fence around the backyard of our first house, we partnered with one of our neighbors and installed a cement block wall.

   Key Tip: *When doing a project that could affect your neighbors, ask for their financial participation. They just might say yes.*

Kitchen Remodel. We've remodeled our kitchens at each of the two homes we've owned. Both times, we purchased the cabinets, and Steve helped install them with Annette's dad and a friend whom we paid. We also primarily used coupons or discounts to purchase and install several appliances.

Key Tip: *Don't be shy about coordinating with your contractor to do some of the work yourself and asking and or paying some skilled friends to help.*

Central Air-Conditioning. With summer temperatures as high as 120 degrees, most houses here in Arizona are equipped with central air-conditioning. We've replaced ours once at each house. The second time, we were familiar with the terminology and knew the questions to ask. We always recommend gathering five to seven bids for major home improvement projects. In this case, the lowest bidder's price was 60 percent less than our trusted air-conditioning service company. Our regular service person knew the reputation and quality workmanship of this company and encouraged us to use them. They were a larger company and needed to keep their crews working during a slow period in the year, and we benefited from their lower bid.

Key Tip: *When you pick a slow season for a particular business, you can often get a better deal.*

Natural Gas Plumbing. We installed natural gas plumbing so we could convert many of our appliances from electric to gas and reduce our electric bill. We researched numerous contractors over several months, then designed the piping layout ourselves and closely supervised the lowest bidder on the job.

Key Tip: *Some projects may require months of research and quotes to finally get a price you're happy with. Don't give up.*

Carpeting. We've done this one twice as well. The first time, Steve and a college buddy installed the carpeting. The second time, the carpet was ordered before we bid on the house. We chose the color but not the quality or the contractor. We didn't know to ask to see a plan for the seam layout, so we had to work through some issues with the contractor.

Key Tip: *Whenever you have carpeting installed, always ask to see the seam layout before they start working.*

Hardwood Flooring. After years of trying to maintain and repair an improperly installed wood floor, Steve and the kids removed the old floor, and we paid an expert to install a new floor properly.

Key Tip: *When something is improperly installed and damaged, trying to maintain and work with the result is sometimes not worth the effort.*

Six Steps for Researching, Hiring, and Paying a Contractor

As you may have guessed, we advocate starting such a project only when the cash is in the bank—never take out a loan. By following our principles for researching, hiring, managing, and paying a contractor, you'll always get much more for your money.

Step 1: Research. Free enterprise can always be used to our advantage. Businesses not only want to make money but also want to keep their employees busy to avoid layoffs. If a particular field is very competitive, savvy researchers can win the bidding wars as prices are driven down to keep workers on the job. Remember, every price is negotiable. The more time you spend on the research phase, the more confident and knowledgeable you will be when it comes to the final negotiations.

Step 2: Initial Contact. We assemble a folder for the project and create a call list of contractors from friends and neighbors. Then we refer to the yellow pages. We avoid companies that have full-page ads in the phone book—usually when companies spend a large amount of money on advertising, their prices are higher.

In your initial phone call, be sure to ask if the company is licensed and bonded. While you might think you can save some money dealing with a small company that isn't licensed and bonded, you have little or no recourse if something should go wrong on the job. Don't skimp on this step—you can save much time and future frustration by eliminating, early on, contractors who don't protect themselves and their customers with the proper business practices.

Never, never—did we say *never*?—hire a company that knocks on your door offering their services . . . for anything. Many of these companies are unethical, and not having the time to check them out could result in disaster for you. This is a serious concern for the elderly, who are often preyed upon by these companies, which will take their money and either not do the job at all or do shoddy work.

Step 3: The Interview. As we meet with each contractor, we take copious notes—usually one to two pages on each one—and store them in the project folder. Our discussions with friends who have had similar work done usually yield a list of questions to ask. As we interview more people, our list of questions grows along with our knowledge of the trade. It's funny to see an unsuspecting contractor raise his eyebrows as Annette asks a trade-specific, technical question he was not expecting to hear from an "uninformed" woman.

Here are some of the questions we ask:

· How long have you been in business?

· How long have you done business in our state? (Usually longer is better, but newer with good references is often less expensive.)

· Will my project require a permit? (If you don't know, you should call your city's building department and find out prior to interviewing anyone. Asking this question will test the contractor's knowledge and honesty. By the way, offering to take your time to go to the city and get the permit can save you some money too. But don't offer this until the price is finalized. Then deduct the cost.)

· Are there any other questions I should be asking? (Most are flattered and want to share their knowledge—and tell you why their product is the best. One roofer spent a good amount of time explaining the different qualities of shingles and various types of tar paper. A kitchen cabinet rep explained the different types of drawer construction—dovetailed versus stapled ends. This same rep also told us to ask about the construction quality of the cabinet boxes. Were they made of plywood or particleboard? Were the drawer guides A, B, or C quality? What type of warranty is offered on the construction and the wood finish? It feels so good to progress from ignorance to a well-informed buyer.)

When we remodeled our second kitchen, we called and met with at least fifteen different cabinet reps or designers over a six-week period. One rep wouldn't quote the job because, according to him, "your budget won't be adequate for a job this size." Silly rep: Annette not only redid the kitchen but also added the wood floors for the amount we had originally budgeted.

Step 4: Use Your Intuition. As you interview prospective candidates, observe them carefully. You can glean a lot of information by the way a person dresses, carries himself, and speaks. Be on the lookout for inconsistencies and promises that sound too good to be true. Also note whether they return phone calls, show up on time, and send information as promised. If they are lax in any of these areas before the sale, they'll likely be worse afterward.

A dear friend who knew an air-conditioning contractor referred him to us but had never used his services. During the interview, we asked about his qualifications, and he said he was licensed. When we checked him out with the State of Arizona's Registrar of Contractors (see step 5), we discovered that his license had been revoked. (In Arizona the Registrar of Contractors is an office that licenses and supervises various types of construction-related contractors. While they may have different names, most states have this type of licensing agency.) When we called him about it, he said that he knew that it was, but since he was thinking of merging his business with another company, it didn't really matter. A lack of integrity in answering a simple question is usually an indication of a lack of integrity in bigger things. He didn't get the job.

We ran into another issue when we were researching windows for our garage to replace openings with security bars. Annette met with a fellow who owned a window business that sold several different national brands. He tried to convince her that his company actually manufactured the windows on his property. He was in his fifties, with dyed blond hair, huge rings on his fingers, fancy clothes, and not a lick of truth in him. Other things he said and did convinced us that he was not the type of person we wanted to deal with. (He did, however, provide us with quite a laugh!)

Usually in a marriage, one spouse is better than the other at "reading" or perceiving a person's character. If you aren't, don't ignore the "I can't explain it, but I just don't feel comfortable with this person" statements that you might hear. It could save you thousands of dollars. If you're widowed or single, before you sign any contract, review the final data with someone you respect who will ask you the tough questions.

Step 5: The Final Decision. When the interviews are complete, we review our notes together and discuss the options. Once we've narrowed it down to a final few, we check with the Registrar of Contractors to see if their licenses are current and if there are any complaints filed against them. We also call the Better Business Bureau to see if they have any unresolved complaints. These organizations won't necessarily give you the same information; that's why it's important to call both.

Then we phone each of the finalists and ask a few more questions. Usually by this point we've received a well-rounded education in the trade we are studying. We discuss the final nitty-gritty details of the project, add in any upgrade costs or other options we might want, and negotiate the final price.

There are always ways to save money in the final negotiation:

· If two companies have similar products but one has a lower price, ask if the other company can match or beat the price.

· Ask if there are any special promotions or sales coming up— sometimes the special price can be authorized early.

· Be sure to ask about delivery charges, tax, and rush charges.

· In the end, ask for everything in writing. Never just go on a handshake, even if the deal is with a friend (if you do, it could mean the end of the friendship). The final estimate should have all the extras and discounts written out. If a company won't put the estimate in writing, eliminate it. If you need more data on your final candidate, ask for three customer references that you can contact.

We don't recommend using the lowest bidder unless you've gathered a pile of positive information and glowing references. Of the four times we did go with the lowest bidder, only two turned out hassle-free. Many times the lowest bidder is either a company that doesn't have excellent workmanship or is struggling to stay afloat and may cut some corners.

Step 6: Payday. Never pay all the money for a job up front. During your final negotiations, you should determine a payment schedule. You should always hold at least 25 percent of the final bill until the job is completed to your satisfaction. If you pay them everything and a problem surfaces at the end, the company is less likely to resolve it.

Getting quality home improvement projects completed only requires you to be expert in one thing, and it's not a trade like plumbing or masonry—it's a skill. Once you master your research skills, you'll be happier, your house will be happier, and you'll come out money ahead every time.

WHAT THE KIDS SAY ABOUT HOUSING

John, twenty-three years old, says, "My goal is to buy a house within the next four years. I currently rent an apartment with a friend of mine; this keeps my expenses lower so I can sock money away in the bank each month. I've found that the most consistent way for me to save is to have the money automatically deducted from my paycheck and deposited right into my savings account."

Abbey, at eight years old, said, "When I get married, I'm going to move to Flagstaff—up in the mountains—and live on a ranch, have lots of kids, and a two-story pink house." (Abbey really likes Barbies.)

WHAT YOU CAN DO NOW ABOUT HOUSING COSTS

TIMID MOUSE:

If you are planning on buying a house, start saving like crazy to accumulate a large down payment. As you get close to your goal, start researching houses for sale in the area where you want to live. The more you research, the more you'll save.

WISE OWL:

Evaluate your current housing situation. If you are in over your head, set up a debt liquidation plan to eliminate your debts (see Chapter 7: Debt). Make sure you read Chapter 3: Budgeting and set up a workable budget so you can start cutting all of your other expenses. If you can't balance your budget, you may need to consider downsizing to something more affordable. Eliminating a huge house payment will help you sleep better at night.

AMAZING ANT:

If you're in the right home for your budget and have no other debt, start cutting expenses so you can pay some extra principal every month. Make sure you ask for a loan history from your mortgage company each year so you can be sure they are allocating your extra principal properly.

SIX

UTILITIES:

Shut the Door,
Turn Out the Lights!

While buying a home is the largest expense most of us will ever experience, keeping that home comfortable can put the squeeze on your budget if you're not careful. According to the U.S. Department of Energy, consumers spend as much as 6 to 12 percent of their gross income on utility bills—and nearly half of this money is spent on heating and cooling. Another chunk of your utility spending is for phone service—including long distance, cell phone, and Internet connections—and these costs can also get out of hand if you don't pay attention to them. If your annual household income is $50,000, the government statistics say you are spending somewhere between $3,000 and $6,000 annually on utilities. That's a lot of dough. And as you may realize by now, anytime there is a major expense, there can be major savings.

We employ lots of cost-saving methods when it comes to utilities. Our home is about 3,500 square feet, and our cost for basic utilities—including phone, gas, electricity, and water / city services—is about half of what many neighbors with comparably sized houses are spending. While all of our ideas may not apply to your climate, we hope that this chapter will inspire you to question your utility expenses and perhaps try several options for keeping some of that money in your pocket.

As with other budget categories, we save a predetermined amount of money from each paycheck to cover our utility expenses. We have calculated our costs on an annual basis and divide the total by 24 to know how much to save from each paycheck. (If you get paid every other week and reconcile your budget every two weeks, you'll want to divide by 26.) Because of our system and the mild Arizona winters, we always accumulate an excess in our utility account as we head toward the summer—usually $500 to $700. This money will be slowly depleted by our higher summer utility costs.

Here in the dry Southwest, our extreme summer temperatures last about five months, so one of our most costly challenges is keeping cool. In other parts of the country, the opposite is true, and winter is the longest and most expensive season of the year. Either way, the same principles apply: we need to be vigilant about finding ways to minimize our utility costs while still maintaining our safety and comfort.

ALTERNATIVE COOLING AND HEATING METHODS HELP YOU SAVE

No matter where you live, there are alternative methods for staying warm and keeping cool. Use what we share as a starting point for researching alternative utility cost-saving methods for the region in which you live.

Chill Out

Evaporative Coolers. Because of our low humidity, for part of the year we can use evaporative coolers instead of air-conditioning. (An evaporative cooler draws outside air over moistened pads and blows the cooled air into the house.) These units cost about 66 percent less to run than conventional central air. After experiencing such significant savings in our first house, having an "evap cooling" system became a priority when we were hunting for our second house. But because they work best when the humidity is low, we can't use them for two months out of our five-month "summer" and have to resort to air-conditioning during July and August.

UpDux. We also learned about a product called UpDux, vents that move some of the cool air in our house up into the attic when the evaporative cooler is running. These UpDux vents keep the house more comfortable because they not only allow air to circulate through the entire house but also cool off the attic considerably, which affects the temperature of the whole house. UpDux only cost about $20 each, and having one in each room of the house helps the evap coolers run more effectively.

Fans. Portable fans and ceiling fans are relatively inexpensive and provide air movement that allows the thermostat to be set a few degrees higher. Between the two houses we've owned, Steve has installed at least eight ceiling fans. Early on, we purchased just based on price—we thought cheaper was better. But after having a couple of fans burn out and hearing the endless *click-click-click* of the cheaper fans, we concluded that larger, better-built motors may cost a little more, but the fan will move more air, last longer, and run more quietly. Just remember to turn them off when you leave the room because they provide no lasting cooling effect. We've found great savings on fans at home improvement stores or discount retailers during end-of-summer sales. These usually aren't advertised sales, just piles of overstocked, deeply discounted items.

Upgrading Your Equipment. If you currently have an older central air-conditioning unit that seems to be either continually running or often in need of repair, it might be more cost-effective to replace it with a newer, high-efficiency one. The U.S. Environmental Protection Agency (EPA) recommends replacing older cooling systems with more efficient Energy Star–rated units, especially if your current unit is more than ten years old. Because technology is constantly improving, and even though many appliances have a life span of thirty years or more, when our major appliances or heating or cooling systems are about twenty years old we start researching the value of replacing them.

According to the EPA, a properly installed Energy Star air-conditioning unit can reduce your cooling costs by up to 20 percent. Our experience supports this theory—and we found that it can extend to saving on heating expenses as well. We replaced two twenty-year-old central air-conditioning/electric heat pump units on our current house. They ran constantly and did not do an adequate job of cooling or heating the house, costing us a boodle on our electricity bill. Also, due to their age, parts frequently wore out and they needed repair regularly. After much research we bought two much more efficient air-conditioning/gas heater units and saw a drastic reduction in our costs for cooling and heating.

We talked to you about getting the best prices for home improvements in Chapter 5: Housing, but we can't emphasize this enough: the more research we do, the more we save. In the case of replacing the central air/gas heaters, we had quotes ranging from $11,000 down to $5,300—for the exact same product.

Programmable Thermostats. These provide a great way to manage your energy usage and cost between $50 and $150. The beauty of a programmable thermostat is that it can be set according to your personal preference and schedule and then left alone to do its job. For example, during the summer you can set it to automatically rise to 82 degrees at 8:00 A.M., if everyone has left for the day, and lower to 78 at 6:00 P.M., when occupants return home. They are most effective for families who leave the house empty during the day but occupy it in the late afternoon and evening hours. A recent study conducted in the Pacific Northwest found that these types of thermostats were effective at reducing energy consumption, provided that the homeowners left them alone. In their small sampling—25 homeowners with programmable thermostats compared to 125 with conventional thermostats—they discovered that the more homeowners adjusted the programmable thermostat, the less money they saved.

Depending on how determined you are, you can really conserve a lot of cash by using such a thermostat. For instance—this next story isn't for everyone, only the stout-hearted and super-thrifty—we have some friends who are more frugal than we are when it comes to their summer electrical usage. They set their programmable thermostat to turn on the air-conditioning unit at five o'clock in the morning. It runs continually for four hours, until nine, when their utility usage rate increases. By that time the temperature in the house has usually dropped to the mid-sixties, and the air conditioner is turned off until the next morning. Because they have extra insulation and use ceiling fans, they stay relatively comfortable throughout the day, although the temperature can get a little warm as the day winds down. Before bed they jump in their swimming pool, cool off, and then go to sleep.

Since we work out of our house, we've decided to become our own programmable thermostat. Our largest electric consumption occurs during the summer when it is humid—usually the months of July and August. During these two months we alternate every couple of hours between the two units (set at 80 degrees) and also use several ceiling or portable fans. The house is kept comfortable and our utility bill is slashed considerably.

Staying Warm

Burn, Baby, Burn. For those of you in colder climates, having a high-efficiency wood-burning stove can supplement your gas or oil heat in the winter and help save money. We visited some friends in Vermont who had installed such a stove. It not only heated the main floor and the upstairs of the house but also warmed water for the water heater *and* ran it through the kitchen baseboards to warm the kitchen.

Buying wood for the stove is an additional cost, of course, but if you keep your eyes open you'll always be able to find free wood discarded by neighbors and landscape crews. For example, whenever we see a neighbor having a tree cut down, we'll ask for the wood and then cut it into pieces that fit in our fireplace. Landscapers are happy about this because it means less material that they have to haul to the dump. This not only provides us with free firewood but keeps material out of our limited landfill space.

EIGHT MORE WAYS TO SAVE ON
HEATING AND COOLING

1. Wear layers in the winter, which lets you keep the thermostat lower. Thick socks help too.

2. Buy a water-heater jacket. They're inexpensive, take about an hour to install, and can reduce heat loss.

3. Close vents in rooms that don't get used. This will force more of the heated or cooled air into other inhabited areas of the house. One of our newsletter readers blocked off the vents in her basement laundry room during the winters because the basement was always warmer due to being underground and because of the warmth created by running her dryer. Also keep the doors closed in unoccupied rooms to minimize the square footage that needs to be heated or cooled.

4. Install self-closing hinges on doors that the kids commonly use. They can be adjusted to prevent pinching of fingers. Having doors close automatically reduces the loss of heat in the winter and cool air in the summer. Plus you'll never again have to yell, "Shut that door! Do you think I work for the power company?"

5. Use compact fluorescent lights for areas where you leave lights on for hours at a time—the laundry room, the kitchen, and the front of the house. They emit less heat, use less electricity, and last longer than standard incandescent bulbs. Prices have steadily been coming down as these types of lights become more popular.

6. Use surge protectors. Plug all computer components into a surge protector/power strip and turn them off with the flick of one switch.

7. Insulate. When installing the UpDux in our old house—1,450 square feet—we discovered that the insulation in the attic was not adequate. It was about three inches thick—the equivalent of R-7 (not very good). We researched blown-in insulation and for about $250 had our attic covered with twelve inches of insulation, which raised the R-value to 28 (way better). We felt the difference immediately not only in our comfort, but in our checkbook.

8. Use other fuels. When we moved into our second home in 1995, all the appliances and the heating and cooling system were electric. Our electric rate was based on peak usage from 9 A.M. to 9 P.M. We had to really watch which appliances were running; otherwise, our electric bill would be astronomical. A couple of years later, during a Realtor's open house two doors down, we noticed that this home had gas appliances. Our previous house had both gas and electric appliances, and we now knew that a combination would save huge amounts of money. So we called the gas company, and they told us that they would extend the gas line to our lot if we convinced our next-door neighbor, who was just starting to build her house, to put in gas also. Our only expense, besides appliances, would be to have a plumber install new gas pipelines to all of the appliances. We gathered quotes and did the math. Sometimes large cash outlays can produce lower living expenses and greater comfort. Since we plan on staying in this house for thirty years and we calculated that in eight to ten years we'd start to see savings, we decided to go ahead with the project. We figured that the only appliances we would

The Pitfalls of Technology: Load Controllers

When we moved into our second house, it was equipped with a load controller. These devices are designed to manage the maximum usage of electricity in an effort to control your utility bill. All of our appliances were electric: water heater, stove, refrigerator, air conditioner/heat pump, washer and dryer. The load controller was attached to most of these appliances—refrigerator excluded. When electrical usage reached a predetermined level, it was programmed to turn off the appliances in a prioritized order. So if the air-conditioning went on while the clothes were in the dryer, the dryer would shut off, leaving wet clothes to sit. If our water heater and some other appliance was running and the air-conditioning started up, it would immediately shut down as a result of too high of an electrical demand. The temperature in the house would begin to rise, and we would begin to swelter. Although the load controller is designed to save money, it just gave us headaches. When we plumbed the house for natural gas and converted the water heater, dryer, and stove from electric to gas, we disconnected the load controller and still enjoyed a great amount of savings.

purchase immediately were a water heater and a used gas dryer. (Who cares if the washer and dryer match?) Other appliances would be replaced over time as they wore out.

REDUCING WATER USAGE

Paying attention to water usage can save you a bundle. For example, we have a small citrus orchard on our property, which had a leaky and in- efficient drip irrigation system in it when we bought the house. We tried to patch it up for a couple of years but finally decided it was time to fix it instead of patch it. Steve planned and rerouted the entire sys- tem to make it more efficient. It was a huge job, but the end result was better fruit, less water used, and a lower water bill.

Even if you don't have an orchard, there are many other things you can do to conserve water.

Time Your Showers

We have three teens who love to take long showers. We've implemented a five-to-ten-minute running-water shower rule, with longer time allot- ted for girls with long hair. We set a timer and knock on the door when the time is up. If knocking doesn't work, we shut off the main water valve to the house. Sure, it sounds drastic, but you can bet that it only happened a couple of times before we got full compliance.

Turn Off the Water When You Don't Need It

Try not to brush your teeth or shave with the water running. You may need to be careful with this one—oftentimes adults have trouble with it. It has the potential to be as controversial as squeezing the tooth- paste from the middle. When we shave, we partially fill the sink with water for rinsing the razor, rather than running the water each time the razor needs to be rinsed.

Put in Low-Flow Showerheads

These units use less water while compensating with higher pressure. You can also put a restrictive rubber washer in your existing shower-head to reduce water flow. Most of these units will cut the average water flow from 3.5 to about 2 gallons per minute. This is a significant savings of water and water heating, and you won't notice much of a difference when you shower.

Fix Dripping Faucets or Leaking Toilets

There are many types of faucets and toilets out there, but most are relatively easy to repair. If you don't know how to do this, go to a home improvement store and ask—they're usually happy to help. You may not do it perfectly the first time, but just think of the money you'll save by not calling a plumber out for this little task. Regarding toilets, if you're hearing water dribbling into the bowl, you may want to check the rubber flapper in the tank (one of the most common sources of leaks is an old flapper), which is inexpensive and easy to replace. These wear out every few years and allow water to seep out of the tank into the bowl. A sure indication is hearing the water occasionally run for a short amount of time to fill the tank when the toilet has not been recently used.

Bottle in the Tank

Speaking of toilets, put a filled water bottle (24 to 32 ounces) in the toilet tank. This will save you an equivalent volume of water on each flush. It can result in significant water savings, especially if you have a large family.

Outside Hose Bibs and Sprinkler Systems

These items need to be checked and maintained regularly. A hose that's used infrequently can drip for months without being noticed. Sprinkler valves, hidden from view, can also waste untold water if they leak. We know, we've learned!

Check for Leaks

If you suspect a water leak because of an unusually high water bill, turn off all faucets in the house and take a stroll to your water meter. If it indicates that water is still being consumed, chances are you've got a leak. Walk around the outside of the house and the perimeter of your property—especially if you have in-ground sprinklers—and look for wet ground.

OTHER WAYS TO SAVE ELECTRICITY AROUND THE HOUSE

In the Kitchen

Refrigerator. Vacuum the coils at least once each year. Dusty coils don't allow the refrigerant to diffuse heat as efficiently and will cause the compressor to run longer.

Freezer. If you don't have a frost-free freezer, defrost it once each year.

Cooking. During the summer months, avoid using your oven so you don't heat up the kitchen (and the house). Use a barbecue grill as much as possible, or make use of a slow cooker outside on the patio or in the garage. We try to save roasts and other big oven meals for the weekends, when electric rates are less expensive, or for the fall and winter months, when the extra heat from the oven helps warm the house.

Dishwasher. Run your dishwasher only when fully loaded. Skip the drying cycle and just allow your dishes to air dry.

Outside the House

Get a Clothesline. We use it to hang sheets, blankets, quilts, and blue jeans. All of these items take longer than most laundry to dry in the dryer. Using the dryer heats up the house, which is okay in the winter but costly during the summer, as the air-conditioning has to run longer to compensate. If you live in a rainy climate, you can put the clothesline in a covered area—under a porch, patio cover, or in a garage. If you live in a wintry climate, your options are pretty much limited to your attic or basement.

The average electric clothes dryer uses 4,000 watts of electricity per hour. Assuming you are charged 10 cents per kilowatt-hour, the cost to run a dryer for one hour is about 40 cents. It may not seem like much, but if you can eliminate one or two loads each week by hanging your clothes out to dry, the money can really add up. Plus your clothes won't shrink as much, *and* you'll save on cooling costs during the summer.

Window Coverings. Shutters, blinds, drapes, and pleated shades—especially on windows that receive direct sunlight on the east and west sides—all can help lower the inside temperature of your house. Awnings are another great shade producer.

Landscaping. If you have a yard or lots of land, strategically plant shade trees on the hottest sides of your house and/or plant evergreens to be used as windbreaks to further insulate during cold weather. Properly placed, trees can alter the inside temperature of your house by 10 to 20 percent.

With a little research, some changed habits, and a diligent attitude you can take charge of your utility costs and save some significant money. Do your homework, but remember to turn out the lights when you're done.

TALK ISN'T CHEAP: SAVING ON YOUR PHONE BILL

For the economically minded, the telephone can be one of the greatest time- and money-saving tools around. But if you're not careful, pressure from sweet-talking salespeople to add multiple services to your calling plan can

Utility Assistance Programs

If you are a senior citizen living on a fixed income or are in a lower income bracket, check with your utility company for a discount or financial assistance program.

double or even triple your monthly phone bill. Having a standard home phone service as well as Internet access and cellular phones can mean that "reaching out to touch someone" could cost you plenty.

Getting to the bottom line on phone service costs can be a consuming task. A few years ago, Steve evaluated his employer's telephone and cellular bills. For years, they had paid whatever the phone, cellular, and long-distance companies charged them. With careful research he was able to cut the company's expenses in half while increasing services.

If you aren't careful, your home phone bills can become bloated just like those at Steve's old company. Recently, we reviewed several financially strapped budgets and discovered monthly phone expenses in excess of $200. If these budgets had been balanced and included regular deposits to savings and investments, we might agree with this expenditure. But folks who tread water financially or need to free up cash to reach other goals should hang up some of these services.

Residential Service

Once an absolute necessity, residential phone service can sometimes be eliminated by people who carry a cell phone wherever they go (assuming they live in an area with good cell phone service). But those of us who still have to "phone home" should scrutinize our bills and evaluate the services.

Calling Features. The number of options and the costs of add-on services vary from state to state. In our area there are no fewer than thirty-two available extras, ranging in price from $1.25 to $9.45 per month. Basic phone service costs us about $14 per month, but add on the taxes, federal charges, and regulatory fees and it totals $24 per month. For an additional $10 each month, we could purchase a package deal that would allow us to choose three features from a list of nine. But is it worth spending an additional $120 each year? We don't think so.

Line Insurance. Most local phone companies offer a service that provides protection for the phone lines inside your home. With fees ranging from $3 to $5 per month, we need to ask, "Is it worth the money?" In all our years of phone ownership, we've had only one line problem, and that was when we were remodeling our kitchen. Steve was extending a phone line to a different wall and somehow knocked out our phone service. We were without a phone for two days. We researched and hired a private company to resolve the problem—total cost $75. Had we carried line insurance from our local provider, we would have paid $180 for five years of protection prior to the problem, and probably would have waited one to two days for help anyway.

Voice Mail. In our minds, an answering machine is the better route. If you don't have an answering machine, you can buy a new phone/answering machine at a discount store for about $30. These machines have a multitude of features, including multiple voice mailboxes and the ability to retrieve messages while you're away from home (we especially appreciate this feature when we're on vacation). You'll recoup the cost of leasing voice mail service in three to six months. Our answering machine is a lifesaver for us. We use it not only to answer the phone when we're gone but also to screen calls when we are home. As a result, we don't need to pay for caller ID. Most solicitors just hang up.

Call Waiting. We don't have it. We keep calls short by using a timer to limit the amount of time kids can stay on the phone. Communication is the key—if we need to use the phone, we ask our teens to drop off for a few minutes, then they can call back whomever they were talking to. If they want to use the phone after 9:00 P.M., they can use our business cell phone, which has unlimited minutes at night.

Unlisted Number. We do pay for one additional feature—an unlisted phone number for $1.68 per month. This cuts down on unwanted telemarketing calls. With the advent of the Do Not Call registry, this service could be eliminated.

· · ·

Evaluate all of your additional phone services. Each one may only seem to cost a little bit each month, but when they are all added together over the course of a year, it can cost you quite a bit. Once you see the total cost, think about whether these services are really worth it. If not, eliminate some of them.

Long Distance

To save on long-distance service, here are several options.

Lock It Up. The first step toward savings is to cancel your long-distance service on your land line. If you eliminate your current carrier, make sure that you can't dial long distance calls by mistake. If you do, your call may be routed through your local carrier and you could be charged up to 25 cents per minute for the call. Our local phone company has locked our phone against long-distance calls inadvertently dialed with a 1 plus the area code.

No Minimum Fees. If you don't like the idea of eliminating long-distance service from your land line, make sure you have a carrier who does not charge a minimum monthly usage fee. There are several Web sites that provide a state-by-state evaluation of numerous long-distance options. Just be aware that some sites promote their specific product and may present a biased view.

Calling Cards. We use long-distance calling cards that we buy at warehouse clubs. We get 650 minutes for just under $20—about 3 cents per minute. No contracts, no additional fees. One newsletter subscriber told us he found a 99-minute phone card at the dollar store—1 cent per minute. The only problem is that you had to use it up in six months.

Use a Cell Phone. If you have cell phone service that gives you free long distance with unlimited night and weekend calls, use it for long distance during those times. Annette has a friend on the East Coast with whom she chats once a month on the weekends using our business cell phone.

1010 Numbers. Also known as 1010 dial-around. These are long-distance services that anyone can use to receive discounted rates—even if you already have an assigned long-distance provider. These companies compute their fees in several ways. As a result, some are better for international calls, others are better for in-state calls, and others are best for state-to-state. Do a Google search for "1010 rate comparison" to see what they charge. Read the fine print and save.

Take Turns Calling. Before we had a cell phone, Annette and her friend took turns calling each month. If money is tight and your friend isn't willing to reciprocate, you may need to look for other options.

Timers. Set a kitchen timer by the phone and pick a reasonable amount of time you want to talk. When the timer rings, graciously wrap up the conversation.

Read the Bill. Watch out for "cramming"—the practice of adding charges to your phone bill that you haven't authorized. Steve caught our cell phone provider adding $5.95 per month for a service that was supposedly included in our plan. We called and received credit for two months of overcharges.

Get Discounts: Lifeline and Link-Up. The FCC Lifeline telephone discount program gives people with low incomes a discount on basic monthly phone service. Lifeline discounts can range from $5.25 to $10.00 per month, depending on your state of residence. Some states give matching discounts, so you may save even more.

Another program, Link-Up America, also for those with lower incomes, pays for a portion of your phone installation or activation fee. For more details on both programs, visit www.lifeline.gov or call your local phone company.

Managing Internet Charges

Dial-up is still the least expensive way to surf the Net at home. If you do a Google search for ISP (Internet Service Provider) price comparison, you'll find many sources for up-to-date pricing. Ask your friends for recommendations on which ISP they use. Also ask about tech support and if the company's billing is consistent. Getting hooked up cheaply loses its appeal if you've got to fight for service and haggle over the bill each month.

But dial-up brings some decisions. Do you pay for a second phone line just for the Internet? The cost of a second phone line might be more than simply subscribing to DSL or cable Internet access. You have to evaluate the annual cost.

You'll want to analyze how often you access the Internet. Do you really need service at home? Many people view Internet access as a necessity. We see it as a luxury, and if your budget groans at the cost, you may want to use free access at your local library.

One of our newsletter subscribers, Kelly from Scottsdale, recently called to cancel her AOL dial-up service because she had subscribed to a high-speed cable Internet provider. The AOL phone rep offered to reduce her monthly fee from $24.95 to $9 if she would just reconsider. She was bewildered at the instant offer but still declined. The rep then offered to reduce it further, to $5 per month. Again she considered, but turned him down. In desperation, the telemarketer made his final offer—$2.95 per month. Kelly was shocked, but because she had some favorite areas available only to AOL subscribers, she agreed to keep the AOL service for $2.95 per month, in addition to her high-speed cable.

The point of this story is that the price isn't always the *price*. Ask for discounts and special deals—you might just be pleasantly surprised.

Cell Phones

Kids and Phones. When John (our oldest) worked at OfficeMax, they offered him a steeply discounted cell phone package. He racked up some hefty bills and even had the phone turned off a couple times—

"Hey, Dad, did you know that if you don't pay your bill, they can actually turn off your service?" The horror stories we've heard of teens racking up hundreds of dollars in overcharges or eating up thousands of shared minutes of a family's plan just make our heads spin. Giving your kid a cell phone without limits is like giving him a blank check. We don't care if "everybody has one"—that argument just doesn't tug at our wallets. Remember, if you're paying for your kid's cell phone, it's your credit rating and budget that are at stake. We also don't recommend co-signing for your kid's cell phone contract for the same reason. We believe kids shouldn't have cell phones until they have a job and can foot the bill themselves. We know other parents feel differently; do what your budget and conscience can afford. You may find a solution for a younger teen wanting a cell phone in the next paragraph.

> ## WHAT THE KIDS SAY ABOUT CELL PHONES
>
> Roy, at age sixteen, said this about cell phones: "Sure, I think having a cell phone would be cool, but I sure don't want to pay $20 or $40 of my money each month for one. Especially now since I started working a regular part-time job, why should I give away four or five hours of work to pay for it when I have other things I'm saving for? Lots of my friends have them and all they do is play games or goof around with them. Plus their parents pay for their phone service—do you really think my parents would do that for me? You've got to be kidding. But, to be honest, I don't need one. If I'm out and need to make a call, there is always someone around who will lend me a phone. It's really not a hassle, and since most of my friends know our family, they understand."

Prepaid Cellular. If you want a cell phone but don't plan on using it very often, research and try a prepaid cell phone plan. Most cell phone companies offer these. The way they work is that you purchase a phone and a certain number of minutes in advance. Once the minutes are used up, you have a choice: recharge the account or stop talking. Usually the minutes you purchase have an expiration date—about three months. Plans and details vary, so read the details carefully and ask lots of questions. Start your research with TracFone nationwide prepaid wireless (800) 323-2366—they were one of the first to offer prepaid cell phone service. You can get a minimal package for as little as $10 per month. You'll pay a little more for the minutes you use, but you won't have a contract or a high monthly payment.

This option makes much better financial sense if you're considering giving your child a cell phone. With a prepaid plan you'll maintain some budgetary control while allowing your teen to feel like she's part of the in-crowd.

Emergencies. The FCC requires that all cell phones—regardless of whether they have a current calling plan—be able to dial 911 and connect. In fact, many domestic violence shelters collect old cell phones specifically for that purpose. So if your cell phone is "just for emergencies," you don't need a calling plan. Just remember to keep the battery charged.

So, what's our bottom line on all this phone-y talk? Anything beyond basic local phone service really is a luxury and needs to be entered into with careful planning and your household budget in mind. It used to be said that talk is cheap, but that was before the advent of the $150 cell phone bill.

WHAT YOU CAN DO NOW ABOUT UTILITIES

TIMID MOUSE:

Pull out your utility bills for the past twelve months and figure out your monthly average costs. Pick three simple changes you can make to save money. For example, put a quart-sized filled water bottle in your toilet to reduce water usage, install weatherstripping around your front and back doors (if you don't know how, ask a clerk at your local home store to explain it), and when making long-distance phone calls, use either a phone card or free weekend cell phone minutes. Make sure you know how your electric rate is calculated and contact your electric provider to see if there is a more beneficial rate plan for your lifestyle.

WISE OWL:

Evaluate your various utility bills and call each company to see if they have other rate plans that better fit your lifestyle and budget—this includes your cell phone and Internet service provider. Come up with a plan for where you can plant trees or shrubs that will help protect your home from extreme temperatures.

AMAZING ANT:

Evaluate the potential cost savings of replacing major appliances, choosing an alternative heating or cooling system, or replacing your window coverings with more energy-efficient ones. Once you're convinced, save the money you need and negotiate the best deal. Do as much of the work yourself as your ability and time allow.

SEVEN

DEBT:

The American Dream
Turns Into a Nightmare

The American dream of a college education and a beautiful house on a tree-lined street, filled with any number of electronic gizmos and conveniences, is quickly becoming a nightmare for millions of households today. This dream, while picturesque, has a price tag. And that price tag is especially burdensome when it is paid for with borrowed money.

Our addiction to credit is alarming. In 1980, Americans' outstanding credit card debt stood at $50 billion. In 2005, that number had risen to a staggering $800 billion. That's nearly $7,200 for every household in America!

It's no wonder that the use of credit is so prevalent. We are barraged with over four billion direct-mail credit solicitations each year—how many did you toss out last week alone? These direct-mail offers for credit must be working, because the total number of credit cards in America now tops 1 billion. That's an average of 4.78 credit cards per adult.

Such easy access to credit can lead those who aren't careful down the path to credit enslavement. Between 60 and 70 percent of credit card holders *don't* pay off their balance each month. Carrying a balance earns the credit card companies millions of dollars in interest each year, money that's coming out of your pocket. While most of us think we can make ends meet "somehow," bankruptcy is an ever-growing trend. In 1990, nonbusiness bankruptcies totaled 718,107. By 2005, the number of nonbusiness bankruptcies almost tripled to a staggering total of 2 million.

Digging out from under a pile of debt is one of the most rewarding accomplishments you can ever achieve. It's not easy, but it's always good. Our method for eliminating debt has worked for hundreds of people, and with determination and patience, it will work for you too.

PLASTIC SURGERY FOR DEBT: NINE STEPS TO GET YOU OUT OF DEBT FOR GOOD!

Have you ever come across an auto accident in which a battered, disoriented victim was walking around in a daze? Asked if he's all right, he stutters, "Y-Yes, I'll be fine." It's obvious that he's hurt, in shock, and needs immediate medical attention, yet he still refuses help. "I'm all right," he insists.

What does a car crash have to do with debt? As we've helped numerous individuals and couples recover from their debt collisions, we've discovered this very analogy was an accurate depiction of their debt-induced condition. These financially strapped folks were walking around in a daze, thinking that this was normal life—checks bouncing, creditors calling, late notices flooding the mailbox, and utility companies shutting off the power and water. "Doesn't everyone live this way? This is just the way life is," they said. We had to retrain their thinking and help them realize this isn't the way it should be. Juggling finances, avoiding creditors, and having a zero balance in your checking account are not healthy habits for financial well-being.

How do we start a recovery program to get out of debt? We suggest a series of steps, none of them particularly easy, but all of them measurable and effective.

1. Acknowledge the Problem

The first step in any recovery program is admitting there is a problem and that you are willing to work toward the solution. Whether you are overspending $100 or $1,000 each month, your recovery begins with a realization that this is not where you want to be. So pause and consider, then decide to start the recovery program in earnest. This path has many bumps you are yet to encounter, but every worthwhile endeavor begins with the first step.

2. Make Your List and Check It Twice

Pull out all your credit card bills, late utility bills, student loans, car payments—any debt whatsoever—and put it on a list. Also include loans from friends and family, rent due to long-forgotten landlords, or anybody you have borrowed from and haven't paid back. Now organize this list *from the smallest amount owed to the largest.* Disregard, for the moment, interest rates and length of the loan—just make the list.

3. Cut Spending to a Bare Minimum

At an accident scene with an unconscious victim, an EMT first checks breathing and then stops any bleeding. We stop the financial "bleeding" by halting all spending that is not absolutely necessary. This can't be done indefinitely, of course, but it is a necessary step in stabilizing your financial condition. The goal in putting a freeze on spending habits is to generate a monthly excess—"working capital," so to speak. Credit cards sink so many people because they are viewed as additional revenue rather than a purchasing convenience. To reverse the trend, you must create extra money to pay down the credit used in the past.

One of the toughest parts to the recovery from "debt-a-holism" is figuring out what's necessary, which often involves saying good-bye to things you've become attached to—cable TV, high-speed Internet access, eating at restaurants, daily newspaper delivery, a lawn service, magazine subscriptions, and dry cleaning, just to name a few.

It takes courage to identify an expense that you're willing to sacrifice. But there is hope. We were coaching Paul and Sara through this very phase. One of their "necessities" was the daily newspaper. Paul just had to have it. When he realized that the $30 he was spending each month could speed up their financial recovery, he finally gave up his habit. A few days later we received a call from Paul. "You guys won't believe this, but I just discovered that every day someone brings the newspaper into the office and leaves it in the break room!" Are you willing to let your own splurges go for a time? Are you willing to look for other options?

4. Put the Cards Away

If you're going to beat the debt problem, you're going to have to change some habits. One key point is that you need to stop looking at your credit cards as a source of extra money. Plain and simple, *you've just got to stop using them.* If you follow our advice in the budgeting chapter, your money will be so well organized that you might never need a credit card again. We've lived since 1982 without using one—okay, we've actually had two. The first one was a Sears card that we used once to get a discount on a dress (we then canceled it). The second one was a Home Depot card which we thought we'd purchase cabinets with when we were remodeling our kitchen (they offered a 10 percent discount), but we never used the card—and have since canceled it. For those of you concerned about credit scores, we can tell you that in spite of our credit card aversion, we have a very high credit score. It can be done, and without even owning a credit card! Paying mortgage, utilities, and insurance bills on time all contribute to a good credit score.

If you carry several credit cards with you on a daily basis, the temptation is always there. The best solution is to cut up the cards and cancel the accounts as you pay the balance on each one. If being cardless makes you squeamish, cancel all but one and keep it stashed away somewhere. If you can't go that far, at least get them out of your wallet. Putting them away in a hard-to-access spot—some people use the freezer—makes the use of the card much more an issue of choice rather than convenience. Author Larry Burkett offers his (tongue-in-cheek) "recipe" for eliminating credit card usage: "Preheat the oven to 350 degrees, place the credit cards on a greased cookie sheet, and insert into the oven for 10 minutes." The bottom line is this: put the cards away and just don't use them anymore!

5. Get More Money

We aren't suggesting a loan, but we are encouraging you to look around your house for unneeded items that can be turned into money. Many people have purchased clothing items that still have price tags on them. *Return 'em.* How about home and garden improvement items that you purchased but never used? *Return 'em.* Got any unused, nifty kitchen appliances still in boxes? *Return 'em.* Yes, it's uncomfortable, and no, you don't want to inconvenience the sales clerk, but can you stand a little discomfort and possible embarrassment to reach the goal of total recovery? Sure you can! This can be accomplished very easily if you still have your receipts.

Selling gently used items can generate cash too. Consider selling them at a garage sale, or sell your larger-ticket items through a newspaper classified ad (some are free), on eBay (with a reserve price for more valuable items), or on Craigslist.com. If you're a novice with the computer, ask one of your kids or a niece, nephew, or grandchild to help you out. All this "found" money should be accumulated in a separate bank account or envelope in your house. Use the money gathered to pay down the smallest debt from your list completed in step 2.

6. Earn More

Is it time for a raise? If you have been doing a good job, and can document your value, then you may want to ask for a raise. If you've been slacking, work harder and smarter, make yourself more valuable to the company, and then ask the question. It's not a quick process, but it can bring some relief.

If you dread going to work every day, do some soul searching, find where your passion lies, and make plans to move into that field. Is it time to just change jobs in the same field? Whip your resume into shape and start circulating it. This isn't one of your first steps and could take some time to accomplish, but any effort you put into earning more income will help.

Please note that we are not saying to go out and get a second job. Many people have the notion that the only way to recover is to work more hours or get a second job. While this will provide more income, it can add stress to an already overwrought family situation. Rather than working more hours, spend time focusing on reducing your household expenses and managing your debt reduction plan.

7. The Battle Plan

You need to pay every creditor something, even if it's just $5. Take whatever monthly surplus you've managed to generate by following the previous steps, and divide it so that every creditor gets a minimal payment (the largest portion paid to the smallest debt) and a little of what you have goes into savings. Using this method, you can usually eliminate the first debt from your list in a relatively short time. Then apply the monthly excess you've created *and* the payment you were allocating to the first debt and pay it to the second debt—all the while still paying something to every other creditor and putting a little bit in savings too. This method will give you emotional satisfaction as you quickly eliminate debt after debt. Rather than feeling like a victim, you'll start to feel like a victor!

Here's a simplified example of what can be

The Family Connection: Handle with Care!

Nicole is a single mom, recently divorced with three kids. She had a decent job but was struggling to work, raise her kids, and manage her money. It took her a while to get the hang of setting up a budget and planning ahead for expenses, but she eventually caught on. The most amazing part of her story was what happened to her family relationships. She and her ex-husband had borrowed money from her parents. It wasn't a lot—about $300—but it had driven a wedge into her relationship with her mom. When we discovered this debt, it was put on the top of the liquidation list. At first her mother didn't want to accept the money she sent each month. Three months later, when Nicole made the final payment, her mother's attitude had completely changed. At first she was amazed to get anything, then encouraged as Nicole displayed her new money management skills. Finally the relationship was completely restored, and Nicole's mother actually moved to the same city just to be closer to her daughter and help with the kids.

done with $7,300 worth of debt and $150 excess each month. To make the math easier to understand, we've eliminated interest charges from the calculations.

Bob and Carol owe money to three different entities: their dentist, a credit card company, and their bank for a car loan. Their minimum monthly payments total $400. But by tightening their belts and eliminating some unnecessary monthly expenses they have freed up an additional $150 each month. They didn't think that this small amount of excess would do much toward eliminating $7,300 worth of debt. Little did they realize the power of the plan we proposed. Here's what it looked like.

COMPANY	TOTAL AMOUNT OWED	MONTHLY PAYMENT	MONTHS LEFT
Dentist	$300	$100	3
Credit card	$1,000	$50	20
Car	$6,000	$250	24

The excess $150 they chiseled out was applied to their debt and to building an emergency savings account. The first month the dentist got $100 and savings $50.

MONTH 1	PAYMENT	DESCRIPTION	BALANCE
Dentist	$200	Regular payment plus $100 excess	$100
Credit card	$50	Regular payment	$950
Car	$250	Regular payment	$5,750
Savings	$50	$50 excess	$50

During the second month, the dentist bill was so low that they didn't need all of the excess, so some was allocated to the credit card payment.

MONTH 2	PAYMENT	DESCRIPTION	BALANCE
Dentist	$100	Final payment	$0
Credit card	$150	Regular payment plus $100 excess	$800
Car	$250	Regular payment	$5,500
Savings	$50	$50 excess	$100

In month three, the original monthly dentist payment was now paid to the credit card company.

MONTH 3	PAYMENT	DESCRIPTION	BALANCE
Credit card	$250	Regular payment plus $200 excess ($100 from the dentist and $100 excess)	$550
Car	$250	Regular payment	$5,250
Savings	$50	$50 excess	$150

By month four they started to see some real progress and were getting excited. The credit card was almost paid off and their savings were starting to build.

MONTH 4	PAYMENT	DESCRIPTION	BALANCE
Credit card	$250	Regular payment plus $200 excess	$300
Car	$250	Regular payment	$5,000
Savings	$50	$50 excess	$200

By month five they could feel the pressure lifting as the credit card balance was on the verge of oblivion.

MONTH 5	PAYMENT	DESCRIPTION	BALANCE
Credit card	$250	Regular payment plus $200 excess	$50
Car	$250	Regular payment	$4,750
Savings	$50	$50 excess	$250

By month six it was time to celebrate and then change their strategy a bit. Since the only debt left was the car, we encouraged them to increase what they were putting into savings. They went from $50 to $150 each month and started to build a strong emergency account.

MONTH 6	PAYMENT	DESCRIPTION	BALANCE
Credit card	$50	Final payment	$0
Car	$350	Regular payment plus $100 from old credit card payment	$4,400
Savings	$150	$150 excess (taken from old credit card payment)	$400

Month seven to month seventeen was a smooth ride as they kept focused on the goal.

MONTH 7	PAYMENT	DESCRIPTION	BALANCE
Car	$400	Regular payment plus $150 excess	$4,000
Savings	$150	$150 excess	$550

Fast-forward ten months. Once the debt was eliminated, Bob and Carol had several choices: start saving for car replacement, increase savings, or enjoy a little of the excess money and have a party. In the end, they decided to take a short beach vacation—and paid cash for it. Then they started a car replacement account and increased their retirement savings.

MONTH 17	PAYMENT	DESCRIPTION	BALANCE
Car	$400	Regular payment plus $150 excess	$0
Savings	$150	$150 excess	$2,050

Their original payment plan would have taken a total of twenty-four months before they were completely out of debt. With our plan they were finished in seventeen months and had over $2,000 saved for emergencies. It's amazing what can be accomplished in a short amount of time with a plan. And most of the time the repayment plan goes even faster than predicted because unexpected money just "shows up." This includes bonuses, gifts, tax refunds, or other windfalls that often come into the life of people who are disciplined financially.

8. Communicate with Your Creditors

If creditors have been hounding you for payment, you need to call them back. But before you do, get to know your rights as a consumer. Study the Fair Credit Collection Practices Act. It sets guidelines and limits for collection agencies and regulates how and when they can approach you to collect a debt. The Federal Trade Commission governs this act. You can call them or visit their Web site, www.ftc.gov, for specific information.

Once you know your rights, call the creditors and communicate your plan. Let them know what you intend to pay—even if it is well below the minimum. Ask them to suspend interest after a couple of months of faithfully executing your plan. You may be amazed at their cooperative nature when you become trustworthy in your communication. If you are able to accumulate a good amount of cash through the liquidation of unneeded items, you might have some success negotiating a reduced payoff with one of your creditors. This negotiation method usually works well when you are delinquent but have had some previous communication with that particular creditor. We have seen creditors willing to reduce the amount owed by 20 to 40 percent when a lump sum payment is offered. In most cases, though, we don't like to pursue this option. We believe that paying what is owed is honest and honorable. Situations where we bend this rule have involved a single parent who has assumed some debts because of a financially irresponsible ex-spouse and is being hounded by creditors.

Why Put Money in Savings?

Why not just put it all on the debt? Great question. The main reason is to build a savings fund so that if some unexpected expense comes about—and believe us, it will—you aren't tempted to pull out the plastic and charge it. We recommend an initial goal of at least $1,000 in an emergency fund. Eventually, as you build your long-term emergency fund, you should accumulate three to six months of living expenses. It may seem an unachievable amount, but little by little it can be built. See Chapter 13: Savings and Investments for more information.

9. The Payoff

An interesting phenomenon will occur as you successfully eliminate a couple of debts from the list. We call it "repayment intoxication." We've seen people so exuberant about eliminating debt that when a bundle of unexpected cash came their way, rather than carefully planning the disbursement of the money by putting some into savings, they paid all of it to their creditors. This may sound good, but neglecting to set aside money in savings makes you susceptible to many unforeseen emergencies. If a large sum of unexpected cash comes in, pause, talk with your spouse, get some counsel, and then act with purpose. Impulsiveness is one of the reasons people end up abusing credit. And impulsiveness in the repayment of debt can be almost as painful.

Keep a journal of dates that "miracles" occurred—unexpected money came in, significant debts are paid off, and especially the moment you celebrate Debt-Free Day. This list will serve as encouragement to complete your course—to finish the fight.

Are you feeling overwhelmed or encouraged? If you're serious about getting out of debt, your emotions will bounce between the two frequently. We have walked this path with scores of people. The wounds from a debt collision can be completely healed with a carefully applied treatment of self-control and focused attention. The prognosis is good; your condition is not fatal. Many have made a complete recovery within eighteen months, and you can too. Once you start your debt elimination plan, you'll be amazed at how good you feel. As you change your spending habits and near your Debt-Free Day, you'll look back on the way you lived previously and never want to go back.

PAID IN FULL!

Rob and Candy had lived the good life. He had a corporate job for a heavy machinery manufacturer that kept them moving all over the world, where they lived in company-provided villas and enjoyed a six-figure income. When the kids got bigger, they decided to slow down and move closer to family. Rob took an early retirement package and with Candy's approval liquidated his retirement plan to start a home improvement business. Within two years, the business had failed, their savings had been depleted, and they owed over $100,000 to suppliers. They found the idea of bankruptcy repulsive, so they contacted all their creditors and told them that they would pay them off "somehow."

We met them soon after their business failure. Rob had taken a job in Arizona as a manager of a heavy equipment rental company and was earning "only" $60,000 annually, as they put it. They thought they were enduring poverty-type wages; we thought they were earning plenty, at that time much more than we did!

After much coaching and encouragement, they did manage to develop a workable budget and a debt repayment plan. They kept paying all of their creditors a few dollars each month. Eventually they received bonuses, which allowed them to accelerate their payments, but they still had a long way to go. About six months after we first met with them, Rob received a job offer as a general manager at a larger company in the Northwest. His salary more than doubled, and after three years they made the final payment to the last creditor. With great emotion, Rob related a phone conversation with that last creditor. "The guy nearly broke down in tears. He said lots of people promise to pay back what they owe, but you're the only one who ever did." As Rob shared his journey from debt to paid in full, he realized that he had done more than pay a debt; he'd earned a lifelong friend.

Another way to guarantee a permanent debt-free recovery is to build your debt resistance. The next section will do just that.

SLOW DOWN, YOU MOVE TOO FAST! FIVE PHRASES THAT WILL INCREASE YOUR DEBT RESISTANCE

"Today only! Buy now! This deal won't last!" You've heard it all before. Ahhh, the high-pressure pitch from a well-dressed salesperson. How can you resist? It really does sound like a great deal, and it *won't* be here tomorrow. You feel the prickly sweat rise on your brow, and then you say, "Oh, okay, I'll buy it."

Stop the tape. Rewind the scenario. It's time to apply economizer thinking and planning to overcome these types of situations in the future.

Do you remember the Simon and Garfunkel tune "The 59th Street Bridge Song (Feelin' Groovy)"? The lyrics go like this: "Slow down, you move too fast / You got to make the morning last." Well, as you read this section, keep humming the song, but substitute the word *money* for *morning*.

Making spontaneous, fast decisions is one of the main ways that we accumulate unmanageable debt. There are those rare occasions when things turn out right, but there is always a period of time where we question the decision and wonder, "What would have happened if I had waited?"

Let's look at a few real-life examples.

Debt Resistance Phrase 1:
"If I Wait and Search, I Can Always Find It for Less"

The birth of a first child is a tremendous milestone in life. It's also a marketer's dream. Naive first-time parents will believe almost anything and spend almost everything to make sure their newborn child is safe and secure. Just before our son John was born, we experienced the high-pressure, guilt-inducing sales techniques of a master salesperson.

We'd received a postcard in the mail inviting us to an evening event at a local baby store. At the event, we could register for prizes, eat some finger foods, and receive important safety information on various childhood products.

When we arrived, the room was packed with other first-time parents-to-be—many just about to give birth. The presenter discussed, among other things, new laws regarding crib safety—the bars could only be so many inches apart, et cetera—and then launched into the main event: high chairs. He demonstrated how inferior the standard four-legged vinyl fold-up high chairs were. They were unstable and could be tipped over with a gentle nudge. They were unsafe—baby's tender fingers could get pinched when putting the tray on. His spiel went on for quite a while. Of course his product was the answer to all these life-threatening problems. Enter the amazing Wonda Chair! (An appropriate fanfare should play here.) It slices, it dices . . . oh, wait, different product. It was the most essential item for our new precious, powdered little genius. And at only $500, quite affordable with their easy payment plan. Of course, if you order tonight, you'll receive your choice of one additional baby accessory at no extra charge. The pressure, guilt, *and* desire were unimaginable. We needed the chair, we wanted the chair . . . but *we couldn't afford the chair*. Even at that early stage in our frugal journey, we refused to sign up for a payment plan. But we went home terrified of the potential dangers lurking in inferior baby products.

Then we realized that with such a strong sales pitch, there were likely to be many other parents who actually bought one of those invaluable chairs. We started watching the classified ads and eventually found a gently used Wonda Chair for $30—no charge for the crusty creamed spinach under the tray. We cleaned it, put it in the kitchen, John was safe and happy—and our wallets were full. A year later we found another one at a garage sale for even less.

Debt Resistance Phrase 2:
"When Borrowing Is Their First Suggestion, 'No' Is My First Reaction"

In 2004, John—the one who grew up safely because of the marvelous used Wonda Chair—was completing his associate's degree in criminal justice at a community college. Over time, his passion had changed from police work to electronics and sound engineering, and he was working part-time at a large church as a sound and lighting technician. A friend suggested that he attend a nine-month audio recording specialty school. The cost: $13,000. The lure was that the school virtually guaranteed prestigious job placement in the music industry.

We took a personalized tour of the campus and were told that there was a waiting list for enrollment. Steve and John interviewed the head recruiter—really a glorified sales rep. He said that the big, high-paying jobs were in larger cities such as Los Angeles, Nashville, or New York. This meant John would need to relocate, but he wasn't ready to consider that option. When we asked about job prospects in Arizona, the recruiter told us that the highest-paying jobs were in larger churches. When John mentioned the church he was working with, the recruiter told him that he was already handling some of the most sophisticated sound equipment in the industry.

We also met with the financial aid coordinator, who spent exactly four minutes punching in numbers on her keyboard and then proceeded to tell John that he qualified for $2,000 worth of scholarship money. Then, fixing her gaze upon Steve, she said, "And the other $11,000 can be signed for by your dad!" Wow, did she ever make a major wrong assumption! Steve told her that we don't do loans, and that if she wanted John to attend her school, she'd have to put forth a lot more effort and maybe even a few more keystrokes.

John thought about it for a few weeks and finally decided against enrolling. Had we made a quick decision, he would be racking up $11,000 worth of debt for a degree that was virtually worthless in his situation.

Debt Resistance Phrase 3:
"I'm Not Signing Right Now; I Need to See More Options Before I Decide"

A single mom related this story about her community college experience. Sandra was returning to school after a recent illness and divorce. Her financial aid advisor was helpful in filling out her Free Application for Federal Student Aid (FAFSA) but then quickly went on autopilot and helped her sign up for thousands of dollars in student loans. The young advisor never thought to help Sandra research scholarships for which she would definitely qualify—as a woman returning to the workplace, in the medical field, with a low income and dependent children, serving as head of the household, the list was endless. But the advisor's attitude was "Just sign on the dotted line; loans are the easiest way for you to pay for your education."

If Sandra had pushed the advisor to tell her about more options, she might have less in outstanding loans to pay off. Remember, it's okay to ask a lot of questions. It's okay to say, "You know, I'm just not comfortable with this. What other options are there?" It's okay to say, "I need to think about this. Can we set another appointment?"

Debt Resistance Phrase 4:

"I'm Not Buying Today, I'm Just Doing Research"

A while back, a friend of ours named Rob decided it was time to complete his degree after years of being out of school. Rob made a phone call to one of those accelerated college degree programs, and by the next day, his books were ordered and he was approved for a series of student loans totaling over $18,000. His original intent was to get information about classes, but the salesperson was so swift and convincing that Rob didn't realize what was happening or that he would be paying for this decision for a long, long time. Be prepared before you enter into any kind of discussion about loans or mortgages, and stick to your guns.

Debt Resistance Phrase 5:

"Don't Rush Me, Before I Sign, I'm Reading Every Word!"

Read the Fine Print. What could be more boring than reading a loan contract? Not much, as far as we are concerned. In 2004, we decided to refinance the remaining balance on our house. We didn't find many people interested in writing a small mortgage. After much research, we eventually secured a line of credit with the house as collateral and dropped our interest rate significantly. A meeting was scheduled at the title company to sign the final papers. We arrived and were informed that the notary was running late. We waited, and when he finally arrived, he told us that he could allow us twenty minutes to sign the papers. That was enough time, he assured us, as it was all standard wording. We were feeling pressured and uneasy. Should we agree to his terms? Nope, not at all. We called our loan officer at the bank and told her we wanted time to read the entire document. The notary departed. Another person in the office waited for us to finish. We read every page, crossed out items we didn't agree to, and finally signed the papers. What risk was there for the notary? None. What risk was there to us? Plenty. When it's your money on the line, you have the right to take your time and read every word. If you don't, your entire financial future could be in jeopardy.

A Lack of Interest Can Be Costly. When mortgage interest rates were at their all-time lowest, a single woman we know named Lisa decided to finally stop renting and search for a townhouse. She was in a hurry. In our area, the housing market was very competitive—houses sold in just a couple of days. She found a mortgage loan agent who guaranteed that with very little down, even her relatively low salary wouldn't keep her out of the market. Unbeknownst to Lisa, the agent was arranging some pretty creative financing to "help" her. Sometime later, when she reviewed her situation, she was shocked to realize that her financing package wasn't what she thought. Her loan agent had set her up with two adjustable-rate mortgages (ARMs). Monthly payments with an adjustable-rate mortgage can fluctuate from month to month. The first was a standard thirty-year ARM, but the second was a line of credit. The payments for the two loans were combined, and Lisa didn't realize that this meant that her payment on the second loan was for interest only. As interest rates rose, the house that Lisa was struggling to buy became more and more unaffordable.

Her dilemma stemmed from moving too quickly, not reading everything, and putting too much trust in a person who would profit from her decisions. If you're inexperienced with loans, ask someone who is more knowledgeable, with no profit motive, to look over the paperwork. There are a lot of slick, seemingly helpful people out there who just want to help themselves by using you.

. . .

> ## WHAT THE KIDS SAY ABOUT DEBT
>
> Becky, age twenty-one, is a prolific saver and careful spender. A few years back, she needed to give a presentation for one of her college classes, and she chose the topic of college students and credit card debt. Becky says, "My professor, who was in his early thirties, was the person most impacted by my presentation. He told me that he was still paying off loans from his college days and even a few credit cards. What surprised me most was that while I was speaking, the majority of the class rolled their eyes and expressed that they were only concerned with spending money, not paying off debt—after all, many of them were using their parents' money! When I'm done with college, it's nice to know that I won't have any college loans to repay. As a matter of fact, I'll have no debt at all and will be able to start my horse business with cash in the bank. Yee-ha!"

Anytime you are confronted with someone who tells you that a decision needs to be made right now or today, just walk away. Taking your time to make well-informed, researched decisions may frustrate those around you—especially when they're on commission—but you and your wallet will be "feelin' groovy."

Now, everybody sing with us: "Slow down, don't move too fast, I'm gonna make my money last."

WHAT YOU CAN DO NOW ABOUT DEBT

TIMID MOUSE:
Make a list of all the money that you owe. Include friends, family, taxes, student loans, car loans, credit cards, and anything else for which you might owe money. List them from the smallest balance to the largest balance along with monthly minimum payments. Once you've completed this list, don't despair—just move on to the Wise Owl category. If credit card debt is crushing you, get some assistance. Call a reputable firm, like Money Management International (1-866-889-9347).

WISE OWL:
Make a list of assets that you can liquidate or return. Stockpile the cash as you sell the items and build your cash surplus. Eliminate a couple of monthly expenses that are keeping you from generating excess money each month.

AMAZING ANT:
Start eliminating debt with a vengeance. Remember that your debt liquidation shouldn't stop with credit cards. Set your focus on paying off school loans and car loans, and then on completely eliminating your mortgage. The freedom you'll experience will be unbelievable, and the sense of joy you'll feel will splash over onto all those around you.

EIGHT

MEDICAL:

Keeping Your Body Healthy and Your Wallet Happy

Health care and insurance costs are assaulting the household budget. Sadly, things are only getting worse as premiums skyrocket and prices rise for medical procedures and prescription drugs. Any governmental attempt to control these costs becomes a major political hot potato, and not much has been done to remedy the problem or to help those in need. It's hard to keep from feeling like a hapless, helpless victim caught in the crossfire. What can an individual citizen do? Our goal in this chapter is to give you some ammunition to deal with the frustrating red tape associated with health insurance benefits. We'll also discuss saving money on prescription drugs as well as share a few ways we've found to minimize our need for visits to the doctor (and with five kids, this is no small task).

Medical insurance offers our first line of protection against physical and financial disaster. If you don't have it, you've got to get it. Some of our newsletter subscribers live in countries with socialized medicine, and procuring insurance there isn't an issue. But if you live in the United States, you must make acquiring medical insurance a top priority. Even if you can afford only catastrophic coverage, which provides just hospitalization with a very high deductible, do it now. If you have health issues that insurance companies deem as "preexisting conditions" and subsequently these conditions are used to exclude you from coverage, you have three options: (1) Find a temporary insurance policy with fewer preexisting-condition restrictions to cover you while you work on cleaning up your history by getting healthy. Or, if you have a health condition that isn't curable, follow the next step. (2) Take a job with a large company that provides nonqualifying medical coverage. Usually bigger corporations and local, state, and federal agencies provide this type of medical insurance. Some companies even offer coverage for employees who work twenty hours per week. (3) If your income is low, check with your state health department for insurance they might offer at reduced rates or free of charge.

NAVIGATING THE MEDICAL MAZE: MANAGING YOUR INSURANCE BENEFITS TO GET WHAT YOU'VE PAID FOR

Dealing with health insurance claims is enough to make anybody sick. It seems to be an endless maze of paperwork, phone calls, corrected bills, letters of rejection, and overcharges. Will they give you the coverage you have paid for? Should you just blindly trust that the insurance companies and medical providers process everything properly? Don't count on it. How can you survive and actually take control of this unhealthy bureaucracy?

Like any family with kids, we've had our share of trips to the emergency room and sick visits to the doctor's office—each accompanied by insurance company explanations of benefits and other associated red tape. Fortunately, we haven't had any serious illnesses other than

Health Care Statistics

According to a U.S. Census bureau report in August of 2005:

- A substantial 15.7 percent of Americans have no health insurance coverage.

- The proportion of those with employer-sponsored health insurance declined from 63.6 percent in 2001 to 59.8 percent in 2005.

- The percentage of those with government-provided health insurance programs rose from 24.7 percent in 2001 to 27.2 percent in 2005.

A 2005 study sponsored by *USA Today*, the Kaiser Family Foundation, and Harvard Medical School revealed:

- A whopping 21 percent of Americans have overdue medical bills.

- Health care costs (excluding health insurance premiums) rank fifth in the household budget, behind housing, transportation, food, and utilities.

Annette's 1999 kidney stone incident (which generated a huge pile of insurance paperwork). Over the years, we have learned a few techniques to help our insurance providers deal fairly with our claims. It's not an easy or quick process, but these methods have kept us from feeling victimized by some massive, insensitive, and incompetent organizations.

Make Sure You Know Your Benefits

Read what is covered and what is excluded. Are only sick visits covered, or are well checks and annual physicals included? If so, is there a dollar limit to the well check? Several years ago we had a policy that would pay a maximum of $100 per year per person for well checks. That amount was definitely not enough for a complete physical exam with all the blood work, and forget about extra testing of any kind. If you know your limits, you can communicate them to your doctor and try to work out the most care for the least amount of money.

Let's take an example. Steve recently went in for an annual physical. Our current, high-deductible insurance policy has a $200 coverage cap for this kind of visit. The doctor wanted Steve to have a complete blood test, including a lipid panel to test his cholesterol. With our policy, all lab work is subject to our very high deductible. Wanting to conserve our medical account funds while keeping a sharp eye on his health, Steve asked the doctor if there were any options for the blood tests. The doctor told him there were two choices for the lipid panel— one was more detailed and more expensive than the other, but either would work. Steve went to the lab and asked for the pricing for both tests. One was about $100 less expensive than the other. He asked the lab for the price our insurance company allowed, knowing that insurance companies often provide policyholders with discounted rates, and that both prices might go down. What transpired was a one-hour series of phone calls to both the insurance company and the lab, with each telling him that the other should be able to give him the discounted total he would pay. In the end, he never received the answer, so he opted for the least expensive test.

The more time you have, the easier it will be to determine what your costs will be and if a specific procedure will be covered. The first place to look is always your benefits book. But sometimes covered procedures aren't listed in your benefits book. Call your provider, speak with a representative, and ask specific questions—speaking to a live voice often clears things up. A few years ago, one of our kids needed occupational therapy. Annette read through our policy book and didn't find any reference to it as a covered expense. She called the insurance company, and sure enough, they had allowances for this service. It had to be preapproved, but that was a small inconvenience for the six months of weekly services that were covered.

You've Got to Follow Up on the Bills

Don't assume that the insurance company and the doctor's office or hospital are talking to each other. We've had our share of trips to the emergency room for broken bones and stitches—the number of bills for a simple procedure can roll in for several months and be mind-boggling. Annette always deals with these bills right away. She calls the insurance company to make sure that they have communicated with the medical provider and that information is getting transferred so that the claim can be properly completed. Calling right away prevents information from getting lost, makes claims move through the system faster, and lets both parties know that you are paying attention.

You never know what can happen. In one instance, Annette found out after several phone calls that the insurance company hadn't received any of the claim information from the doctor's office. After several repeat calls to both the doctor and the insurance company, it was discovered that the doctor's office personnel didn't know how to operate the fax machine properly, and the faxes weren't reaching the insurance company. While this kind of fax malfunction rarely happens (we hope), many times transmittals, claim forms, or other important documentation has been "lost" or "not received" by the insurance company. Make sure you follow up, and by all means save a copy of everything you submit!

Take Names and Write Notes

We keep all information on smaller, more routine claims in a general medical claims folder. For larger claims, we create a separate file folder to contain all the ensuing paperwork: we staple a sheet of loose-leaf paper to the inside front cover and track all phone communication on that sheet. We take names—some people won't give their last name, so Annette has learned to ask, "Are you the only Mary in the office?" If not, she'll ask for the first letter of her last name. We try to get direct phone numbers to avoid the unending "Please push one for customer service . . . two for . . ." menu choices. We also note the time and date of the call. If we find a particularly helpful person, we build a relationship with that individual and make him or her our primary point of contact. Having one person who actually knows you and your case history will save loads of time and get you answers faster than if you're an unfamiliar customer. This method of record keeping has paid off numerous times. We've been able to document dates, the number of contacts, and how often our calls went unreturned. People are amazed at the detailed information we are able to produce: "Two weeks ago, on May 12, I spoke with Mary about our bill. She said . . ."

Always Keep Your Records

In our state, hospitals have up to six years from date of service to review their records and correct their bills. This means that we could receive a corrected invoice today—with higher charges—for services rendered six years ago! It's not good business, but unfortunately health care providers have lobbied and manipulated the legislative system to protect themselves. This particular loophole applies only to private health care and not to Medicare patients.

Here's a painful example. The 1999 kidney stone Annette experienced took more than four years to be resolved. It started with us unknowingly going to a hospital that was no longer covered under our insurance plan. We went there because we didn't know what was wrong with Annette; she was in pain, and this hospital was where her ob-gyn performed all his surgeries. After Steve negotiated with our insurance carrier, they agreed to cover the whole incident as if the hospital were a preferred provider organization (PPO). Two years after we thought all the checks were sent and the account paid off, the hospital audited its files. It was determined that we owed them $341 more. We checked all our records and calculated that, according to what the hospital originally billed—both the insurance company and us—that the hospital had been *overpaid*. The hospital disagreed and contended that they had underbilled us. As a result, they could correct their billing and collect the balance "owed." Steve was angry. What kind of business is allowed to bill you, collect your money, and then decide years later to modify the bill and try to collect more?

So we fought back. Steve called the state attorney general, who referred him to the state Department of Health Services. There he learned about the laws governing insurance and hospital contracts. Contract law allows hospitals the option of correcting and collecting bills for up to six years, and you can't do anything about it. There are companies that offer to audit hospital collections at no charge except to receive a commission on any amounts they can find and collect on. Hospitals have nothing to lose, so they allow the auditors to review their records, and the patients receive these belated "presents." Our contact at the Arizona Department of Health informed us of all this gloomy news but then was kind enough to redirect our efforts. He told Steve to stop dealing with the billing department and go directly to the office of the hospital's chief financial officer. We should once again explain our story and offer a discounted settlement.

Steve politely but firmly approached the CFO and explained our observation of the bad business practices, the unreturned calls, and the unacceptable lapse in billing time. By being persistent and working up the chain of command, we finally received a resolution to our dilemma. The CFO was grateful for the detailed information we gave him about the billing and collection practices of his organization. We received not only a zero balance on our account but a personal apology from the CFO himself.

Oh, by the way, we did ask for a receipt as proof of the zero balance. We didn't want to leave anything to chance. This is a practice that we haven't always done, but as a result of this experience it now has become a regular request that we make. Always ask for the proof of your balance in writing.

Interestingly, about one month before we received the hospital's revised bill for Annette's kidney stone, Steve was in a clean-it-up and throw-it-out mood. He had come across the stack of kidney stone bills and insurance company explanations of benefits (EOBs) and wanted to throw them out. Luckily, Annette just didn't feel comfortable with that idea, so they were filed once again. Many experts recommend keeping these types of receipts indefinitely.

Some may say that the amount of time it took to fight this battle wasn't worth it. Yes, there are times when throwing in the towel is a better use of time and money, but in this situation we were dealing with, in our opinion, a large amount of money and a matter of integrity and principle. Be resolute, polite, and diplomatic. Learn the chain of authority for the organization, and be persistent—it will pay off.

As economizers, we believe the goal of freeing up money and time isn't just for the purpose of self-gratification. If you have time, help someone who is struggling through the medical maze—widows and widowers who are grappling with the loss of a spouse after a prolonged illness, single moms with sick children. Dealing with daily life is about all they can do. Ignoring the medical bills can only compound their grief and worry with financial distress. Offer to help them find their way.

We hope you don't feel like giving up! Once you experience some of the successes associated with dealing proactively with your medical bills, you'll likely be ready for your next battle—dealing with the cost of prescription drugs.

GIVE ME MORPHINE! ELEVEN WAYS TO SAVE ON PRESCRIPTION DRUGS

Do you remember Bill Cosby's routine about childbirth? To aid his understanding of what childbirth feels like, his wife tells him to grab his bottom lip . . . and pull it over his head. Later, he recounts her experience in the delivery room where, after trying the pain-reducing breathing techniques she has learned, in desperation she cries out, "Give me morphine!"

Paying for prescription drugs today, especially for those with chronic conditions, has become as painful as childbirth. Think this is a minor issue? Think again. According to a 2005 study by the Kaiser Family Foundation and the Harvard School of Public Health, 51 percent of Americans currently take prescription drugs on a daily basis. Since 1993, the retail price of prescription drugs has increased by 7.5 percent each year—almost triple the average inflation rate. A Georgetown University Center for an Aging Society survey reveals that people ages thirty-five to sixty-four pay about $500 out of pocket per year on prescriptions, while seniors ages sixty-five to eighty will shell out over $800 each. Of course expenses increase with more severe conditions such as diabetes, heart disease, hypertension, and cancer. This is money above and beyond what insurance and/or Medicare covers, and these numbers don't appear to be declining.

These costs are particularly burdensome for folks who are retired or on fixed incomes. There are no simple solutions, but many options exist for reducing or eliminating excessive drug costs. Just as it takes a great deal of time to manage your insurance benefits, reducing your prescription drug expenditures may also require significant time, copious notes, and a detailed filing system. Even if you aren't yet retired, keep reading—many of these ideas may benefit you also. And some significant elders in your life may need your assistance as they wrestle with these increasing costs.

1. Drugstore Alternatives

Judy from Scottsdale, Arizona, sent us her strategy for saving on prescriptions: "There are several places on the Internet to buy prescriptions, but I don't feel comfortable about that. I've found Costco or Sam's Club to be my next best bargain. They carry the medications I need at almost half the price. For one particular prescription, I was paying $12.87 per month at my local drugstore and now I pay $7.32 at

Sam's Club for the exact same medication. I've also learned that Costco's online price guide is not the same as their price in store. I've found our local pricing to be better, so I always call first. Another bonus is that these pharmacies are open to the public—if you don't have a membership card you can still access their services!" (According to Costco personnel, membership is not required to make purchases at either the in-store or online pharmacy.)

Make a list of your medications and call the warehouse clubs, grocery stores, and drugstores. Always get the name of the person you speak with, and make note of the prices. If the medication and dosage are the same and you don't have to travel a greater distance, go with the least expensive option.

2. Saving the Co-Pay

Fran Ferguson, a longtime newsletter subscriber and dear friend, has this suggestion: "If you have prescription coverage with a co-pay as part of your health insurance, ask your doctor to write your prescription for a three-month supply. If you make the purchase this way, you'll pay only one co-pay rather than three at the pharmacy. Sometimes you can just ask the pharmacist for a three-month supply." Check your insurance plan for prescription limitations.

3. Generics and Alternative Drugs

A few years ago, while on vacation in Texas, our son John became ill with bacterial pneumonia. We went to a medical clinic where his condition was diagnosed and a prescription authorized. The young doctor prescribed a new antibiotic that cost more than $100 for the dosage he required. We countered the doctor's recommendation and asked for erythromycin—an older but effective antibiotic. (With five kids, we've learned a lot about antibiotics!) He consented and we paid $18 for the prescription. Yes, John recovered just fine. If you have the time to research or have had numerous prescriptions for antibiotics, you may want to create a list of inexpensive antibiotics along with which illnesses they are most effective in treating. Include prices so that you are fully prepared to challenge a doctor's recommendations with sound arguments. The following Web site and book may help: www.crbestbuy drugs.com, a free site run by *Consumer Reports,* where you can research safe alternatives to commonly prescribed drugs. The site reports on several categories of drugs and offers common alternatives that will usually save you money. Each category is presented in a brief format with a longer report available as a PDF download.

You may also want to purchase the latest edition of *The Essential Guide to Prescription Drugs* by James Rybacki, Pharm.D.—an incredibly valuable research source that has been used for more than twenty-five years by readers interested in obtaining as much information as possible about the medicines they take. This book is revised each year and provides a wealth of information that can help you control or lower your prescription and medical costs. It also provides specific information regarding the benefits versus the risks of each medication, all the different names of each drug, principal uses of the drug, how the drug works, and precautions for those over the age of sixty. This will arm you with knowledge and enable you to ask well-informed questions to get what you really need—and what you can afford.

4. Double It and Cut It

Another strategy is to ask your doctor to order your prescription at double the dosage so you can cut or split the tablet in half with a pill splitter. In many cases, the double-strength prescription will cost the same amount as the half-strength one. This simple step is practiced by many people who have cut their drug costs in half. Please check with your doctor or pharmacist before making this decision. According to a consumer medical research group, splitting certain types of pills may compromise their effectiveness.

5. **Expiration Dates**

Money-saving consumer advocate Clark Howard encourages listeners of his daily radio program to disregard expiration dates on medication. He says that the military tested "tons of expired drugs and found out that they were still effective." Steve researched Howard's assertions and found several documented stories and studies stating that most solid-form medications (i.e., pills), properly stored (dark space, dry and cool), will maintain up to 90 percent of their potency for as long as ten to fifteen years beyond the posted expiration date! Specific drugs that aren't recommended for long-term storage are nitroglycerine, insulin, and some liquid antibiotics.

Some states require pharmacists to place an expiration date on newly dispensed prescriptions that is one year earlier than the date on the bulk package from which they are dispensed. Apparently, expiration dates are questionable.

Our friend Dr. Kevin Ludwig, who is a missionary doctor in Papua New Guinea, regularly receives donations of expired medications for use in his clinic. He says that most medications can be stored for years, losing only a small fraction of their potency. The stories he tells of lives he's saved would astonish you. If you're uncomfortable with this idea, do your own research (start with a Google search on "military expired drug testing") and draw your own conclusions.

6. **Free Samples**

Drug companies flood doctors' offices with free samples. When you're heading to the doctor's office, do what Annette does. Bring a canvas tote bag and a list of over-the-counter medications you need to stock your medicine cabinet. This same principle holds true for prescription drugs.

Just ask! You may be pleasantly surprised. Right after our son John recovered from his bout with pneumonia, Annette came down with the same thing. We were back home from our vacation and went to our family practice doctor. He's known us for years and understands and supports our frugal ways. He went to his supply closet and dispensed a sufficient dosage of the antibiotic to bring Annette back to full health.

7. Canada

Steve's parents have been purchasing prescriptions from Canada for several years. This is not a guaranteed way to save—you've got to know your prices to be sure that you're getting a deal. Some medication savings are substantial, while others are not. Steve's parents' favorite source is Universal Drug of Canada—www.universaldrugstore.com, (866) 456-2456. His folks mail their prescriptions and payment to the company, and the drugs are returned by mail. They have a friend whose order was delayed because a customs inspector returned it to the distributor, but for the most part, their experience has been trouble-free.

There are some unscrupulous Canadian or supposedly Canadian drug companies—Steve's folks came across one who told them not to worry if they didn't have a prescription because the company would write one for them! Beware: if they are willing to be dishonest in this portion of their business, what else might they lie about?

Recent reports accuse drugs from Canada of being of lesser or questionable quality, and the FDA appears to be sowing doubts about quality control of drugs purchased from international sources. Many drug companies are either owned by or located in countries other than the United States. Is it possible that the major U.S. drug manufacturers are applying pressure on the FDA to protect their profits? Do what is best for your budget and health.

Okay, now that we've got the easy stuff out of the way, it's time to dive into murkier waters. The savings realized here will depend on a number of factors: how careful you are with research, your income level, and how willing you are to fill out and follow up with paperwork.

8. Discount Plans

Numerous prescription drug discount cards entitle the user to a savings of 20 to 55 percent. Some of these programs are run through your state's Medicaid program, and others are private company programs. Membership in some of these programs is free, while others charge an annual fee. Most of these programs will be eliminated or radically changed with the advent of Medicare Part D. (See the next section.) Annette's mom and dad once joined Arizona's Copper Rx program, which provides discounts of up to 55 percent off generic drugs and 20 percent off brand-name drugs. They found, as they researched prices, that Costco's pharmacy—which doesn't honor the discount card—had lower prices across the board than participating pharmacies.

9. Medicare Part D

This program was initiated in January 2006. Medicare recipients can add prescription drug coverage to their current program. Because the scope of this program is so broad, it can be rather complex. But if you are a Medicare recipient and in a lower income bracket—with an annual income under $11,500 for individuals or $23,000 for a couple—there is a good chance you can have the prescription drug premiums lowered or waived and have your co-pay reduced to $1 for generic drugs and $3 for brand-name drugs. When in doubt, fill out their paperwork—it could save you tons of money.

For seniors who have slightly higher incomes and/or supplemental insurance, apply for Medicare Part D and check with your insurance provider for information about your specific coverage. There is a set enrollment period—it is currently scheduled for November 15 through December 31 each year. Remember, like any other government program, if it gets too confusing, just take two aspirin and call a doctor in the morning.

10. Patient Assistance Programs (PAPs)

One final and extremely helpful way to save on prescription drugs is actually offered by the drug manufacturers themselves. Most manufacturers have put together programs, based on varying qualifications, for lower-income or uninsured people, or those with no prescription drug coverage, to receive steep discounts or free medications.

Each company has a different way to figure eligibility. A friend of ours named Kent shared his experience in researching several PAPs to help his mother manage her prescription drug costs. He told us some programs require proof of eligibility every quarter, some only once each year. Most of the people he spoke with were very patient, but it wasn't easy to get the exact qualifications for each program. Specific information on who can qualify and what the income thresholds are was also hard to come by in literature and on Web sites. (For example, some PAPs consider complete household income, while others consider only the patient's personal income. This can make a big difference if you have elderly parents living in your home.) He needed quite a bit of persistence to get definitive information.

In most cases, the application forms are submitted through your doctor. Medications are delivered to your doctor's office and you must pick them up there. If you have a lower income and need a specific brand-name medication, the patient assistance programs seem to be the best deal out there.

Be aware that there are several service companies that you may be referred to that will offer to fill out and submit the paperwork directly to the drug manufacturer PAPs on your behalf. Of course, they charge—ranging from a small fee per prescription to a monthly fee to keep you signed up. We don't recommend this option. If you need help, ask your doctor's office, a relative, or a friend for assistance.

11. Getting Healthy

We have received several letters from readers who swear by practicing healthy habits. We strongly encourage this too. Many have overcome major health issues and are a living testimony to their willingness to practice healthy disciplines. Could you be one of those who could totally eliminate the cost of prescription drugs by practicing healthy habits? According to a 2004 article in *Forbes* magazine, multiple studies now reveal that lifestyle changes can provide the same, if not better, results than prescription drugs in some cases. This article compared treatments for high cholesterol, hypertension, thinning bones, anxiety and depression, chronic pain, and insomnia. This trend of moving from pills to lifestyle change is growing as more health care professionals see beneficial results. Ask your physician if this is a possibility in your situation. If it is, pursue it with a passion. Being weaned off a prescription drug dependency not only will save you money but will give you courage to zealously tackle other seemingly insurmountable issues in your life. Read more about this in the next section.

Monthly drug costs can be suffocating, but aggressively pursuing lower costs and other money-saving solutions can make financial "breathing" a little easier. If your prescription costs are sucking up a significant portion of your monthly income, now is the time do something about it. Call your doctor, get online, or hit the library. Research will get you the answers you need to save a bundle of cash—and that's not a hard pill to swallow.

HEALTHY BY THE OUNCE: TEN SIMPLE HABITS TO KEEP YOU HEALTHY

We are amazed at the number of people who run to the doctor for a case of sniffles or dash to the emergency room for a sore throat. The key to keeping medical costs down—and healthy living up—is expanding your knowledge of medical conditions and how your body functions. No one will care for you, or your family, as much as you do.

Some people think that knowledge just won't make a difference in how well or how long they will live. To these skeptics we offer the following information. According to the National Vital Statistics Report of 2004, the average life expectancy in America in 1900 was just 47.3 years! That is barely middle-aged today. Today's newborns can expect to live well into their eighties. How is it possible that we have added over thirty years to our life expectancy? It's much better medical knowledge and care combined with increased personal knowledge and better habits. After all, medical practitioners can give us diagnosis, instruction, and medications, but it is up to us to live out the day-to-day habits that will get us well and keep us living longer.

Here are ten inexpensive things we do to get healthy and stay healthy.

Please note: The examples given here are not designed to provide personal medical advice, but are shared to encourage you to learn about alternative options to treating everyday health issues. Please consult your medical doctor or naturopathic physician before making any changes to your medical treatment.

1. Drink It In

Our bodies are about 70 percent water. Water carries nutrients through our body, keeps body systems operating, and flushes out toxins. Next to oxygen, water is the most important element for life. Most experts say that at least 64 ounces of water is needed each day. Many people think that the water contained in drinks such as fruit juice, coffee, cocoa, or soda meets the daily requirement, but the added sugar, stimulants, and unpronounceable chemicals don't promote good health. And some drinks contain so much sodium they actually work against hydrating our bodies. Our family consumes soda, coffee, and fruit juices only on special occasions (which also saves us the cost of buying them for everyday use).

We encourage our kids to take a water bottle with them whenever they're outside playing, riding in the car, or doing other activities away from home. Of course, being thrifty, we don't make a habit of purchasing prefilled water bottles at the grocery store. We have several refillable bottles that we use. There is one caution with this idea—the bottles can harbor germs. We make sure that we regularly wash them out with a bottle brush in soapy water and bleach to kill any bacteria that may be lurking in the bottle or cap.

2. Soap It Up

Don't underestimate the value of soap and water. Whenever we return home from a public place, the first thing we do is wash our hands. Once a month, or more often if someone is sick, one of the kids is sent on doorknob, light switch, and telephone patrol. Armed with a rag and some liquid disinfectant, he or she wipes down these frequently touched items to kill the germs. Imagine the impact on the flu season if every school and office had hand sanitizer available for everyone to use.

3. See the Light

A Mayo Clinic Community Health bulletin stated, "Natural sunlight helps your body produce vitamin D, which is critical to the development of healthy bones and teeth and helps prevent osteoporosis. Getting as little as 10 to 15 minutes of natural sunshine three times a week may be sufficient. Sunshine is necessary for the absorption of vitamin D and calcium." With more adults and children spending extended amounts of time indoors these days, it's easy to forget the simple benefits of a daily dose of sunshine. Of course, balance is important—get too much and you're a candidate for skin cancer.

4. One, Two, Three

We all talk about exercise, but how often do we really test out our body's six hundred muscles? Medical experts stress that exercise, combined with proper rest and nutrition, is one of the most important ways to stay healthy. Try walking around your neighborhood; it's a great time to talk to neighbors. Walking at a mall during extreme weather is a good idea—if you leave your wallet at home.

If you don't think you'll stick with it, get together with a friend or look for inexpensive classes at a community college, church, or YMCA. The key is to do something regularly (and cheaply). Don't rush out and buy an expensive piece of equipment that will collect dust and become a garage-sale bargain. First look for one you can borrow or try at a workout facility. Remember, there are lots of ways to get exercise that don't cost a penny.

5. Germs Beware

Bleach is a powerful disinfectant. Used judiciously and carefully, it can keep many germs at bay. One summer when Steve was in high school he worked in a gymnastics camp kitchen, in trade for camp fees. To keep the kitchen sanitary, they would add a couple of glugs of bleach to the scalding water used to scrub the pots and pans. Bleach was also added to the water for mopping the floors to kill germs and keep the kids at camp healthier.

Today, we use a glug of bleach in our dishwater when cleaning pots and pans (we wear rubber gloves). We also use a 10 percent bleach-and-water solution to wipe down toys and other items purchased at garage sales and thrift stores. We keep the same solution in a spray bottle in the shower to spray on and sponge off the walls a couple of times each week to stop mildew.

6. Consider Herbs and Natural Remedies

This area can be controversial, but the science of nutrition and natural remedies has been growing and improving over the past twenty years. We've noticed an interesting change in the attitude of our medical doctors toward herbal/natural remedies. Previously antagonistic or disbelieving, their attitudes are now more accepting and embracing.

We use a few herbs to treat conditions in our family. Colds are treated with echinacea, grape seed extract, and/or colloidal silver (a natural antibiotic). Vitamin E oil speeds healing of cuts and scrapes. And, while not an herbal cure, gargling with hot salt water does wonders for killing off a sore throat—1 teaspoon salt to 4 ounces of water.

We've found we can beat most mild infections that come our way. As a result, our visits to the doctor and use of antibiotics have been cut way down (no more office visits for a sore throat). One of our most consulted reference guides is the book *Prescription for Nutritional Healing,* by Phyllis Balch, C.N.C. You'll find great suggestions for common and unusual diseases and conditions.

7. Avoid Antibiotics

We realize there are times in life when antibiotics are an absolute necessity. However, many doctors are quick to prescribe them before determining the cause of an infection. Antibiotics kill bacteria—good and bad—but they are ineffective against viruses. And they're not cheap! When taking antibiotics, we've learned to also take large doses of acidophilus, which bolsters our body's production of the good bacteria we need to function properly. There are many types of acidophilus available at health and grocery stores—capsule form, chewable, and lactose free. You'll have to do your own price research to find the best deals in your area.

Now we're going to get really personal.

8. KYBO

For those of you who never experienced camp life, KYBO stands for "keep your bowels operating." As a camp counselor, Steve had to give the nurse a daily report on the "regularity" of the kids in his cabin. The nurse monitored the entire camp and made decisions on dietary changes necessary to keep the campers "moving." Steve knew that there were problems with regularity when stewed prunes showed up on the breakfast menu.

Paying attention to our own bowels is no less important. We monitor our kids and modify their diets if their bowels become sluggish. As important as it is to eat healthy foods, it's just as important to eliminate the waste properly. In order to correct some personal health issues, we've read a mountain of material and learned how to go from really irregular to regular. So we've picked up a few tips on how to introduce natural fiber into our diets.

- A couple of prunes each day can improve the performance of your bowels.

- Adding wheat bran to ground-beef dishes and other foods increases fiber intake.

- Another natural helper is psyllium hulls, available in capsule form from most health food stores. For irritable bowel syndrome, it slows activity down and promotes healing. For constipation, it adds fiber and helps things to keep moving. Don't ask us how or why it works, but it can accomplish both and is truly amazing.

9. Be a Learner

When Annette was pregnant with our first baby, she compiled a list of ten to fifteen questions to ask the doctor during her monthly visits. At first he bristled at her inquisitiveness—normally patients accepted his word as gospel and left him alone. But over time, he came to expect the questions. By the seventh month, he would chuckle and ask Annette what questions were on her list. According to Bernie Siegel, M.D., in his book *Love, Medicine and Miracles,* patients who are a "pain in the butt" generally get better faster. They ask questions, challenge doctors' ideas, and basically take responsibility for their medical care. You need to do the same.

> ## WHAT THE KIDS SAY ABOUT GETTING HEALTHY
>
> Joseph, age fourteen, says, "When I was little I had really bad asthma. If I got sick, it would take a week or more for me to recover. Mom has learned a lot about helping me beat asthma. The herbs and vitamins she gives me keep me healthy so I can play the sports I love. Now if I get sick, it only lasts a couple of days and doesn't turn into asthma. I can play baseball and other sports all year long."

Read as much as you can about conditions you experience. If your kids have asthma, become an asthma expert. Do you have back problems? Read, investigate, and try different things. Being able to treat your condition at home saves time, money, and stress. You'll be surprised where you find solutions. It might be a radio program, a Web site, a used book at a thrift store, or numerous other possibilities.

10. Book It

What better place to invest than in your own well-being? The library holds great resources. Ask friends for titles of books they have found helpful. Start with basic health reference books, then grow your library to include volumes about your specific health issues. Ask your doctor for materials to help you understand your condition better.

Ounce by ounce, book by book, we can improve our health. While daunting at the outset, research can become extremely fulfilling as you discover better ways to deal with the specific problems that have plagued you.

WHAT YOU CAN DO ABOUT YOUR HEALTH NOW

TIMID MOUSE:

If you don't have health insurance, get it! Whether it is state-funded, individual, or picked up through a part-time job, this is a critical leg of your financial table. Read through your health insurance coverage and take notes. Make hand washing a priority in your home.

WISE OWL:

Next time you're in your doctor's office, bring a bag and ask for free samples of over-the-counter medications. Go through your house and disinfect all of the doorknobs, light switches, and phones.

AMAZING ANT:

Start researching natural alternatives for common ailments in your household. Develop some lifestyle changes that will result in healthier living. Pick one or two of the habits in the section "Healthy by the Ounce" and master them—then keep going and don't look back. Start building your library of health reference books, focusing on researching natural remedies for common ailments.

NINE

CLOTHING:

Looking Better, Spending Less

Do you think that being frugal means dressing in clothes that are decades old, threadbare, and strangely colored? Or do you believe that in order to be well dressed, you need to spend a lot of money? Both of these assumptions are false. This chapter will introduce so many ideas that when you're finished, we hope you'll be convinced that you can look terrific and wear stylish clothes without spending a fortune.

For America's Cheapest Family, living better in the clothing realm means buying the best-quality clothes for the lowest price. Achieving this goal is not impossible, as a matter of fact; it's so easy to find great deals on good-looking clothes that one of our struggles is keeping our closets from becoming overstuffed.

Former Filipino first lady Imelda Marcos's 1,200 pairs of shoes are synonymous with excess. But in truth, we all have our excesses, and for many of us, that's our clothes closet. Just look at new homes these days with their massive walk-in closets—is it possible that as Americans we have more than we really need?

Recent newspaper articles on thrift store donations show that, as a society, we are donating thousands of tons of used clothing, some barely worn, for resale. The disposal of clothing in Seattle, Washington, had become such a landfill problem—30,000 tons per year—that in

2003 they initiated a program to encourage donation of clothes rather than disposal. Visit any garage sale and you'll see piles of clothes, some with retail tags still on, being sold for pennies on the dollar.

Indeed, for those in financial distress, the clothing budget is one of the easiest to eliminate. Most of us could easily go quite some time without purchasing any clothing except socks and underwear. If you have kids, however, going a year without purchasing any clothes is unrealistic. Either way, at some point you'll have to outfit everyone, and while building or rebuilding a wardrobe isn't a quick job, it can be done well and inexpensively.

There is no realistic gauge for what an average family spends on clothes. There are just too many variables to create a credible average. The Bureau of Labor Statistics reports that the average single guy spends $836 per year on clothes (an average of $70 each month), while the average single woman spends $1,108 ($92 each month). The same report suggests that a family's apparel purchases will consume 3 to 5 percent of take-home pay. And as the kids get older, the cost to keep each child clothed increases. But have no fear—we've got plenty of tips for dealing with kids' clothes as well as your own.

We will break down this tapestry of clothes shopping into two parts: wardrobe building for adults and winning the price and style battle with your kids. In both cases you'll discover that with a little planning you'll end up with an eye-catching closet.

BUILDING A BETTER WARDROBE FOR LESS

Women usually love what they buy, yet hate two-thirds of what is in their closets.

—MIGNON MCLAUGHLIN

We've simplified and improved our wardrobes inexpensively by using three main techniques: color draping and evaluation, organization, and careful wardrobe building.

Evaluate Your Clothes by Color

Have you ever purchased an article of clothing that looked nice in the store, then never wore it again because it didn't look the same when you put it on at home? This can happen if you aren't sure what colors are flattering on you and if you shop impulsively, without a plan. An informative book called *Color Me Beautiful* helped us in this area. Author Carole Jackson has developed a system of grouping people into four color types or "seasons," winter, spring, summer, and fall, based on hair and eye color as well as skin tone and color. Her system, known as "color draping," got its name from taking large swatches of different-colored fabrics and draping them over your shoulder to see which colors went best with various skin tones and hair colors. The theories were initially developed for women, but men and children can use them as well.

Jackson provides a recommended color-draping palette for each season: certain colors will look great on one person but terrible on someone with different skin and hair color. Once Annette, who is a "winter," understood Jackson's concept of color draping, she purged her wardrobe of all unflattering colors. When she evaluated what remained, she realized that these were the outfits in which she actually received the most compliments. Motivated by Annette's success, Steve, who is a "summer," also discarded many unflattering colors from his collection and started a wardrobe rebuilding process.

When in doubt, wear red.

—Bill Blass

This understanding has made clothes shopping much faster and easier. We simply don't consider any article of clothing that doesn't fit within our color palettes. Much of Annette's wardrobe consists of Christmas red, black, royal purple, royal blue, navy blue, turquoise, maroon, emerald green, hot pink, pale pink, and pale blue. Steve's palette mostly includes red, maroon, blue, black, cool gray, emerald green, and white.

The end result of knowing which colors look best on us is that we wear everything we have in our closet—unless, of course, it shrinks or we expand.

Keep It Organized

Organizing clothes in your closet or dresser is essential to saving money. In our closet, we hang clothes by type and color. This makes finding a particular top or pair of pants quicker and easier. It also makes assessing wardrobe needs trouble-free. We hang all long-sleeve shirts in one section and short-sleeve tops in another, arranged by color. Suits, pants, skirts, and dresses are also organized in the same fashion. Double closet bars on one side of our closet allow us more efficient storage for shorter items, such as shirts and pants. Steve hangs his dress pants from their cuffs using wooden clamp-type hangers—this eliminates wrinkles across the knees.

Building a Wardrobe

Starting with a few basic colors and styles can give you a mix-and-match system that will achieve a maximum number of different outfits from a minimum number of components. Neutral colors work well as a foundation to your wardrobe. For example, Annette has three pairs of Dockers-type slacks: navy, black, and khaki (beige)—this last color is okay for her if not worn near her face. She also has three pairs of shorts and three skirts in the same colors as her slacks. With a couple of pairs of denim jeans in blue and black, she's got a great start for a basic casual wardrobe. Obviously, if you work in an office environment you'll have different basics, but the same principle applies: build with neutrals and accent with select colors. Annette avoids prints in her wardrobe with the exception of a few dresses, as they are harder to mix and match. Prints are also less flattering when trying to hide a few extra pounds. Annette also picks straight-line skirts and blouses that are long and worn outside of her pants and skirts.

Steve's basics were different because he worked in an office environment. He needed some basic suits (gray and blue), a blue blazer, a few pairs of dress slacks, and some solid-colored dress shirts (white, blue, and one pink). He also built a more casual collection of Dockers and polo shirts.

We follow the same guidelines with shoes. Steve has two pairs of dress shoes (cordovan and black), three pairs of casual shoes, two pairs of sneakers, and one pair of hiking boots. Annette has four different colors of pumps (white, beige, navy, and black), along with three colors of flats (brown, navy, and black), two pairs of sneakers, and one pair of hiking boots. If you want to keep your dress shoes looking their best, keep them on a shoe tree.

Dry Cleaning Costs

We try to avoid items that need dry cleaning. While a dress or outfit may be a steal at a consignment or thrift store, if it isn't machine- or hand-washable, we avoid it. We must consider not only the cost of dry cleaning but also the time involved in dropping off and picking up the item. If you're building a business wardrobe and you must have suits that require dry cleaning, make sure you have money set aside in your budget for these expenses.

Classic Styles

Fashion designers are constantly changing what's in and what's out. Why? For two reasons: one is to make money, and the other is to keep their jobs. As economizers, we shun trendy fashions. Not only does the latest rage not flatter our aging, gravity-challenged bodies, but fad clothing requires constant updating and shopping. In our minds, it's just not worth the effort or the money.

In his book *Dress for Success,* John Malloy encourages the purchasing of classic fashions. He promotes avoiding extremes—large lapels, trendy colors, high or low waists, baggy pants. If you do go trendy, you'll have to revamp your wardrobe every couple of years. With classic styles, you can still look smashing and get more mileage out of your clothing budget. You can, however, create some trendy outfits by using classic styles and adding trendy accessories. These could include earrings, socks, belts, purses, scarves, hats, or whatever else is in style at the moment. This way when the trend changes you're only eliminating a $5 accessory instead of a more expensive item such as a blouse.

THE $1,000 JAW DROP

Years ago, when Steve was working for a graphics studio as a designer and account rep, we were referred to a woman who was starting a wardrobe consulting business in which most of her clientele was higher-income women. Not only would Liz help a client by color-draping her and evaluating her current wardrobe, she would also sell her unwanted clothes. This eventually led to the establishment of a great little consignment shop called Regal Rags, which is chock-full of incredible deals on high-end fashions.

Early in the life of Liz's business, the husband of one of her clients wanted her to resell several of his unwanted suits. Steve happened to call Liz at the right time, and the suits happened to be the right size—no alterations required. Out of the several available, only one color fit into Steve's wardrobe—black. We thought that $80 was a fair price for this smooth, shiny wool suit, especially because it had satin-lined pants. Ooh, we'd never seen satin-lined pants before!

Several weeks later, Steve wore the suit to a client meeting with the head of recruiting for a large international company. After the meeting, Tom walked up to Steve and fingered the lapel of his jacket, saying, "Where did you get this suit? Look at the lift in the shoulders! Who is the maker?" Steve replied that he had just gotten it from a friend. Tom gingerly pulled open the jacket and read the label.

"Armani!" he exclaimed, staring slack-jawed at Steve. "You have an Armani suit! Do you know what these cost?"

"Nope," Steve replied honestly.

Tom continued, "Why, that suit is worth at least $1,000!"

Now it was time for Steve's jaw to drop. To think that we stumbled upon the find of a lifetime and only thought that it was a good deal!

Shop Smart

After completing our closet evaluation and organization, we created a list of items we were missing and posted it in the closet so we could easily add to it. No, we didn't run out to the mall and start shopping . . . *you know us better than that!* If you rush out to buy, you'll usually spend more money. We were in no hurry, so we started our hunting at thrift stores.

We have a multilevel hierarchy of stores when we shop for clothes—this includes our clothes and clothes for the kids.

- **Small thrift stores.** We start at a couple of our favorite thrift stores. If we're looking for casual clothes such as jeans, Dockers, or polo shirts, our first option is almost always a small thrift store—Family Attic Treasures—that benefits an adoption agency. They have a smaller selection but offer quality clothes, low prices, and a friendly staff to boot. For those who haven't visited a thrift store lately or doubt thrift store quality, you really ought to take a second look. The industry has undergone an overhaul in the last twenty years. Because of today's consumerism, an abundance of high-quality clothing and household items is now available in these stores. The stores themselves are cleaner, are better organized, and definitely have more convenient hours than garage sales (see our thoughts on those below). This type of thrift store is everywhere, from rural communities to large metropolitan areas. Some of them may be dives, but don't give up on the whole concept without visiting several. You'll eventually find a gem like ours and fall in love with the people, the bargains, and the way they do business.

- **Bigger thrift stores.** Our second line of attack is Savers Thrift Department Stores (Value Village in some states), which are located in more than two hundred places in the United States, Canada, and Australia (www.savers.com). These stores are huge—filling space about the size of a large grocery store. All of their clothes are organized by type, size, and color, which makes getting what we need much easier. They also have every season of apparel displayed all year long, so, for example, you could buy shorts in the wintertime if you needed to. In our area Goodwill has recently upgraded their stores to compete with Savers. You may also want to check out Salvation Army and Disabled American Veterans thrift stores. Just be aware that in some of these stores you may have to dig for your treasures and give them a thorough washing when you get them home.

- **Consignment stores.** If we can't find what we want in the thrift stores, we go to our favorite high-end consignment store, A Second Look. With over twenty thousand people consigning clothes and housewares here, this store has become so well known that people travel from all over the country to walk its aisles. The used clothing market has improved greatly all over the country, so there is likely to be a great resource like this in a city near you. Check the yellow pages, search online, and ask around.

- **Discount retailers.** Usually after the first three options, we find what we need. If not, then we go to discount retailers such as Ross or Marshall's. If Annette is looking for a dress and hasn't found what she wants at the other stores, she can usually find a nice new one for between $20 and $30. Steve also finds great deals on dress socks and ties here.

- **Retail closeout stores.** We've tried places like Nordstrom Rack, which sells overstock and returns for those particular stores. But we found that while we could pick up some bargains in these stores, we had to wade through so much merchandise—some previously owned and damaged—that it ended up being too time-consuming. Plus the prices weren't all that great—a little more than we would pay from our first four options. Not to mention that the stores were usually really crowded, nothing is returnable, and the checkout lines were very long.

The following resources may require more time, effort, or driving, but you may just stumble upon the greatest killer deals of the century.

- **Garage sales.** What about garage sales? You might think that we'd be raving about them, and we agree that there are bargains to be found, but there is a trade-off: you have to spend a lot of time driving from sale to sale. We've discovered that most of our garage sale outings take about four hours. Even with a list in hand and asking for specific items at each garage sale, we often don't find what we are looking for (although we often come away with stuff we didn't know we needed). Because adult clothing is too hit-or-miss, we won't shop garage sales if this is all we're looking for, and here's why: you have to stumble upon a sale where the person selling his or her clothes is the same size as you, and there is only a slight possibility of this happening. And even if you do, what about finding styles and colors that you like? That's much less probable. Using half the time, we can usually hit two thrift stores or consignment stores, where our chances for success are much greater.

- **Rummage sales.** Church rummage sales or club benefit sales, where a large volume of donated items from various families is for sale, is a much surer way to find great deals on clothing that fits. The key is that they usually have clothing from a huge number of people, not just one or two. We once stumbled upon a great deal for Steve at a grade-school rummage sale. He found four virtually brand-new Lands' End fitted white dress shirts. Years earlier Annette had purchased a couple of these as a Christmas present for Steve and spent $35 each—we picked up these treasures for $2 each.

- **End-of-season sales.** Another place to pick up some real deals is a high-end retail store at their end-of-season sales. Years ago Steve bought some wonderfully tailored wool dress slacks with satin lining for $45, marked down from $120. Sometimes those clearance racks can contain some real bargains.

- **Friends.** Over the years we've been the recipient of many bags of hand-me-downs from thoughtful friends and relatives who have kids a few steps ahead of ours. We've also received bags of clothes from other adults who have cleaned out their closets and remembered us. We take what we can use from the clothes given to us and pass along the rest. Many of our friends know that we can usually find someone who can use what they're getting rid of.

Shopping at thrift and discount stores has its pitfalls. Even with a list in hand, we still pick up some impulse items (although far fewer than without a list). There are also those occasional unnoticed flaws on previously worn items—stains, missing buttons, worn crotches, and broken zippers—that we sometimes miss when we're buying. We've learned to check the clothes carefully. And there *are* times when we walk away empty-handed. But the same thing can happen at the mall. Still, staying focused with your "hit list" will result in the greatest savings, the quickest shopping, and the most fantastic wardrobe you've ever had.

This focused hunt paid off in a big way when Roy (then age fifteen) needed a tuxedo for his performances in the community concert band. We'd been searching halfheartedly for several months and hadn't found one at either thrift or consignment stores. There was no way were going to pay retail for one (and we knew that we could find one for less than the cost of a one-time rental), so as his first concert date approached, we anxiously kept looking. With only one week left before the concert, Steve and Roy planned a final shopping trip, working through our used clothing store hierarchy. Steve's tux jacket fit Roy, so at the very least all they needed to find was a pair of pants. They hit pay dirt at the second store, where they found a pair of tux pants that didn't even need to be altered. The price was even better, only $16! The decision to piece together a tux was the best option for Roy, since he is still growing.

Starting from Scratch

When our daughter Becky started working her first job, she needed to update her college wardrobe—basically blue jeans—to business casual. So we headed to thrift and consignment stores to find a variety of Dockers and nice shirts. Becky purchased four pairs of slacks and about ten different shirts for less than $70. Together, Annette and Becky created a mix-and-match chart listing each combination of pants and shirt—over thirty outfits total. When Becky dresses, bleary-eyed, early in the morning, consulting the chart has made it much quicker and easier. This is a great trick for those guys who are color-matching-challenged—it really takes the guesswork out of dressing well.

Vacation Blunder and Recovery

A few years back we headed to Colorado for vacation and to attend a conference. We enjoy having our family dress in color-coordinated attire; it's fun and the identical clothing makes it easier to spot one another should we get separated. During the week before we left, Annette reviewed outfits for each of the kids to wear. Steve followed the plan pretty well but didn't pack a red shirt for one of the color-coordinated days. When we discovered his wardrobe deficiency, the kids didn't miss the chance to tease him. "Dad, *you* didn't pack everything you needed!"

During one of our driving outings we passed a Savers thrift store and went in for a visit. Steve found a great-looking red Chaps polo shirt for $5. It then occurred to us, as we looked around the store, that thrift stores are just about everywhere. Even forgetting clothing on a vacation isn't an excuse to go out and spend money at a retail store!

The thrift store was a gold mine. We discovered lots of souvenirs that the kids were able to afford—Colorado shirts and Colorado Rockies baseball hats that they wouldn't have chosen to pay retail for in a gift shop. There was even a large selection of coats, hiking boots, and other winter outerwear—rare finds in our Phoenix stores, but items we sometimes need.

Better Dressed, Better Treatment

Another great tip from *Dress for Success* is that the better you dress, the better you are treated. John Malloy shares a study he commissioned in which men dressed in a suit and tie asked strangers at an airport for change for a cab. The better-dressed gentlemen received more money more often than those who wore a suit with no tie and an open-collared shirt. We've experienced something similar when we've returned unwanted items at a store. If we are nicely dressed, we always receive better treatment.

Applying a planned approach to building and managing our wardrobes has saved us gobs of money and time, and it will do the same for you too. And if you have kids, keeping them clothed doesn't have to be a hopelessly expensive battle. With our five kids we've had lots of practice in this area—keep reading.

KIDS' CLOTHING WARS: ELEVEN WAYS TO WIN THE BATTLES OF COST AND STYLE

Often interviewers ask us how we manage to maintain a thrifty lifestyle and still have happy, well-dressed kids. Indeed, our kids *do* dress well and feel good about the clothes they buy and wear, and they don't break our bank doing it. But for many families, the battle over kids' clothing rages on. Faced with peer pressure, movies, TV, and ubiquitous ads, how can you dress your kids well while spending less money?

According to the U.S. Department of Labor's Consumer Expenditure Survey, the average American spends $370 to $1,090 per child per year for clothing. The lower figure is for clothing an infant and the higher cost represents keeping a trendy teen clad in the latest duds. Interestingly, the price of clothes keeps increasing while many styles are decreasing the amount of the body they cover—pay more, get less. This is a battle for your hard-earned cash. If you join the opposition, you'll spend $100 for one pair of the latest shoes or "in vogue," ratty-looking jeans. If you fight for the Frugal Alliance, you'll spend less money and help your kids create a great-looking, complete wardrobe that lasts more than one season.

We refuse to play into the retail realm's hands. Pushing new must-have fashions every few months, they announce higher prices and flaunt immodest or grungy styles as the norm. A war-experienced soldier won't fight such an enemy on their terms. He'll make his own rules based on his strengths. So we'll fight this war on two fronts: the spending front (getting quality clothing inexpensively) and the style front (convincing kids to dress nicely). Here are our strategies.

Spending: Getting Quality Clothes Inexpensively

1. Start Young. Dressing infants through preschoolers is fairly easy. They'll wear whatever Mom picks out, regardless of style or color. At this stage, the concern is how quickly they outgrow their clothes. The least expensive way to purchase clothes for kids in this age group is at garage sales. You can usually find piles of outfits for $1 or less. At benefit or church rummage sales with lots of kids' clothes, we've been able to negotiate for a bag full of clothes for as little as $2.

Planning several sizes ahead helps you avoid paying retail prices too. Coming up with a logical storage system (more about this below) will keep you from overbuying. This strategy will also help you find what you need quicker. Then when the child outgrows the clothes, you can either store them for your younger kids to wear in the future or pass them to others. We've enjoyed watching our younger two boys' excited faces as they grow into the clothes that their "cool" older brother wore. Of course, each kid has different tastes, so some clothes go back into storage until the next one comes along. One final advantage of buying in advance is that it eliminates the stress of dressing your little cherub for church only to find she's jumped two sizes and has nothing nice to wear.

2. Cultivating Hand-Me-Downs. As we mentioned in the adult section, sharing or trading clothes with others is a wonderful way to keep your costs down and to build relationships. You can't just come out and ask people to swap their kids' clothes. But we've found that if we offer to pass them a bag of clothes that might fit one of their kids, they'll often reciprocate later. Many times people pass us clothes because their kids are older than ours and they know that we'll gratefully receive them. We can't trade clothes with them, but we can give back to them in other ways. Inevitably, as our kids outgrow clothes and we pass them on to others, more bags arrive. We pick the clothes that we think will look best on our kids and pass on the rest. Most moms are extremely grateful to have a bag of "new" clothes.

How to find such a network? One friend shared that she stumbled upon a garage sale in her neighborhood where the family was selling clothes that fit her two boys perfectly. She developed a relationship with the family, and then made an agreement to buy their future hand-me-downs at a reasonable price.

3. Have a Storage System. This is an absolute necessity. If you save the clothes but can't find them when you need them, you've wasted the effort and will end up spending more money. We store clothes, sorted by size, in similar-sized boxes. We keep most of them in the garage, but if space is limited, you can store them in the tops of closets or under beds. Annette keeps a card file with one index card per box of clothes. The index card lists the box number, the contents, and where it is stored.

Keep in mind when you store clothes that there are some things that don't store well. Elastic waistbands may disintegrate depending on storage temperature and the amount of time they are stored. Also, if the clothes aren't perfectly clean when they are put into storage, stains are much harder to remove several years later.

4. Have a Shopping Plan. We consider clothes shopping for kids to be something like a specal ops military strike—get in, find what we need, and get out. Just like when we hunt for clothes for ourselves, we visit certain stores depending on the need. If we're looking for casual clothes, such as jeans, Dockers, or polo shirts, our first option is our favorite small thrift store. Our second line of attack is Savers, where Becky recently went to update her winter work wardrobe. Her careful shopping netted her three blazers, one skirt suit, two pairs of slacks, and four shirts, all for about $50! If we're looking for dress clothes for the kids, we are more likely to find what we need at A Second Look, a consignment store in our area that's great for higher-end, more stylish dress clothes.

You may have to try a couple of different stores in your area until you hit pay dirt, but once you find a good source, it will be another great weapon in your arsenal to manage your kids' clothing expenses.

5. Review Clothes. Keeping track of your kids' clothing needs can be difficult. Annette compiles a list of needed clothes (dress, play, underwear, and outerwear) twice yearly—when she switches the kids' wardrobes from summer to winter in October, and again in April when she switches from winter back to summer. With our hand-me-down supply, the lists are usually relatively short. Typically we need to go shopping at stores for just a few items. And because we go early in the season, we can easily find what we need.

Another advantage of this semiannual wardrobe review is the elimination of the bloated closet and drawer syndrome. Without constant evaluation, the kids' clothing collection will grow exponentially—usually as a result of birthdays, holidays, hand-me-downs, and great deals at thrift stores.

Keeping a list of needed clothes can also help immensely when it comes to planning ahead (our next step) as you carry the lists with you and check off items as they are purchased.

6. Plan Ahead. We've all seen the end-of-season closeout ads, and they're not just for adults! The selection may be limited, but the prices can't be beat. Shopping nine months to one year in advance can be a daunting task, especially if you have several kids, but this strategy has garnered us great savings. One summer sixteen-year-old Roy entered an essay contest and won a $100 gift certificate to Tilly's, a California-based teen clothing store. He could have easily spent the money on one or two in-season items. Instead, when he shopped the first week in November, he checked the clearance tables, where he scored five pairs of nice shorts, one swimming suit, and two "really cool" short-sleeve shirts, all to be saved for the spring. Even if he grows taller, the shorts will still fit.

There have even been a few times where Annette has shopped three or four years in advance. These situations occurred when she spied a fantastic bargain on a beautiful dress for either Becky or Abbey. The hardest part was waiting until it fit properly. But watching the anticipation grow as the girls fell in love with the dresses was a lot of fun for us as parents.

7. Simplify the Wardrobe. Putting limits on your kids' wardrobe is essential—it will help you determine when enough is enough.

We keep it pretty simple: they all own a couple of pairs of blue jeans, Dockers-type pants, and dress pants. The girls have several seasonal dresses, and the boys each have a suit and a couple of dress shirts. Additionally, they each have several pairs of shorts and a number of T-shirts. During the summer, our older kids, ages eight and above, sleep in boxer shorts and T-shirts. In the winter, the girls have warmer PJs, but the boys sleep in sweatshirts and sweatpants.

With a pared-down wardrobe, it's important to help the kids rotate their clothes so they don't end up wearing—and wearing out—just one pair of favorite pants. Our "Payday" system for the kids (Chapter 12: Kids and Money) includes regular dresser-drawer inspections to make sure their clothes are kept neat and orderly.

Style: Convincing the Kids to Dress Nicely

8. Give 'Em Choices. As kids get older, they want to have a say in the clothes they wear. In our family, the parents (i.e., Mom) always have veto power. Years ago Annette attended a seminar that presented the idea of "shared control." This helpful concept reduces skirmishes over clothing and works like this: the parent picks out two or three acceptable clothing choices, and the young child gets to make the final selection. They feel empowered, but you have control. By the time our kids are teenagers, they have a pretty good idea of what types of clothing are appropriate for most situations.

9. Give 'Em Limits. Some parents tell us that they have to choose their battles carefully and that fighting over clothes just isn't worth it. "Hogwash!" is our response. If we as parents aren't going to take a stand, who will? Will aunts, uncles, grandparents, pastors, coaches, or school administrators take the time to hold the line with our kids? Is it fair to expect them to?

On the positive side, we've seen the trend turning as many school administrators are realizing that this clothing nonsense has gone too far. We need leaders in our kids' lives who set limits. We recently chatted with a high school math teacher who shared a newly enacted policy at her school. Because so many girls were coming to school with grossly immodest clothing, the principal's office now keeps a box of extra-large T-shirts on hand, which are distributed to inappropriately dressed students. Our kids' drama instructor also set a clothing policy: no spaghetti straps or bare midriffs for girls, and no low-rider pants with visible underwear for the boys. We need to support and encourage these values. But ultimately, we need to realize that it is our responsibility as parents to set and hold the standards. We also need to return to our own parents' decree, harsh as it may sound: "I don't care what everyone else is wearing; you're not wearing that."

10. Don't Give 'Em Money. Our kids start buying their clothes at around age eleven—sometimes younger, depending on their desire and maturity. The money they earn is part of our Payday system, which starts at age five. At eleven, the "teen syndrome" hasn't yet hit in full force. We have the opportunity to teach and influence the choices they make with their money, and we help them find bargains at garage sales and thrift or consignment stores. Because they are spending their own money, they become much more careful in what they buy. This system totally eliminates the whining for expensive designer sneakers or other clothes. Try it—you'll likely be pleasantly surprised by the results.

If by chance the kids run low on their clothing money and have a real need, we will contribute to their clothing purchase. But, honestly, this situation has rarely occurred.

Another family we know uses a different

Holiday Clothing Hullabaloo

It was Christmastime 2005. Abbey was eleven years old and seriously struggling with this question: None of her cousins get dressed up nicely for Christmas Eve at Nana and Grandpa's house, so why should she?

We made this a topic of discussion at the dinner table one night. Annette stated her reason: we don't have to follow the cultural trend of dressing down. Just because the majority may choose a particular trend doesn't mean we have to do the same. Steve said that Christmas is a very special celebration and warranted dressing nicely—and especially because Nana loves to make Christmas Eve a memorable time for the whole family.

Becky, who's nine years older than Abbey, chimed in, "Yeah, I agree with Mom. I'm going to wear my new two-piece plaid skirt suit that I just got for a great price."

Roy and Joseph said, "It's okay with us, we'll wear our black Dockers, white turtlenecks, and red sweaters."

Finally Abbey agreed, saying, "*Okay, I'll get dressed up! I might even wear a skirt.*"

Now that's teamwork at its best: parents being supported by older siblings who influence the younger ones in a positive way. Oh, that it would always happen this way!

system. The parents set a limit on what they will spend for a particular clothing item. If a child wants to purchase something more expensive than the parents' limit, he or she is responsible for paying the difference from his or her own savings or earnings. Making your kids active participants in the buying process will be a positive step in leading them to financial independence.

11. Give 'Em Love. One of the most important weapons in our armament is love. Balancing a hard line on clothes with a soft line on hugs, laughter, and fun family times will give resilience to your relationships and your rules. Remember, your kids are not the enemy; the trendy attitudes are. Standing firm against peer-pressure-induced attitudes while still loving the child is a tough balancing act, but it can be accomplished.

CUTTING CLOTHING COSTS WITH SIX SIMPLE STRATEGIES

Pat Rowley, a subscriber from Erie, Pennsylvania, has a plan for combating peer pressure for purchasing the latest clothing styles for her kids—and herself.

> I don't buy my children the latest trends in clothing at retail price. I find them trendy clothes along with classic fashions at upscale secondhand stores in the area. It took some time and effort to find the stores, but now that I have, I shop there regularly. Here in Erie, there is one store that sells just used name-brand clothing and footwear for teens. Another great store is called Once Upon a Child—a great place to purchase used baby and children's clothes. I purchase used professional business attire and classic styles for women at a store called My Sister's Closet. With a little digging you can even find great deals at Goodwill, City Mission, and Salvation Army thrift stores. Why would anyone pay retail?

Donna Brooks, a subscriber from Chambersburg, Pennsylvania, describes her five saving strategies for clothing her family inexpensively:

Consignment strategy. A consignment store nearby takes many of our unneeded clothing items. I tell my kids that any money they make from selling their own clothes is theirs to spend on other clothes from the consignment store or Goodwill store. I have even purchased brand-new items at garage sales for 10 cents or 25 cents and then taken them to the consignment store to sell. Even with their cut taken out, I receive far more than I could by selling them at my own garage sale.

Thrift store bulk bag sale. Our Salvation Army thrift store often has $6-per-bag sale days. Plus, when I use a $1 coupon they distribute, I can get a sack full of clothing for only $5! Anything that doesn't fit someone in the family goes to the consignment store. So there is very little risk in picking up clothes without trying them on.

Return policy. Some area thrift stores allow me to return clothes if they don't fit. If I see a deal for my kids, I can buy it, take it home, and have them try it on. Anything that doesn't fit goes back—or to the consignment store. I can move faster and pick up the deal when I see it if the kids aren't with me.

Digging for deals. I've found a great resource for clothing in our area called Gabriel Brothers—www.gabrielbrothers.com. (They have more than a hundred stores in eight eastern states. Thirty-one stores have the Gabriel Brothers name, and another seventy-one stores bear the Rugged Wearhouse brand.) Some clothing is slightly damaged, some better and some worse. But I've gotten clothing there with very minimal damage—hard to spot—for a steal! You can't be in a hurry, though, because you've got to leave time to hunt through piles and racks of clothes to find the best deals.

WHAT THE KIDS SAY ABOUT CLOTHING

Our older daughter, Becky, has been raised shopping in thrift stores. She says, "My friends are constantly trying to 'rehabilitate' me. They invite me to go to the mall with them and try to convince me to spend my hard-earned money for retail-priced merchandise. I come home laughing at the amount of money *they* spend on stuff I can find at thrift or consignment stores for *sooo* much less."

Becky has a great-looking wardrobe, which always garners her compliments. Her greatest finds have been a full-length Pendleton wool coat for 99 cents and several gorgeous formal gowns purchased for less than $20 each.

Shoes. I have purchased various sizes of shoes at yard sales (only if they're brand-new) years ahead of when they will fit one of our kids. I do this mostly with tennis shoes or snow boots. When my kids are ready for the shoes, I go to my cache and pull out a new pair. Anything that doesn't fit goes to someone else who can use them—cousins or friends. I'll only take a chance on shoes like this if I can get them dirt-cheap!

WHAT YOU CAN DO NOW ABOUT CLOTHING

TIMID MOUSE:

For you, the easiest way to save is to stay out of the stores. Don't go shopping . . . period. See how you can make the clothing you have work for your daily and work needs. Reorganize your clothes closet by color and type, as described earlier. Mend anything that needs a button, hem, or new elastic. For your kids, start the older ones buying some or all of their own clothes.

WISE OWL:

For yourself, evaluate your wardrobe. Read up on color draping and figure out what colors and styles look best on you. Then get rid of the stuff you won't wear, don't wear, or shouldn't wear. Compile a list of what you're lacking. If you have the money saved for buying more clothes, check out thrift or consignment stores to find the items you need. For your kids, commit to evaluating your children's wardrobe at least twice during the next year (spring/summer and fall/winter). Pass on what doesn't fit and make a list of things they need. If your kids are younger, hit the garage sales. Otherwise, try thrift and consignment stores.

AMAZING ANT:

For you, start rebuilding your wardrobe, making sure you have basic colors and classic styles included. Research thrift and consignment stores in your area to develop your own ranking system for where to buy the different types of clothes that you need. For your kids, stand firm when their clothing desires exceed your household clothing budget. Make clothing styles a topic of discussion with your kids around the dinner table.

TEN

ENTERTAINMENT & RECREATION:

Finding Fun for Free

What are you willing to pay for fun and entertainment? If you're like other families, it seems that there is no end to the things you can find to spend your discretionary income on. It's so easy to drop a significant amount of money on recreational activities. Many people we've talked to think that they just can't whittle down these expenses and still have a good time. But we challenge that notion.

Consider what you'd pay (without discounts) for the following: a professional sporting event, a concert, a museum visit, a trip to the zoo, a first-run movie, or a Renaissance festival. Add to those admission fees the price of gas, parking, meals, and souvenirs, and the outing can quickly burn a hole in your wallet. Even simple activities such as bowling, ice-skating, roller-skating, or miniature golf can deplete your recreation budget if you're not careful.

We are convinced that meaningful memories can be created with little or no cost if you just know where to look. Whether it's a date night, family get-together, or outing, we've found oodles of ways to have an enjoyable time without dropping a lot of cash.

RECREATION IDEAS THAT WON'T WRECK THE BUDGET

Some of our suggestions in this chapter may sound like things a kid would do. Well, it seems that kids do know how to have fun—with anything from a cardboard box to a bucket of water. Have we become so sophisticated that we have forgotten the simple pleasures that can bring immense enjoyment to our lives? Please read these ideas with an open mind and perhaps, just perhaps, you'll discover a wonderful new youthfulness and save some money in the process. We want to jog your mind so that you can start thinking of recreation in a different way. We'll throw out lots of ideas but leave the specific details up to you.

Holiday Recreation

If you're looking for inspiration, just check your wall calendar.

- **New Year's Eve.** We always host a party. We invite families with kids our kids' ages, and everyone brings food so our preparation is minimal. We play Charades, have a White Elephant gift exchange, and throw confetti at midnight.

- **Martin Luther King Jr. Day.** This is an opportune time to visit a museum of black history and culture and to learn about the history of slavery and segregation in our country. Many cities host breakfasts or luncheons to celebrate Dr. King's impact on society.

- **Valentine's Day.** We don't usually do a date night on Valentine's Day—it's too crowded and most restaurants won't accept coupons that night. So we go out the prior or following night, when they're less crowded. If you enjoy making homemade cards, they are always appreciated. An outdoor mall near our home hosts a "Lovers' Lane" with free horse-drawn carriage rides, chocolate tasting, and dancing to big-band music.

- The Jewish festival of **Purim**—which precedes Passover—provides an opportunity for a costume party based on a wonderful story about beautiful Queen Esther and how she courageously saved her people from a massacre. We attended such a party—it was fun and we'll never forget it!

· **Passover.** Many families celebrate this holiday with a traditional Passover Seder. It's a terrific recounting of the biblical history of when the Israelites were freed from Egyptian slavery. If you're not Jewish, there's lots of information on the Internet, or you can ask one of your Jewish friends for help.

· **Easter.** Many churches host musicals celebrating these occasions. It's also a great time to color hard-boiled eggs and have an Easter egg hunt (we use plastic eggs and fill them with candy and coins). One year we blew out raw eggs (Becky got dizzy) and then swirled them in model-car paint floating on water. They turned out beautiful, and we fill a pretty crystal bowl with them each spring.

· **Mother's Day.** Consider a special breakfast, cards from the kids, or a favorite dinner cooked by someone other than Mom. Even if you don't have a mother, you can take the time to say thanks to an older woman who has influenced your life.

· **Memorial Day.** The three-day weekend of Memorial Day provides an ideal opportunity to host a barbecue, cheer for our troops at a parade, visit a veterans' cemetery and place flags on the graves, and attend a church picnic or one of many other commemorative events. For many years Annette's extended family (over thirty-five of us) all got together and raced little Pinewood Derby cars—the kind that the Cub Scouts race. This was done in honor of the Indy 500 race, which occurs on this weekend. It was a hoot! We even had news cameras from a local TV station show up one year to watch this crazy family fun, and it aired on the local evening news that night.

· **Father's Day.** Celebrate Father's Day in June with the dads in your life or visit a man of character who has influenced your life. One year Annette and the kids sent Steve on a treasure hunt . . . looking for the rest of the family. It started with a note left at home directing him to go to our favorite Chinese buffet to pick up egg rolls (his favorite appetizer). John was waiting there and gave him the next clue. John and Steve drove to a restaurant (where kids ate free with an adult meal) to meet the rest of the family. After dinner Steve was blindfolded and taken to his favorite ice cream shop for dessert. It was a smashing success, especially for the kids—they love fooling good old Dad.

· **Fourth of July.** Time for fireworks and picnics! One of our favorite memories is celebrating Independence Day in a small Arizona mountain town that was celebrating the holiday as a town for the first time. The veterans' band played, reminiscent of the Mayberry town band from the *Andy Griffith Show*. The fireworks were spectacular, the people friendly, and the weather cool. Recently we've found a spot near a golf course lake to sit on the grass and watch a fireworks display. We bring a boom box and play patriotic music while we ooh and ahh at the dazzling skyward spectacle.

· **Labor Day.** A three-day weekend for camping, barbecues, or just lounging around.

· **Halloween.** Why not act like a kid? Plan your Halloween costume early in October, which alleviates stress and allows you to find better deals as you gather the materials you need to make your costume. At the end of the month, you can don your costume and go visit neighbors. You'll be surprised how much fun it is to go door to door and talk with laughing friends. You could also try planning a costume party or attending a harvest festival.

· **Thanksgiving.** On this holiday we reach out to people who have no family in town. We shoot fake turkeys with BB guns, play the card game Spoons, and eat lots of pie. If everyone who attends helps out by bringing a side dish and you purchase your turkey during the two weeks before Thanksgiving (on sale), this meal can be prepared for just a few dollars.

· **December.** There are lots of free or inexpensive recreation activities in December. Most high schools and colleges host holiday concerts. There are always free church-sponsored musicals. Community productions of *A Christmas Carol* or *The Nutcracker* often offer free admission with a donation to Toys for Tots or a food bank. Our Christmas season wouldn't be complete without a night of driving around with hot cocoa and fresh cookies to admire the beautiful Christmas lights decorating the houses in our area.

Date Night/Dining Out

Dinner dates don't have to be expensive. We love to use the Entertainment Book with its two-for-one coupons. These are readily available in most cities, or visit www.entertainment.com for more details. You can also find some great coupons in your mailbox or newspaper—don't throw that junk mail away! Of course we read the coupon carefully, as some are only for lunch or have specified days of usage (such as Monday through Thursday), and most of them only discount the entrée, not appetizers or drinks. So we drink water with a slice of lemon.

Remember that some restaurants are known for large portions, so consider splitting an entrée and saving some money. Some restaurants also have early-bird specials—discounted meals if you dine in before the dinner rush.

Dining In

A few years back some friends of ours were in the midst of digging their way out of debt and getting their finances under control. Bob and Carol had made it through the toughest part of getting caught up with bills and balancing their budget. Finally there was a little breathing room. How much, you ask? Well, after they had allocated money to all of their necessities and savings, they had exactly $10 available for recreation. Only $10! What fun could you have with a measly $10?

This is where commitment and creativity really play an important role in creating memorable recreation. They discussed their options. With four young kids at home, a babysitter just wasn't an option. Finally, they decided that what they really wanted was a quiet dinner alone. So they fed the kids early and got them settled in bed. Then Bob ran out and picked up a great Chinese carry-out dinner for two.

When he returned, Carol had the table set, the lights dimmed, and the candles lit. Sitting close together at their kitchen table, they enjoyed their date. Later Carol confided in Annette that she'd enjoyed that dinner more than any date in their past. Why? It's simple. They knew that all of their expenses for the near future were covered. Money was saved in the bank, and even though they only had $10 to spend on dinner, they knew that there would be no regrets for spending that money and that they could totally relax and enjoy it!

Isn't that what recreation is all about—relaxation and enjoyment?

Annual Local Activities

Every community offers events that occur on a yearly basis. It seems there is something special every week of the year, and many are free. Keeping a watchful eye on your local newspaper calendar of events will give you plenty of ideas for things to do. Another great resource is the AAA *Tour Book* for your state or your local Convention and Visitors' Bureau. They list activities city by city. Just be sure to verify all the information before planning an outing.

In our area we have:

· A hot-air balloon race in January.

· A huge used-book sale at a large coliseum in downtown Phoenix in February. People line up for hours before the doors open to ensure they get first dibs on some great titles.

· Several free horse shows in February and March.

· An open house at a state wildlife rehabilitation center in spring and fall. The first time we attended, we were amazed to learn about numerous creatures that we hadn't realized lived in our desert.

· A myriad of college and high school spring concerts and recitals in May. Subscribers Beth and Curtis from Spokane, Washington, suggest, "Most universities publish dates and times of their recitals in the local newspaper or online. One of our most enjoyable evenings was spent in a university recital hall listening to a solo tuba recital. It was memorable and quite entertaining—and, best of all, it was absolutely free." If you ever get the opportunity to hear one of our military bands perform, don't miss it. They are phenomenal—and free, too.

· The Arizona State Fair every October.

· Scout-O-Rama in November—this is a huge event where Cub Scouts and Boy Scouts display scout skills and hands-on activities for kids and adults. You could experience amateur rocketry, delicious Dutch-oven cooking, obstacle courses, plant conservation information, native wildlife demonstrations, and so much more.

Readers Chime in

The longer you practice thrifty habits, the more ways you'll find to make saving money actually fun. Here are a bunch of great ideas from other super-frugal subscribers:

Giving and Receiving

Volunteering can provide you with free recreation too. Our daughter Becky regularly volunteers at the All-Arabian Horse Show in Scottsdale. Her few hours of donated labor provide her with free parking and passes to several daytime events. We've also volunteered at our local botanical garden during their annual luminaria holiday festival. We received free admission, heard excellent music, and helped usher for a wonderful event.

Books, Art, and Movies. Erin McGever from Phoenix, Arizona, says, "Try the public library for books about travel, hobbies, or home decorating. We've learned a lot about one another and the world this way. We also check out local art galleries for free festivals where they even serve free treats. Dollar theaters work well if you don't mind seeing a movie a few weeks after everyone else has."

Free Ideas. Lisa Marchinkewicz of Hudsonville, Missouri, says, "Our family goes camping often. This last January, we went to a free RV show. We paid $3 for parking and spent at least half a day there. It was good to think about summer again, and we picked up some great ideas for how to modify our camper to better suit our needs."

Save on Books and Save on Dinner. Hazel Cotton from Texarkana, Texas, says, "We leave our checkbook and credit card at home and then visit a large bookstore nearby. If we find a book we really like and our public library doesn't have it, we'll do an interlibrary loan. If we like the library book enough to own it, we'll purchase it. If we can't get it through the library, we'll think about it for at least a week before deciding whether we'll buy it. Once a month we go out to a nice restaurant with a coupon and usually spend $25, including a tip."

Give me an *F,* Give me an *R,* Give me two *E*'s. Curtis and Beth from Spokane, Washington, say, "Don't forget about attending your local high school sporting events—most are absolutely free! Also visit your city, county, and state parks. Many will have free admission. Take a walk, climb a tree, climb a hill, or roll down one. Don't forget about neighborliness. We had one evening of great fun with several of our neighbors on our street. One person brought their hammer dulcimer, another brought spoons, and I [Curtis] brought my banjo. We laughed and sang and had a night we'll never forget."

Substantial Fun, Done for Cheap. Doreen Hallman from Phoenix, Arizona, encourages family game nights. "For years we have done a monthly game night with friends and their kids. It usually consists of a host couple and two other families preferably with kids the same age. Little kids can be put down to sleep and you don't need a babysitter. Everyone brings substantial hors d'oeuvres, which become dinner for the night."

Volunteering for Fun and . . . Free Stuff. Hazel Cotton from Texarkana, Texas, adds, "Last September our local museum hosted its annual arts and crafts festival. I found that by volunteering at the museum, I could get free passes for us. Once we were at the festival we found all sorts of free stuff like pens and bottled water, etc. We ate a large breakfast so we were not tempted to buy the expensive food at the festival. Also one of our local hospitals had an event offering free health screenings. We went to this event also, enjoyed ourselves, and didn't spend a dime."

Seasonal Ideas

We've already covered holidays, but there's always plenty to do even if Christmas was last week. Unique activities are associated with each season of the year. No matter where you live, wonderful seasonal activities can capture your imagination and your heart. Of course, many of these ideas are limited by your geographic location—ice-fishing in the Arizona desert, for example, just won't work!

But as the weather cools in the fall in other parts of the country, you'll have different options. Consider apple picking, making annual holiday preparations (such as buying gifts and wrapping them, crafting gifts, addressing Christmas cards, taking your annual Christmas picture, and making food and guest lists for parties you'll host in December), going on a hayride, taking walks in the park, and raking a humongous pile of leaves and jumping into it—you'll laugh and feel like a kid again.

During the winter, you could pull out that ice-fishing pole in the northern states, or you could enjoy sledding, ice-skating, Christmas caroling, building snow forts, reading aloud a favorite book together by a crackling fire, or having a snowball fight. In warm-weather states such as Arizona and Florida, picking citrus, hiking, or playing tennis can be fun.

In springtime, outdoor dates or family activities could include visiting an arboretum, strawberry picking, bird watching, or hiking through fields of wildflowers, the forest, the desert, or mountain trails. We especially enjoy this season, as our citrus trees are in full bloom—nothing compares to taking a walk while the smell of fresh citrus blossoms waft through the air and hundreds of butterflies dart about.

And then there's summer, the season of sun and fun.

School's Out for Summer—Yikes!

It's June and school's out . . . what do you do to help your kids have healthy fun? Is it a night at the movies, a visit to an amusement park, or an afternoon at the mall? How much will that cost you? Perhaps you might want to consider tackling a large project, learning a new skill, or participating in community service. These activities can also be fun and more rewarding.

But be careful of overkill. We've seen parents sign their kids up for a crushing load of summer activities that have both parent and child exhausted (and broke) by summer's end. Are expensive camps, clinics, and planned activities all there is to having summertime fun? Spending gobs of money to keep your kids entertained isn't necessarily the solution. We have included a list of suggestions—most of which we've done—to stimulate your thinking.

Don't think, however, that these ideas are just for kids! As we said earlier, kids often know how to have fun in a way that adults don't, and we think folks of any age will get some enjoyment out of these ideas.

We know that if both parents are working, your options are more limited, but there are still activities that you can do together. Consider setting up a kind of co-op with a couple of other working families and coordinating days off to do activities with the kids.

Libraries. Most public libraries have summer reading programs. We have signed our kids up for three different reading programs, and they've earned prizes from each one, from pencils and other little trinkets to movie and restaurant coupons and even Major League Baseball tickets. Even if your library doesn't have a reading program, a trip there once every week or two offers free fun: libraries often schedule story times, clowns, magicians, and other kid-friendly entertainment, and some even have adult-oriented lectures and demonstrations. And remember that libraries lend more than just books. They have movies (including documentaries), books on tape, magazines, and even music.

Note: Watch the renewal date. Checking out large quantities of books can be a budget buster if you miss the due date. Our libraries allow phone or Internet renewal, which makes it much easier to avoid fines. If you have a regularly scheduled time to go to the library, it makes missing due dates less of a problem.

Museums. People often think of museums as great places to visit. While they can be very educational, we've found that they can also be over-stimulating, especially to young children. We try to limit our time there to no more than four hours. Some museums schedule occasional free days. Contact your local museums to see what they offer.

Entertainment Books. We've also found that the Entertainment Books, which are much less expensive to purchase during the summer because they are halfway through their expiration period, often offer two-for-one coupons for local museums and other attractions. Check them out online at www.entertainment.com.

Quiet Time. We schedule a couple of afternoons each week from 2 to 4 P.M. as reading or artwork time. Even Mom needs a break, and staying inside during the heat of the day can be refreshing.

Movies. We don't live our lives in front of the TV, but during the summer we'll schedule a weekly time to watch a movie borrowed from a friend or the library for some excellent "edutainment." Disney classics like *Old Yeller, Swiss Family Robinson, Treasure Island, The Apple Dumpling Gang, Homeward Bound,* and many others are wonderful to watch. Also, historical movies hold our kids' attention, educate them, and provide better role models and heroes than most of today's movies—*Davy Crockett, Johnny Tremain,* and Gary Cooper in *Sergeant York* are just a few examples.

Volunteer. Don't neglect this wonderful avenue of service, which we believe should be instilled in kids at a very young age. Many charitable organizations have age limits due to liability, so if you have young children, visiting nursing homes or helping at a church may be the only outlets available to you. If you have teens, many nonprofit organizations can use their help. Check out food banks, soup kitchens, city parks and recreation areas, Habitat for Humanity and other low-income housing organizations, animal shelters, and rescue organizations. Don't neglect the needs of those in your neighborhood, such as widows and senior citizens. We've done yard work as a family for our sweet neighbor Martha, and it was a blessing for her and all of our kids. We've learned of numerous volunteer opportunities from our involvement in Boy Scouts and their focus on community service. Volunteering as a family is a great way to stretch your comfort zone and to see parts of the world and society that you normally wouldn't be exposed to.

Field Trips. As a home-schooling family, we've taken lots of field trips and discovered that museums aren't the only interesting destinations. Remember that many businesses love to have families and groups tour their facilities. We try to pick destinations that fit with our kids' interests, and we have visited all but a couple of the following:

- A candy factory
- A vineyard
- A miniature-horse ranch
- An urban farm
- A dairy farm
- An airplane hangar
- A smaller noncommercial airport
- Krispy Kreme doughnut "factory"
- The Arizona Game and Fish Department
- An ice factory—a great place to go during the summer
- Courthouses
- Television studios
- Radio stations
- Newspapers
- Our state, city, or town legislators
- Bowling alleys behind the scenes
- An auto body shop
- Waste management facilities or recycling plants
- Historic sites such as Native American villages, pioneer towns, Revolutionary War and Civil War reenactments, army

forts, or homes of and memorials to famous Americans, such as Kit Carson's log cabin, Booker T. Washington's lab, the residences of Molly Brown or Thomas Edison, and various presidential libraries and war hero memorials

If you get a few families together, you can each plan an activity and rotate the responsibility from one week to the next. It lightens the load and provides great family interaction.

Outdoors. When the weather is pleasant, spending time outdoors is wonderful and provides great opportunities for exercise and a little bit of science too. Many botanical gardens and arboretums have fascinating exhibits and trails. Numerous state and city parks or forests also include interesting features and exhibits. Don't forget hiking in the woods, Rollerblading through a park, biking, flying a kite, or picnicking.

Maybe you're partial to the water. Try boating at an urban lake, waterskiing or just riding with a friend who has a boat, camping, or hosting barbecues with juicy corn on the cob and watermelon. Beaches also provide a healthy atmosphere for hours of exploring and discovery, and don't forget swimming—we do lots of this. One of our favorite mini-dates is to escape to our pool and sit and talk after the kids are in bed.

Many cities also sponsor music festivals or provide free outdoor concerts—check your newspaper for listings.

Maybe it's time to start a garden. Digging in the dirt, amending the soil, planting, and then harvesting in early fall can be a productive way to spend time this summer. Check out the book *Square Foot Gardening* or visit www.squarefootgardening.com for simple gardening ideas.

The Real World. We think it's important to invest in teaching our kids real-life skills. Why not plan some house projects? Try cleaning up and reorganizing bedroom closets, cleaning out the garage or toolshed, ironing and mending clothes, or organizing linen and bathroom closets. We've also taught our kids to help with menu planning, grocery shopping, and meal preparation. When our youngest, Abbey, was seven years old, she was determined to prepare an entire meal she found in her Beanie Baby cookbook. We all pitched in, and the memories and photos still bring her a proud sense of accomplishment. She prepared piggies in blankets (small hot dog pieces wrapped in pieces of dinner rolls), fruit kabobs, and cookie cupcakes. It was a smashing success.

If you have the inclination and it's not too far to travel, research your state or county fair. You and your kids may enter artwork and craft projects. We have spent many a summer's day working on these. We've done this for years, and the kids always feel a deep sense of accomplishment when they receive ribbons and prize money.

GAME PLAN FOR A FAIR DEAL

We are often asked to describe our system for evaluating and procuring great deals—a sort of checklist or procedure manual for saving money. Unfortunately, there's no one way to do it. Occasionally we stumble onto a great deal, but most times it takes time, research, and patience. We'll share a story of one of our recent recreational bargains as an illustration of these principles in action.

Take Me to the Fair

It was time for our annual excursion to the Arizona State Fair, where we always see the exhibits, ride the Ferris wheel and roller coasters, eat overpriced food, and generally have a great time.

Normally admission to our state fair is $9.50 for adults and $4.50 for kids. Between Annette, Steve, Becky, Roy, Joseph, and Abbey, it would cost us $47 just to get through the gate. Add to that another $8 for parking and $25 for each of the kids to have a special unlimited-ride wristband and we've created a spending binge of epic proportions—more than $150, not including food. All of this for a few hours of fun in the sun. Aware of the retail cost, we made the decision to go to the fair... but we *knew* we could do it for less! Read on and we'll explain.

> ## WHAT THE KIDS SAY ABOUT RECREATION
>
> Daughter Becky, now twenty-one, has lived through much of our early years of learning to be frugal. She remembers some great birthday parties where we had a clown or petting zoo come to our house. As time went on, we learned to find less expensive ways to make birthdays fun. "One of my favorite birthdays was when I helped Mom and Dad plan a mall scavenger hunt for my party. It was a blast. I think it was especially fun for me to put in the time planning the party and then to see my friends have a really good time."

Know the Playing Field

One of the first keys to finding a great deal is to *gather data*—learn the rules, restrictions, and secrets of the field you're playing on. You might visit various Web sites, talk with knowledgeable friends, and read consumer magazines or newspaper articles.

In this case, visiting the state fair Web site and calling their main office provided most of the information we needed. We took lots of notes and discovered that a multitude of admission and ride discounts were available. These details may not seem pertinent to your pursuit of saving a few bucks, but in reality, sometimes the hardest part of getting a real deal is sifting through piles of information in search of that one nugget of gold. Here's what we discovered:

- Admission discounts offered:
  - *Dollar Days* There were two days when admission to the fair was one dollar per person. *Cost: $6.*
  - *FREE for Schools* Public, private, and home school field-trip groups are given free admission and parking. This option requires an extensive registration process. We belong to a home school co-op and in past years had used this option. School groups are also allowed to bring in their own food, which can be a major cost savings. However, this year, the restrictions regarding which days school groups could attend just didn't work out with our schedule.
  - *FREE Admission* Macy's department stores sponsored two special Monday admission deals. For the first 96 minutes that the gates were open, people could get in for free. Unfortunately these specials didn't fit with our schedule either.

- Ride discounts offered:
  - *Ten for $10* There were three days when the fair offered a ride special of ten rides for $10. But this promotion fell on days when admission discounts weren't offered, so the savings were a wash.
  - *Wristband Days* The fair offered unlimited-ride passes for $25 per person on five days of its run. In previous years, when the price

was lower, the kids had paid for half the price of their wristbands and we paid the other half. But we had discovered that even if we arrived at the fair early, the large number of people standing in lines limited the number of rides the kids could get. In an eight-hour period they could ride ten to fifteen rides, including multiple times through fun houses that had no lines. And, of course, the most desirable, dizzying, and stomach-churning rides always had the longest lines. We ruled out this option because we weren't going to arrive at the fair until early evening.

- *Read and Ride* Each year kids five to fourteen years old are offered three free ride tickets if they write three short book reports. Since we have two kids in that age category, they qualified to receive six free ride coupons—which they were "encouraged" to share with the rest of us, meaning that each of us could ride one ride. We also had some tickets left over from last year that were honored as well. *Cost: $0.*

- **Parking discount offered:**
  - In an effort to minimize parking lot congestion, the fair administrators offered free parking to those who were willing to park in a distant lot and take a free shuttle bus to the entrance gate. *Cost: $0.*

Make Your Game Plan

Once we gathered all the data, we reviewed our schedule along with the older kids' college class schedules, weighed the costs and number of hours we could spend at the fair . . . *and promptly took two aspirin for a headache.* Once we recovered, we drew up our game plan.

Reviewing all of your collected data can be a daunting task. Give yourself time and maybe even ask someone else to help review the information—especially if it's an expensive decision that you are considering. Steve is great at gathering materials but gets bogged down at this point. Annette is great at cutting through it all and boiling it down to a few simple choices.

We decided to go on opening day:

Admission $6. It was a one-dollar admission day, so we spent a total of $6.

Rides Six free ride tickets which the two youngest had earned with book reports. Those, combined with what we already had, enabled us each to take two free rides.

Parking Parking was free, as we decided to try the distant lot and shuttle bus deal.

Broken Plays and Bonus Yardage

But even the best-planned plays can hit a snag. In our case, the night started badly because the shuttle bus drivers, who had been flown in from out of state, got lost going from the fair to our distant free parking lot. We stood in line for an hour waiting for the bus to arrive. When we finally arrived at the fairgrounds, the place was wall-to-wall people. It took a while, but we eventually got the kids to every ride that they wanted.

Sometimes, in spite of excellent research and careful planning, the unexpected occurs. You've got to deal with a broken play or unexpected interference, and this can be upsetting. But the likelihood of this happening is greatly minimized with careful planning. And the more often you attend the same function or research the same types of opportunities, the better you'll be at it and the more success you'll experience. And you never know what kind of bonuses you'll find.

As the night progressed, we walked through several exhibition halls and saw some prize-winning cattle, turkeys, and rabbits. But the best part of the fair was a totally serendipitous pleasure. While walking from one exhibit hall to another, we came across a music pavilion with an excellent band playing music from the sixties. They dressed in costumes of the singers they were imitating—the Beatles, the Rolling Stones, Tom Jones, and Engelbert Humper-whatever. Amazingly, they sounded very authentic, but their Beatles renditions, in particular, were hilarious. Our kids couldn't stop laughing at their drummer's Ringo Starr impersonation. He donned a large fake nose and long-haired wig and continuously bobbed and swayed his head as he pounded out the rhythm on the drums. It was truly the highlight of the night.

In the End Zone

Our attempt to get a "fair deal" wasn't a total bust. We spent a total of only $6, and while we experienced a few disappointments, we did take home one major highlight that we still speak of to this day. As we look back, we realize a couple things: we should have spent $8 and parked in the fair parking lot. But we could have spent much more money going on a different day and had the same experience or even a worse one. After a thorough family evaluation, we decided to chalk this one up under the win column.

PLAN, PLAN, AND PLAN SOME MORE

We encourage you to gather data, evaluate the information, and plan carefully. If you have the time, use it to your advantage to ask more questions, and you're sure to find more ways to save. As you can see, fun recreational activities can be found just about everywhere you look. Sure, it may take some planning, but how many memorable activities have you experienced that "just happened" without any preparation? The time you invest in the important relationships in your life will pay huge dividends. And remember, your investment of time doesn't necessarily mean a huge investment of money too—*you can still have lots of fun while spending less!*

WHAT YOU CAN DO NOW ABOUT RECREATION

TIMID MOUSE:
Pick one time over the next month that you can set aside for recreation. Then pick up the newspaper, visitors' bureau guide for your state or city, and try a new free activity or take some time to play a game together as a family.

WISE OWL:
Pick a holiday or other family celebration and spend a few weeks working with the rest of the family to come up with ideas that would make it a terrific celebration without much expense.

AMAZING ANT:
Make finding free entertainment a game and set a goal to cut your recreation costs in half this year. Be sure to include others in your fun events, and when you come across a real crowd-pleaser, be sure to tell us about it too!

When the kids ask for money to go out and have some fun, encourage them to host a game night, use a coupon, or look for something to do that is free. With some prior planning they can create some great times for themselves and their friends. (Make sure your kids are earning their own money from chores at home when they are between eight and fifteen years old—Chapter 12: Kids and Money—or from a part-time job as they become working age.)

ELEVEN

VACATIONS:

Getting Away Without Debt Regret

What do you remember most about your childhood family vacations—the places you visited, the things you did, or the people you were with? We remember playing in the woods, visiting historical sites, standing on scenic vistas, and spending time with fun relatives. Now think back to your last vacation as an adult. What are your most enduring memories—the sites and people, or the credit card bills that haunted your mailbox for months and months afterward? Vacations should be events that build positive interactions and create long-lasting, fun-filled memories, not short weeks that stress you out because they're breaking the bank.

In the first section of this chapter we'll share various inexpensive vacation options—many of which we've done. In the second section we'll chronicle an eighteen-day mega-vacation we took to Washington, D.C., and beyond. The American Automobile Association (AAA) says that the D.C. area is the second most expensive vacation destination in the United States (Hawaii is the priciest), but we were able to significantly beat the averages for money spent. And even though we kept the cost down, we still saw as many sights as our feet could stand and had a wonderful family time.

According to the 2004 American Express Leisure Travel Index, the average American family will spend $2,962 on their annual vacation, including airfare, lodging, meals, souvenirs, and other vacation expenses. Some sources would have us believe that the "mouse amusement park" is one of the only ways to have a truly memorable family vacation with kids. While we like amusement parks, there are so many other great destinations in our country where we can have a terrific experience and learn about our heroic ancestors that we just don't want to limit our choices to a couple of themed playgrounds. And besides, any way you slice it, following the "normal" vacation path is going to cost you, and if you intend to spend the average amount, you'll need to be saving a little over $200 each month to fund it. If that price is a little too steep, keep reading.

We've always made our vacation plans based on what money we have already saved in our vacation budget account. If the account was low for a particular year, we found options that fit the funds we had saved. When we plan a longer, more expensive vacation, we sock away extra money we've come across, or we have a garage sale to help build the fund before the vacation. (See Chapter 7: Debt for more ideas on raising money.) If your vacation funds are limited, or if you just want to reach other goals with that money, here is your opportunity to exercise creativity rather than your credit card.

THE VALUE OF HOME VACATIONS

We've taken "home vacations" several times, and through them have created some of our greatest family memories. One of the keys to a home vacation is balance: we schedule a mix of activities and home projects so the time off doesn't feel like our normal time at home. We alternate days of sleeping in and relaxing at home with full days of activities, and we usually plan two or three field trips or day trips for the week.

Many of us live near attractions that would make tourists drool, but because they're so close and we are so busy working, we don't take the time to enjoy the treasures in our own backyards. Annette grew up on Long Island, for example, and never visited the Statue of Liberty.

Not until after we were married and went back to New York to visit friends and relatives did she finally tour this landmark.

We haven't made the same mistake in Arizona. We've visited the Ceretta Candy Factory, the Desert Botanical Garden's Butterfly Pavilion, the Wildlife World Zoo, the Mystery Castle, the Pueblo Grande Museum and Indian Ruins, the Arizona State Fair, the Hall of Flame Museum of Firefighting, a Krispy Kreme for a doughnut tour, an organic farm in Scottsdale, the Jerome copper mine, Oak Creek Canyon, the Grand Canyon, and the Civil War reenactment at Picacho Peak State Park. Whew, that's some list! Some of the activities may sound familiar if you've read the recreation chapter—indeed, quite often a home vacation can be built out of weekend plans that you've always been meaning to try but never quite had enough time for!

We're sure your area has just as much to offer. Make a list of the sights in your city and surrounding area. Contact the local Convention and Visitors' Bureau or Chamber of Commerce and have them send you brochures and pamphlets on your local attractions. Visit AAA if you have a membership, and pick up a tour book for your state. Research other possibilities at your public library—you're certain to find a treasure trove of information written by local authors. Check the local paper for events occurring the week you've planned to vacation. Many museums select one day each month to be free to the public—find the day and plan your vacation accordingly. You'll be amazed at the wide array of options available.

Great Home Vacation Accomplishments

Completing a home improvement project during a week of vacation may sound illogical, but it can really be a stress reliever. You know, one of those necessary projects that has been on the "to-do" list for years, the kind of thing that you've avoided because it just isn't going to be fun. Sure, it won't be fun if it takes up your entire weekend, but if you've got fun activities scheduled around it and less pressure to finish quickly, it can be satisfying.

Here's one example that sticks in our minds. We have a citrus orchard with thirty trees. Some time ago we ran into a problem—the trees weren't growing well because the irrigation system wasn't operating correctly. But reworking the system was a huge task, and the thought of doing it over several weekends was overwhelming. So we scheduled it for a home vacation week and mixed in some recreational activities to make the work more bearable. Now when we walk in the orchard, we see new growth, healthy trees, and large delicious fruit to enjoy.

Other projects we've tackled include establishing new garden beds, cutting down or trimming trees, cleaning out filing cabinets, and building storage room shelves. Your list might include putting photos in photo albums, cleaning out closets, baking a huge batch of cookies, or, if money is tight, gathering unneeded stuff from the house and having a garage sale at the end of the week. Whatever is on your long-term to-do list, review it, discuss it, and make plans to conquer it—you just might end your vacation feeling like you've really accomplished something.

By their very nature home vacations can eliminate huge travel and lodging costs, but don't forget about the food savings. A traveling vacation often means that almost all of your meals will be eaten at restaurants. When you're at home, however, you have the option of eating out, buying prepared meals, or cooking at home.

Home Recreation Ideas

Cook a special meal. How about a complete turkey dinner or some other family favorite? Make it Thanksgiving in June.

Borrow or Rent a Movie or Two. Pick an oldie—it's okay to introduce the kids to a black-and-white hero. Or find a newer release that the whole family will enjoy. Prepare some popcorn, turn out the lights, and treat the whole adventure like an in-house movie theater.

Go Bowling. Bowling alleys often have discounted rates—call for information. If you live near a university, their bowling fees are often much less than the commercial lanes, and the lanes are usually smoke-free.

Try Backyard Camping. This is always fun, especially for little kids. Set up the tent, have a campfire—and use your own bathroom! During Christmas break each year, we usually "camp out" in front of our fireplace. Sleeping bags are lined up, and we all fall asleep to the crackling of the logs on the fire.

Play Miniature Golf. Two-for-one coupons are great deals and can be found in the coupon mailers in your mailbox or the Entertainment Book for your area. We've laughed ourselves silly watching inexperienced golfers (us) hit balls over holes that weren't the ones we were aiming for.

Go to Discount Theaters. Look around your area for discounted, off-first-run movie theaters—you'll save a boodle. If you're dying to see a new release, try a matinee—you're on vacation anyway! They aren't crowded and usually less expensive.

Enjoy Game Days. Pull out the card and board games. It's relaxing (sometimes) and builds relationships. Monopoly, Risk, Apples to Apples, Uno, and Mille Bornes are among our favorites. Steve has even introduced the kids to a discontinued game he played in college: The American Dream, which you can still find on eBay. The kids have a blast!

Have Christmas in July. Do some Christmas shopping at thrift stores. Our kids love it because they get so much more for their money, and come December you'll have a lot less to worry about.

Take a Free Tour. Many significant historic sites, state capitols, and colleges or universities provide free tours. Don't forget candy factories, dairies, and other private companies in your area.

Keep It a Secret

We don't tell friends or the office where we will be; we just say we're un-available. This keeps our vacation week from becoming full of phone calls and daily distractions. Certainly don't check your e-mail.

Home vacations don't have to be a boring or second-rate alterna-tive to a "real" vacation, and when you review your bills, you may be a whole lot happier.

INEXPENSIVE OUT-OF-TOWN VACATIONS

Planning and research can make out-of-town travel affordable too. Even if you have the money saved, these ideas will help you stretch it further. We will focus on driving vacations and several lodging options.

Camping

This is one of the least expensive options for getting out of town. Author Gary Smalley believes that camping vacations are one of the best ways to build family unity because "something always goes wrong." These "wrong" things become the stuff of family history and laugh-inducing legends that will be told and retold for years to come. We've certainly found this to be the case—when our son John was seven, he wandered off a hiking trail at our campground outside of San Diego and got lost in a thorny patch of shrubs, a story we've recounted ever since—even funnier now because he's an accomplished hiker and Eagle Scout.

Go to the library and get a listing of national or state parks in your area that allow camping. These locations are usually reasonably priced. Consider purchasing a National Parks Pass—$50 per year for a family or $10 for seniors (who can include children and grandchildren for free), which allows year-round entrance to the parks. Yes, there are campsites with showers for those of you who, like Annette, want more of the comforts of home in the wild. Ask your camping friends about places they have found to be picturesque. And if you don't have camping gear already, ask around: there are bound to be avid campers in your circle of relations who can lend you equipment or who would love to go with you. Note: If you borrow camping equipment, always return it cleaner and in better shape than when you got it.

College Dorms

Consider this option instead of a hotel. Many small colleges rent out their dorm rooms during the summer; some even set aside a few during the school year, usually for people taking campus tours. Years ago we stayed at a college in San Diego located right on the beach! There are numerous options from New York to Hawaii—that's right, Hawaii, for only $40 per couple per night. (Check out Hawaiian Mission Academy at www.hma4u.org.) You'll have to make some phone calls and do some digging, but the savings can be significant. Don't forget that if you have children, exposing them to different colleges can help them develop a vision for higher education.

Borrow a Cabin

Most of us know someone who owns a cabin. If money is tight, ask if you can use it for a few days. It may cost you utilities or a small fee, but you may stumble into a fabulous retreat. Be sensitive, leave it neater than you found it, and always provide a thank-you gift.

Discounted Hotels

There are always bargains to be found. If you need a hotel room, research, research, research, and keep those questions coming. Ask for discounts (AAA, senior citizen, weekend, weekday, etc.). Ask if they charge for parking. Ask if they provide a free breakfast. As we researched a recent vacation, we were amazed at the range of what different hotels considered a continental breakfast. For about the same room price, we encountered everything from sweet rolls and coffee to a full hot breakfast buffet with fresh fruit. If you have a large family like ours, these all-you-can-eat meals can save you a considerable amount of money.

FOOD FOR THE TRIP

Here are a few strategies we use to keep food costs down while traveling:

- **Breakfast foods.** Bring bagels, fresh fruit, instant oatmeal, and hot cocoa. Most hotels provide coffeemakers to heat up water. Some have in-room refrigerators for storing leftovers and other food—buy a carton of milk and some cereal and you've got your own continental breakfast right there.

- **Snacks.** To curb the impulse for pricey fast food or gas station goodies, bring plenty of snacks, such as pretzels, cookies, raisins, apples, carrots, crackers, trail mix, and beef jerky (homemade, of course).

- **Drinks.** We drink water in the car—no stains or sticky spills to clean up!

- **Bring a slow cooker and canned meals.** Pack soup, stew, and chili. Turn on the slow cooker in the morning and return to a nice hot meal. We always set ours on a bathroom counter if we are leaving the hotel for several hours, and we have never had a problem with the cleaning staff bothering it.

- **Fast food.** We look for inexpensive burger places that offer $1 specials and can feed all of us for about $15. Knowing that the burger thing will get old, we'll mix in fried chicken, pizza, and our favorite, Chinese food. All-you-can-eat restaurants are great if you're traveling with teens—and often have a great salad bar for a healthier option. Pick up local circulars and look for coupons or purchase an Entertainment Book if you are going to be in the area for several days (during the summer they are half price). Remember that grocery stores usually have ready-made sandwiches and salads to go.

While we always try to eat a balanced meal and usually avoid fast food, we view vacations as a time when we can let down our guard and not be so concerned with eating healthy. (Although it's always a relief to get back to Scottsdale and eat Annette's good home cookin').

· **Pack a cooler.** When we drive, we take our large 48-quart cooler with us. It's great for taking food from home and for storing any leftovers from restaurant meals later in the trip. Ice is easy to find (free at most hotels). Bring plenty of plastic storage bags to keep stuff from getting soggy.

ACTIVITIES ON THE ROAD

If you have a long car ride, plan in advance and pack:

· **Books on tape** (free from the public library). There are some great titles for family listening.

· **Books** for individual and group reading.

· **Art supplies.** Try sticker books and coloring books to occupy your kids' time. Or if you really want to think ahead, bring old Christmas cards for the kids to cut up with fancy edging scissors, to be used as holiday gift tags.

· **Games.** Magnetic travel versions such as checkers, chess, and Othello are great.

· **Journals** for recording travel experiences.

· **Music.** Each of the kids has his or her favorite type of music, so we let them bring CDs or tapes to share with everyone.

"EDU-VACATION"

Wherever we travel, we try to encourage some of the kids' interests. Roy wants to be an aerospace engineer, so when we were in Texas, we visited

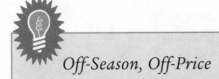

Off-Season, Off-Price

Vacations just aren't fun if you pay too much money or have to wait in long lines with hundreds of other travelers. Home-schooling our kids had its distinct advantages when it came to vacation planning. Because we weren't in the public school system, we could travel during off seasons. We fondly remember a trip to a major theme park where there was easy parking, no lines for the rides, and no crowds to fight through.

Whenever possible, consider off-season vacations. Go completely opposite, such as staying at a ski resort in the summer. If you can vacation at the end of summer, right before school starts, you can scoop up some great deals. Beach vacations in September are great. The water is still warm even though the air temperature may be cooler. But the best thing is that you're not fighting crowds for beach space or parking. Call several lodging facilities at desired destinations six months to a year before you intend to visit. Ask when their off-season rates begin and try to plan your trip accordingly.

Beverly and Howard Clarke, subscribers from Hollywood, Florida, wrote this: "Schedule your trip for the weekend *after* a major holiday. The merchants and hotels are always glad to see you, and many times prices are lower."

If you have some flexibility in your vacation timing and can go off-season, you can have a great time and great savings.

the Houston Space Center. He was in awe as we toured the facility and had the opportunity to discuss NASA internships with the staff. John is involved in sound engineering, so we visited Uncle Greg's office, the PBS station at Texas A&M. Creating a vision in our kids is another important part of our vacations.

If your kids are nearing college age, visiting various college campuses as you traverse the country can help them become more focused on their goals. Becky thought she wanted to attend Colorado State University because of their well-known equine program, so a campus tour was included in our vacation itinerary that year.

If you have vacation time, don't neglect using it to develop fun-filled retreats that fit your family, encourage deeper relationships, and keep your budget healthy! You can create wonderful lasting memories without the lingering regret of debt.

GOLD MEDAL VACATIONS

In June 2005, we celebrated with our daughter Becky as she was presented with a Congressional Award gold medal during a ceremony in Washington, D.C. We planned the longest vacation we've ever taken (eighteen days) around this special event. Just for a point of reference, we checked out what the experts thought our vacation should cost. The AAA travel survey told us that a family of four should expect to spend $441 each day for food and lodging while in D.C. That breaks down to $110.25 per person per day. Taking this average figure, our family of six (John was working full-time and couldn't take vacation days at this time) should have spent—are you ready for a laugh?—$11,907 for our eighteen-day trip. Wow, that'll stop your heart for a while. Their figures didn't even include transportation, admissions, or rental car. "Experts" and "averages" make us giggle. We're hoping that after you read what we did, you'll be giggling too. Rather than giving you a boring travelogue or a recounting of the many U-turns we made while attempting to navigate the capital, we've boiled down the salient money-saving details of this trip into six categories.

SIX WAYS TO SAVE ON VACATION

1. Plan What You Can, But Be Ready to Change

One of the main tenets for economizing is advanced planning. Spontaneity, while fun, is usually costly. Our eighteen-day trek was originally planned to include ten people—our family of six and both sets of grandparents. We started researching tours, lodging, and airfare three months prior to the trip. We consulted AAA tour books and maps, visited numerous Web sites for sightseeing information, and called car rental companies, congressional offices, hotels, and airlines. We had it all figured out—or so we thought. In the last weeks before the trip, many of the plans had to be changed, as both sets of grandparents experienced some major health issues and had to cancel their participation. As a result, the two weeks before we left were incredibly hectic—we were holding a budgeting seminar, making hospital visits, rearranging many of our travel plans, and packing, so by the time we fell into our airplane seats exhausted, we were ready for a vacation!

2. Transportation

Our first idea had been to drive to the East Coast. We did a cost comparison of driving versus flying. Driving our van four thousand miles, including gas, lodging, and food on the road for four days each way, cost about $1,700. Flying, with discounted fares and renting a car, ended up costing about the same amount but saved us eight full days and allowed us more time to see the sights and visit friends and family.

After we decided on flying, we made numerous phone calls to various airlines and adjusted our departure date to get maximum savings. It turned out that if we left on a weekday and returned on a Sunday night we got the best deal. We ended up making reservations with Southwest Airlines and booked our flights seventy-five days in advance. Even with increases in airfares, you can still find some bargain rates if you are flying out of a major city and willing to shop around (and early). Our round-trip fares were $198 per person.

3. Lodging

Initially, rather than staying in hotel rooms, Steve thought that we could find some alternative lodging arrangements in the D.C. area. Had we been traveling in a smaller group, either without kids or grandparents, there were a few options that looked good. Staying at YMCA and Boy Scout camps would have cost our entire group only $25 to $35 per night (that's a real deal), and several would have rented us accommodations at very reasonable prices had we been traveling any other time than the summer. Two of the several universities near D.C. that Steve called offered to let us stay in their dorm rooms. American University charged $45 per night, linens included, although due to the room size, we would have needed three rooms for our crew. We thought this price was fairly reasonable but didn't stay there because we ended up getting an even better deal. Washington Bible College was also an option, but our family would have been split up in the men's and women's dorms, and we would have rather stayed together. Our last option was to avail ourselves of Annette's brother's Marriott employee discount at $50 per night per room—which included a hot continental breakfast. This was our least expensive option at $100 per night for two rooms, which would accommodate our entire group. But we would have been staying about thirty-five miles from D.C.

We'd love to tell you that our research garnered us the best deal for a warm clean room in D.C., but we can't. Annette's dad is a consummate credit card point wheeler-dealer. He had accumulated several hundred thousand points through credit cards and time-shares that he owns, and he decided to cash in enough of his points to get two hotel rooms at a Fairfield Inn (with a hot continental breakfast) for ten days. The plan was that he would pay for the rooms with his points, and we would pay for two midsized rental cars, food, and gas for the entire trip. Sometimes unexpected opportunities arise—we considered this a chance to essentially barter/share expenses, which created a plan that would benefit everyone involved. When he ended up in the hospital just before the trip, he changed the hotel reservations to our name and gifted us with the points—the room rate should have been $110 per room per day. Thanks, Dad!

But, regardless of whether you have a point-accumulating father, low rates are still available for lodging—especially since it's likely you don't have quite as complicated a group as we did! If you have the attitude that hotels are not the destination, as we do, you focus your search on a clean room, a safe facility, and (if the price is right) a continental breakfast.

Most hotels have laundry facilities, which are usually overpriced. But if you bring your own laundry detergent, it can reduce the cost and allow you to pack fewer clothes. Be careful, though! The dryer the hotel provided didn't dry our clothes—even after two full cycles. We speculated that the dryer vent was clogged, and when we told the manager, she offered to do our next load of wash in the hotel laundry facilities at no charge. We took her up on her offer. This was a mistake. It was a load of colored clothes, some of them weren't colorfast, and they came back a completely different color. We concluded that hotels are accustomed to just washing white linens in very hot water. Basically our load was boiled clean, and as a result, Joseph's black hiking shorts are now sort of a dark green. Even though several items were discolored, everything was still wearable. Since we don't pay that much for our clothes (another benefit of buying clothes inexpensively is that there's less heartache when something like this happens) and none of the discolored items were dress clothes, we chalked this one up to experience and laughed about it.

4. Car Rental Games

We needed a rental car for seventeen days. With a group of eight to transport (our group of six and Annette's parents; Steve's parents planned to drive their own car from Chicago), we needed either a minivan or a full-size van. But when we saw that the price for renting either would be well over $2,300 ($135 per day), we were stopped short—we didn't expect to spend that much. After much discussion and research, we found it was much less expensive to rent two midsized cars from Avis; Steve would drive one and Annette's dad would drive the other. The kids would take turns riding with Grandpa and Nana. The total cost for seventeen days: $588, by using Costco's discount with Avis. This was the deal we were looking for.

But when our driving group size shrank from eight down to six, we had to really work hard to come up with a new plan. Now we didn't need two midsized cars, but one wouldn't accommodate us. You may ask why we didn't stick with the two-car deal, as we had already planned to pay for the whole cost of the car ourselves anyway. Well, we planned on doing about two thousand miles of driving up and down the coast, and we didn't want to be locked into both of us *having* to drive. If she has a choice, Annette would rather not drive in totally unknown territory. Cramming into one car—we knew it would be a tight fit—would allow us to always have one person to navigate and to trade off driving responsibilities when necessary.

So Steve researched minivans again, and still found them to be over 300 percent more than a midsized car. Our only other option was to get a full-size car that seated six people. After several phone calls, we made our deal with Budget—Avis wouldn't accept a debit card to reserve the car, and remember, we just don't use credit cards. We found that the retail price for renting a Grand Marquis would have been about $900, but with an AAA discount it dropped to $700. Now, watch these next tricks carefully. If we used our Entertainment Book, along with a couple of coupons, and made two separate reservations, our total cost plummeted to $550. We made one reservation for three days and used an upgrade coupon to guarantee a six-passenger vehicle. Then we made a separate reservation for the following two-week period and used a 20-percent-off coupon (this saved us about $120). It did mean that we had to trade in the first car after three days, but we were in the D.C. area anyway, so it wasn't a big deal. Most car rental companies will only allow you to use one coupon per reservation, so breaking up our rental saved us quite a bit.

We also saw some additional savings from only using one car. It made finding parking places much easier, especially in D.C., and saved a bundle on gas. We calculated that even if the midsized cars each got 30 miles to the gallon, driving two of them everywhere would be the equivalent of 15 mpg. The Mercury Marquis we rented, even fully loaded, delivered 25 mpg on the highway.

5. Saving on Food

We used several strategies to keep food costs under control and still have a fun time.

- **Continental breakfast.** We talked a little about this earlier, but with teenagers, this was a godsend. Fairfield Inn provided a great breakfast that even included fresh hot waffles. But it didn't include hot eggs, and after a few days, Annette had an over-easy hankering. So one morning we visited a Denny's and everyone ordered a $3.99 Grand Slam breakfast with eggs cooked just the way they wanted them. Most hotel brochures or Web sites don't give specific descriptions of the type of continental breakfast served, so making a brief phone call directly to the property can give you the information you need to plan your breakfast meals.

- **Eating out for less.** We ordered a D.C. and Maryland-area Entertainment Book a couple of weeks prior to our trip. During the summer the price is 50 percent off retail, so the book cost $15, including shipping. This little book saved us over $325, between the rental car discounts and food coupons we used. Once we purchased two large boxes of fried chicken for $15—half price with an Entertainment Book coupon. This fed us for two meals—we kept the leftovers on ice, of course. Several times over the course of the trip we stopped for McDonald's 99-cent burgers and some fries, no coupons needed. A couple of times we used Entertainment Book coupons to purchase pizza. We also stopped a few times for our family favorite, Chinese. One place was all-you-can-eat—whew, were they glad to see us leave!

· **Slow cooker.** As we drove to various destinations the first couple of days, we kept our eyes peeled for a thrift store where we could purchase an inexpensive slow cooker—lugging our own onto the plane was impractical, as it would have been too bulky and we already had a large amount of luggage. We knew, as a result of doing a little Internet research, that there were a number of thrift stores in the D.C. area. And we were fairly certain that we could find what we needed for a good price. Indeed, we did find a slow cooker for $5, and then stopped at a nearby grocery store to purchase enough canned food for three meals—chicken chowder, beef stew, and SpaghettiOs. The wonderful thing about the slow cooker is that dinner was ready to eat when we walked in the door—not a bad deal when our teenage boys were famished. We also bought some healthy snacks, including fresh fruit, raisins, and crackers, all for about $28.

· **Planned menu.** Just as she does at home, Annette looked at our proposed schedule and together we penciled in when we would eat out, eat in, or eat fast food. This allowed us to plan a couple of special dinners that we knew the kids would enjoy, and kept us from getting caught off guard and having to pay through the nose.

· **Drinks and snacks.** We always carry water bottles with us, but every once in a while it's nice to stop for a treat—and a little jolt of caffeine. But rather than stop at a gas station with a convenience store attached to it and pay $1 to $1.89 for each person to get a soda, we stopped at a grocery store. The deli counter often provides cups with ice, and we purchased a two-liter bottle of soda for 79 cents. On one particular day, it was so hot that we splurged on ice cream sandwiches for everyone. One box of six did the trick—and yes, they were on sale. A quick junk food stop for less than $6. We also used the clean restrooms while we were there.

6. Saving on Sights and Activities

- **National Parks Pass.** This pass is a great value, as we mentioned earlier: $50 per year for a family or $10 for seniors. Most park admissions are between $5 and $8 for adults, so for our group of six it saved us over $70 in retail admission prices—and could still be used for another eleven months. The nice thing about the pass is that it allows your whole family in, regardless of age and total number. Since Becky had just turned twenty, she would have had to pay adult admission, but with the pass, she was included for free. If you are a single, it will probably be less expensive to just pay retail admission to the parks, unless you plan on visiting a great number of them in one year's time.

- **Congressional aid.** Admission to most of the monuments and museums in the D.C. area is free. Some require you to stand in line to get tickets, so we had to plan our schedule to allow us to be at the right place early enough to get tickets before they ran out. Another way to get some of the better tours for free is through the office of your senator or representative—tickets for tours of the Capitol, the Kennedy Center for the Performing Arts, the White House, and a few others are obtained through their offices. But learn from our mistake here. We had heard that White House tours were hard to come by, so we asked three different representatives' offices for ten tickets. About a month before the trip, we were offered seven passes by one office, but we turned them down because at that time our group size was eight. We continued following up with the other offices in hopes of getting all eight. It turned out that we should have taken the seven. We later discovered that very few requests for tickets are honored—as a result, we ended up looking at the White House through black wrought-iron fencing as a gentle drizzle urged us to hurry back to our car.

· **Guided tours.** We learned an important lesson at Fort McHenry in Baltimore. This was the location of a battle between the British and Americans during the War of 1812 that inspired Francis Scott Key to pen the words to our national anthem. We decided to participate in a half-hour ranger guided tour. This tour was sort of like watching a bad movie and hoping that it would get better . . . but it never did. One hour later the kids were rolling their eyes and begging us to move on. Our tour guide meant well, but rather than taking us through the fort and weaving his story as we saw the sights, he had us sit in two different grassy areas and attempted to dramatize the battle for an hour. By the time we left the fort, it was too late to make it to the next sight we had wanted to see. We found ourselves in the same situation in the Library of Congress. Our tour guide reveled in describing, in great detail, the artistic and spiritual meaning of the naked women painted on the ceilings and the naked statues carved into the staircases. After enduring two rooms of his in-depth descriptions, we ditched him and enjoyed our own exploration of the beautiful building. The highlight of our trip was not even included in the guided tour: a room dedicated to Bob Hope and full of audio and video clips, along with letters he'd written or received and scripts that he had used. So here's the lesson we learned: if the guide is a bore, do your own tour.

· **Don't believe all you read.** We did much of our pre-trip planning using the AAA *Tour Book*. While AAA usually does a great job, their book is made one year in advance of publication. You need to verify all information once you are in the area. Oftentimes we discovered changes in admission requirements, tour times, and prices. (We used our cell phone a number of times to verify information rather than the hotel phone, which may have carried extra charges.) If you want more reliable info in advance, state offices of tourism will send out free brochures that cover a multitude of attractions and have more detailed maps and other more current information. Most offices of tourism have toll-free numbers, so you can contact them months in advance to aid in your planning. And don't forget to try the Internet—we found out online about several free military band concerts in D.C. Kids can be a great help with the research too.

· **Timing.** Another area we could have done better in was parking. We visited one out-of-D.C. sight on the weekend. In hindsight it would have been better to be in D.C. on the weekends, because all the parking meters are free and most of the attractions we were interested in were open. We didn't fare too badly, though—there were several weekday two-hour meters that were available after 9:30 A.M. The only stipulation was that your car had to be off the street by rush hour, 4:30 P.M. This was a good time to go for an early dinner at a side street restaurant or visit an attraction out of the downtown area and return after 6:30 P.M., when street parking was once again free. So a couple of the evenings we returned after rush hour and visited the memorials on the Mall, which are beautifully illumined at night.

· **Travel with kids.** Vacations can be a stressful time for kids as well as adults. We always have the kids load their backpacks full of activities and books to keep them occupied during flights and

WHAT THE KIDS SAY ABOUT VACATIONS

Abbey, age twelve, says, "Our vacations are always fun. It's great to go sightseeing, get away from home, and spend time together with our family. I wish we could bring our dogs with us—because they're part of the family too—but my mom always says we can't. Months before we leave on vacation, I start saving my money so I can buy my own souvenirs and other things I want. When we went on our D.C. trip, I had $50 saved and spent almost all of it in two weeks! I bought postcards, a special Fort McHenry patriotic purse, astronaut ice cream at the Smithsonian, some handmade soap at Jamestown, and rock candy at Williamsburg. There's more, but I can't remember it all. Oh, I almost forgot, I bought a few Christmas presents for my brothers and sister—but you can't tell them about it!"

long car rides. For the younger kids, when they weren't yet reading, we'd pack larger storybooks that contain multiple stories, books on tape, and some new toys that are kept hidden until they are "required." Having a few surprises (toys, books, snacks, or other favorite things) for those whiny moments on a long trip can be a perfect distraction to a younger child. Having a few prepurchased special items also eliminates the need for many overpriced souvenirs. The older kids really enjoy reading, so a few months prior to the trip we encouraged them to read biographies pertaining to American history, making the sights they saw come alive. You can do this for any region you're visiting—just check used-book stores for relevant titles, or hit your library.

· **Souvenir savings.** Every day hundreds of flags are raised over the U.S. Capitol to be sent to individuals who have requested them. Anyone can contact their senator or representative and request one be flown for them. The cost ranges from $13 to about $22. We ordered one for Becky to commemorate her special day and award. If you keep your eyes peeled, you'll find other inexpensive, unusual, and very memorable souvenirs. Be sure to check the clearance tables in every gift shop (you'll likely find a reasonably priced memento). Since our kids spend their own money on souvenirs, they tend to buy things like pencils, pens, key chains, patches, and keepsake ornaments. When we visited the Bureau of Engraving, Annette bought a bag of shredded dollar bills (for about $3). The bag had enough material to fill several empty glass ornament balls that she had at home. They made lovely souvenir ornaments for the family.

In the end, our eighteen-day sojourn to the East Coast cost us about $2,700, including airfare, rental car, food, and admissions. If we had added hotel costs for the first ten days ($1,760), for a total of $4,460, our expenses still would have been far below the AAA-calculated total of $11,907. (We stayed with a friend and relatives for the last eight days.)

Vacations are no reason to go into debt. Read, research, and don't be afraid to think differently. You'll find that you too can beat the experts—and probably have more fun—when it comes to planning and paying for your vacation.

WHAT YOU CAN DO NOW ABOUT VACATION SPENDING

TIMID MOUSE:

Start thinking about your vacation today. Calculate how much money you will have saved when vacation time rolls around. Make your plans based on what you have, and give your credit cards a break. Consider a home vacation this year.

WISE OWL:

Look back over the past and calculate how much you've spent annually on vacations. From that number develop a monthly amount that you need to save in advance to fund your vacation(s). Try some alternative vacations: camping, borrowing a friend's cabin, or a volunteer service project.

AMAZING ANT:

With your money saved in advance of your vacation, go and have a good time. While on vacation, use your frugal methods to see how much of your vacation money you can leave unspent by finding deals at your destination—free food at continental breakfasts, souvenirs at swap meets or flea markets, and discounted hotels.

TWELVE

KIDS AND MONEY:

Teaching Kids About Money Isn't Kid Stuff

If you have kids, you already know that they can add significantly to your bills, and the "experts" say that it will take a small fortune to raise children from infancy through young-adulthood. In the 2004 report *Expenditures on Children and Families*, the U.S. Department of Agriculture estimates that we should expect to spend about $261,000 to raise each child from birth through age seventeen. That's right, and this number doesn't include college expenses! As with most statistics we encounter, we disagree. Kids don't have to cost over a quarter of a million dollars to raise. Better yet, they can be part of the solution to minimize expenses, especially if you take a proactive approach to teaching them about earning, saving, and spending money when they are young.

If you think this topic has no relevance to getting right on the money, think again. Madison Avenue has done the research, and your little cherub is in their crosshairs. Market researchers have long studied the findings of James McNeal, a retired professor from Texas A&M University who's considered by many to be the godfather of marketing to kids. His research indicates that kids not only spend their own money—estimates hover around $29 billion for kids ages four to twelve—but also influence family spending to the tune of about $290 billion each year. What does that mean in family terms? According to the 2000 census, there are currently about 41 million kids ages five to fourteen in the United States. This means that each one had some sort of controlling influence over about $7,073 this last year—that's $589 each month. From which cereals you buy to the kind of car you drive, the marketing gurus think that "Junior" has a say.

Whether the "experts" are right on the money or not, we all know that our kids' desires are important to us. But how much they actually cost is very negotiable.

Training kids to be wise about the use of money will take time, but it is worth every minute you put into it. If you start young and act consistently, the struggles will be fewer, and you'll proudly watch your child develop excellent money-handling skills. If you wait until Junior is in high school, your battle may be more difficult, but it can still be won.

And the rewards are huge: we want to spare our kids the pain and humiliation of financial distress. We want them to leave home with a firm financial footing—not necessarily with lots of money in the bank, but with the ability to manage their earnings and spending with habits that they have learned and practiced since they were little.

TRAINING MONEYSMART KIDS

We have a theory that child discipline is more about parents being disciplined than anything else. How does discipline relate to kids and money? To put it simply, if our kids are going to learn how to handle money, *we* must be disciplined in *our* approach to handling money and consistent in teaching them about it.

We aren't the most disciplined people in the world. Just like everyone, we have struggles in certain areas of life, but during more than twenty-four years of marriage and raising five kids, we've learned a thing or two about teaching our kids to handle money.

We didn't start out knowing the perfect way to transfer our economizing values, but over time, as our MoneySmart Kids system evolved, the kids caught our vision too. All of our kids have been taught to handle money from a young age. They've all learned to work hard and discovered that extra work results in extra rewards.

Our exact system may not work for every family, but here are seven principles that can help you successfully train your kids to be responsible with money.

Principle 1: Be an Example

If you ask just about anyone who is struggling financially "What did your parents teach you about handling money?" inevitably the response will be "Nothing" or "They were frugal, but we didn't talk about it much" or "They taught me to save, but nothing else." But where can a kid learn to handle money, and who is going to teach it? Is it going to be in school or church? It's not likely. As parents, it's up to us to impart money lessons, and that starts with getting your own financial house in order.

From a very young age the kids were aware that we had a spending plan. They heard us discuss purchases and saw us saving in advance for things we wanted to buy or do. The point is, we have been doing the things that we expect our kids to do. "Do as I say, not as I do" just won't fly with kids. Being an example in financial discipline is the first step toward training your kids to be responsible with money. If you're not budgeting your money you can't expect that your kids will either.

Principle 2: Search for a System

Maybe you've tried a money training technique that failed, or maybe you're looking for ways to improve your existing method. The key is that you've got to have a plan, an understandable system, that works for you and your kids. If you don't have one, keep looking, reading, modifying, and asking other families what they are doing to train their kids, and you'll eventually come up with a system perfectly suited for you.

In 1987, when our eldest child, John, was four years old, we started with a three-cup system. We literally had three Styrofoam cups and labeled them "Give," "Save," and "Spend." We didn't give John an allowance because we didn't believe that paying him just for being part of the family was a realistic life principle, but we did pay him for extra chores he did around the house. Then we helped him divide that money into his cups. And when he received gifts of money for birthdays or holidays, they were divided, too—if we remembered to remind him.

Eventually we decided to try something else, and chose Crown Financial Ministries' "My Giving Bank," a plastic bank with three compartments: "Give," "Bank," and "Store." We now recommend this type of bank for younger kids, from two to six years old. But as John grew older and his stash of money increased, this bank became too difficult to use. It was hard to get specific amounts of money out of the bank, and with continued deposits it became heavy and cumbersome to carry around. Not to mention that there was no way to know how much money was in the bank and no tracking system for when money was deposited or taken out.

Principle 3: **Consistency Counts**

What we discovered with our rudimentary attempts was that a system needed more than mechanics to be successful. Whether it was Styrofoam cups, plastic banks, or fancy envelopes, success was dependent on our participation and training.

Our first system with the cups didn't work because we were inconsistent. As John received or earned money, we'd often forget to help divide it into his cups. Another problem was that we didn't have a regularly scheduled time each week to implement our plan. We can't expect kids to learn a discipline from an undisciplined approach. The same thing happened with the three-part "My Giving Bank." The bank is a wonderful tool, but tools in the hands of an untrained operator are not very effective.

We finally discovered that if we were going to be successful in teaching our kids about money, we needed to devote more time to researching a workable system and more effort in consistently making time each week to implement it.

Principle 4: **Encouraging New Habits**

Steve discovered our current system while listening to a book on tape from the library—*Three Steps to a Strong Family* by Richard and Linda Eyre. The book outlined Family Traditions (we had some), Family Laws (we had those also), and a Family Economy (that's what we were missing).Their system included daily accountability for habits they wanted to reinforce in their children, and weekly rewards of "pay" that gave the kids money to manage. It seemed so practical and easy to use that we decided to try it. While we initially implemented their system exactly as they did, over time we realized that we needed to personalize it so it would work better for our family and lifestyle. Every family will have different habits and attitudes that they want to emphasize. Identifying the ones you want to focus on will be a key to making both kids and parents enjoy the system.

We've called our system MoneySmart Kids since 1995, but our kids just call it Payday. The system is based on earning points during four portions of each day. These "portions" were habits or activities that we deemed as important for our family: Morning Point, Chore Point, School Point, and Round-up Point. They can earn four points each weekday and three points on Saturday, totaling twenty-three points for meeting all of the objectives. Sunday is our family day, so no chores are done and no points are given. Here's a more detailed description.

Kids Want to Learn

When John was about nine, he was saving his money to buy a BMX bike. We started looking at the newspaper ads, but the prices advertised far exceeded the $60 that he had saved. So we decided to look at garage sales. It took only two weekends of looking before he found his treasure—a chrome BMX Predator bike with aluminum cranks and a racing seat, for exactly $60. He was in his glory.

A couple of weeks later we had some friends over to talk about their finances. John came over to tell Kurt and Gracie about his recent purchase and his smart shopping. They were really encouraging and wanted to see this prized possession. Later, Kurt told John that they had purchased an almost identical bike for their son, Todd, for about $300.

Soon after Kurt and Gracie left, John sidled up to Annette and said, "No wonder they're asking you to help them with their money. They spent $300 for the same bike that I bought for $60!"

A few days after that, John came to both of us and asked, "When are you going to teach me finances like you do with all these other people?" That really surprised and motivated us to come up with a system to train our kids to manage their money.

Morning Point. We wanted to encourage the kids to get up and moving each morning. A child earns this point when he or she has gotten dressed, combed his or her hair, fixed the bed, and eaten breakfast. But the child must do all of this without being nagged and with a good attitude. Argue and you lose your morning point. Don't finish your breakfast or don't make your bed—no point!

Chore Point. Each kid (beyond eighteen months) has some age- and ability-appropriate chores. To help us recall the regularly occurring chores, we created a list of over fifty of them and posted it on our bulletin board. Each morning the kids are assigned two or three chores to complete. For younger kids, some of these include unloading part of the dishwasher, watering plants, emptying wastebaskets, setting the table, and dragging the laundry basket to the washer. For older kids, it's helping prepare dinner, changing lightbulbs, sweeping/vacuuming floors, mowing the lawn, taking out the trash, and our all-time favorite, baking chocolate chip cookies—this earns a lot of extra points.

The job(s) must be done completely and in a timely manner. Of course, kids don't just inherit the ability to do these things; we must first teach them how to do the job (again and again), and then inspect their work each time. The purpose of checking up on them is to help our kids be successful while encouraging them to learn to work hard. Who wants to do a job that no one reviews? We lavish plenty of praise for a job well done—especially in the learning phase—and instruct when it could be done better. When chores are done completely, without complaining, they've earned point number two!

School Point. We home-school our kids; if you don't, you may apply this point to homework, studying, or some other self-improvement habit you want to reinforce. Our problem was that the kids would argue about doing some subjects, take too long to complete others, or do incomplete work. If they complete all of their schoolwork with a good attitude, point number three is earned.

Round-up Point. When we started our Payday system, five kids and two adults occupied our house. We got the kids together and calculated that if we each left three things "to put away later," by the end of the day there would be twenty-one items to clean up. So we created the Round-up Point. Before the kids get dessert, they go through the house and pick up anything they've left out during the day. This can backfire with the "I didn't leave that out" argument, so a toy gets left on the floor for days. As a result, sometimes we do Team Round-up—everyone works in one room until everything is put away, then we move to the next room. This is the best way to clean and build unity. We also tie getting ready for bed and going to sleep with the Round-up Point. A kid who violates lights-out forfeits his or her Round-up Point.

Time Cards. Each week we print out a "time card" for the kids to record their points. Each child's name and the week's dates are written at the top, and there is one square for each day with each of the four points listed on it. The kids circle the points they've earned, confirm it with Mom or Dad, and then write in the total. Steve signs off on the total each day at breakfast. If they forget to have him sign the time card, no points for the day. Of course, we give much assistance to the younger kids and a day or two grace period if a particular week is hectic.

Extra Points. A kid can negotiate for extra points by seeing a job that needs to be done and completing it without being told. Or the child can consult the chore chart and get approval to do an extra chore listed there. For example, vacuuming the car is 3 points, brushing the dogs is 2 points, sweeping the floor is 1 point, and cleaning up a younger sibling's mess is 2 points. We want to encourage them to look around, see a need, and do something about it. What's the payoff? If they earn at least 2 extra points per week—25 points total—they earn *double pay!* Most employers pay bonuses to employees who go above and beyond the call of duty, and so do we.

Principle 5: Determine What to Pay

From what we've been reading and hearing, the price tag of kids' allowances is getting way out of control. A recent article in *Money* magazine reported that the average weekly allowance for a "tweener"—a kid age nine to fourteen—is $9.15. And if you really want to see stars, just take a look at the average weekly allowance for a typical teenager. According to a survey conducted by Nickelodeon with Youth Intelligence, they're being given $50 each week just for living and breathing—that's $2,400 per year! We think a system based on working and earning is far more beneficial for a child and his parents.

Developing a fair compensation system is crucial. Pay them too much, and they have no incentive to learn to do more because they'll be rolling in the dough. In addition, paying too much initially can get pretty expensive, and as they get older and ask for raises it could be tough to maintain the structure of the system. But pay them too little and the system will have little value to them. What to do?

In our system, younger kids earn 5 cents per point, and all their money goes into their three-container bank. Sometime between the ages of six and eight, depending on their work and math ability, their pay doubles to 10 cents per point, and once they reach twelve years of age, it increases to 20 cents. This age and money schedule should be adjusted depending on the maturity and ability of each child.

Here are some examples of what it could cost you per week:

1. 10 cents per point (ages six to ten)
   23 points × 10 cents = $2.30
   25 points × 20 cents (double pay bonus applied) = $5.00

2. 15 cents per point (ages ten to twelve)
   23 points × 15 cents = $3.45
   25 points × 30 cents (double pay bonus applied) = $7.50

3. 20 cents per point (ages twelve and up)
   23 points × 20 cents = $4.60
   25 points × 40 cents (double pay bonus applied) = $10.00

This may seem like a lot of money, but isn't it worth $500 per year—what it would cost you for one child at 20 cents per point—to train your child in healthy work and money management habits?

Every Sunday evening after dinner, it's Payday time. We sit around the dining room table with the cash box and all the kids pull out their banks or envelopes. We total points for the week and disperse the pay. We check the math on their envelopes just to make sure they haven't lost track of anything. It's a great time for affirmation and discussing the consequences of good and poor decisions.

Principle 6: **Reality Spending**

There is a problem with giving kids money and allowing them to spend it on whatever tickles their fancy: it's just not real life! Wouldn't it be great if we had no taxes withheld from our paychecks and no bills to pay—whew, we could have fun with all that money. Having kids participate in paying their own living expenses helps them feel more self-responsible and grown up. Plus it minimizes the cold slap of reality once they are truly out on their own.

We teach our kids to divide their money using percentages. The younger kids divvy up their money three ways: Give, 10 percent; Save, 20 percent; and Spend, 70 percent. We are here to help them plan out their purchases, and we encourage them to keep a "wish list" of things they want to buy. It minimizes impulse spending and helps to develop planning and evaluating skills, especially when faced with a "must-have" purchase without adequate funds in the envelope. Great things start to happen as they evaluate their purchases. They're learning practical life and math skills along with financial responsibility.

At age twelve, they're ready for a little more reality, so they begin purchasing their own clothes, and the percentages change: Give, 10 percent; Save, 20 percent; Clothes, 40 percent; Spend, 30 percent. Once they accumulate about $100 for clothing, they can reduce the percentage required—but if they go shopping and their clothing money is reduced below that threshold, then the percentage goes back up. Our kids love shopping at thrift and consignment stores, where they can usually bring home bargains—the mall has little appeal, because it would consume too much of *their* money! But if something unexpected should happen and they need a particular clothing item and don't have all the money for it, we'll help them out. In all of our years of working this system with our kids we've only had to help out a handful of times—particularly when our teenage boys were going through major growth spurts.

The Envelopes. We originally started with 6-by-9-inch open-ended paper envelopes, and each kid began with three: Give, Save, and Spend (Clothes was added later). The kids would put their money, receipts, and deposit slips in the designated envelopes. On the outside of the envelopes we drew lines and columns for them to record the date of a transaction, a brief description of the item purchased or amount deposited, the amount, and finally the running total. The total on the outside of the envelope equaled the cash inside the envelope.

As time went on, the envelopes became very worn. Eventually the coins fell out through holes in the sides and bottoms of the envelopes, but we taped and repaired until we discovered Tyvek envelopes. They are a plastic-like paper, reinforced with nylon, and are virtually indestructible. We also put two smaller envelopes inside—cash envelopes from our local bank, given to us for free. One envelope holds the money and the second is for receipts. The kids also keep a short pencil tucked in for recording purchases.

There have been a couple of times when envelopes have been left someplace. Since we put each child's first name and our home phone number on the top (and perhaps because there was kid-like scrawling on the ledger portion of the envelope) the envelope and all of the money has always been returned. It was truly heartwarming to receive a phone call saying: "Hello, this is Marcia, and I think I have a child's money envelope here."

Building Savings. Learning to save for the future or in advance for anticipated purchases is an important habit to teach our kids. If they can learn this at a young age, the credit card problems of our culture will never haunt their lives. Our kids have quickly realized that little bits of money add up. As they faithfully put 20 percent of their weekly "earnings" in their "Save" envelope, that money really starts to add up too.

Eventually we take them to the bank to open up their very own savings account—that's a big day. Both parents are signers on the account to make deposits and withdrawals easier. When the total in that envelope reaches $30, we plan a trip to the bank for a deposit.

Principle 7: Cheer Their Independence

It can be frightening to see our kids grow more and more independent, yet isn't it what we really want? It's the most wonderful thing to see our kids make a large purchase after having planned, saved, and researched. We love watching them reach goals, but the greatest benefit is in what it does to their character. They know that they can work and save to purchase anything that they want—well, almost anything. The list of things they've purchased with their own money is endless: expensive baseball bats, radio-controlled planes, collectable model horses, custom Barbie clothes, and even cars (the real kind with engines and insurance bills) when our older kids become young adults.

Through all of this, they've learned the value of waiting—waiting while they save the money for an important purchase, and waiting until they find the best bargain possible. The only thing we don't make them wait for is to tell other family members about a great deal they just found.

Any kids' money system you employ must encourage and reward good decisions. Cheer for their success and be there for them when they hit a bump in the road. We searched for a workable system for our

---

WHAT THE KIDS SAY ABOUT OUR MONEYSMART KIDS SYSTEM

Roy, now seventeen years old, has been capitalizing on our MoneySmart Kids system since he was five. Here's his evaluation of the system. "I really like the freedom I have by earning my own money. If I want to buy something really expensive, I have to discuss it with Mom and Dad first. They ask me lots of questions—sometimes too many. A few years ago, I wanted to spend $70 to buy a K'nex Screaming Serpent roller coaster kit. They didn't think it was a good idea because I would probably get bored with it after I put it together. But I kept thinking about it and came back to them a couple more times with more reasons why I thought it would be a good purchase. Finally they gave in and let me buy it. Okay, I hate to admit this, but I spent one whole day putting the kit together and about two days playing with it. After that I decided I wasn't very interested in watching it go around and around on the track. I like toys and projects that I can interact with—just watching isn't much fun for me. So now the kit is back in its box, in the garage, waiting for our next garage sale. We were recently at a used book fair and a couple of people were actually selling used Screaming Serpent kits for about $40. *I hope I can make that much on it when I sell it.*"

family for eleven years. It takes time and perseverance to find and fine-tune a system that works. But once you do, you will be amazed at the return on your investment of time and money. Remember the key to it all is parents being disciplined. If you consistently manage the system, you'll experience the same joy we do as your kids come running when you call out, "It's Payday time!"

WHAT YOU CAN DO NOW ABOUT KIDS AND MONEY

TIMID MOUSE:
This week evaluate what you're doing to teach your kids to manage their money. Start a program for the kids that links household responsibilities with earning money. If you haven't yet started a budgeting system for yourself, now is the time. Kids will imitate what you demonstrate.

WISE OWL:
Evaluate the allowance system you are currently using. Is it helping your kids develop real-life money management skills? If not, make the changes necessary to plug those holes. Help your kids develop a wish list for things that they want to start saving their money for and eventually purchase.

AMAZING ANT:
Encourage your older kids to set some long-term goals, such as saving money for auto insurance (if they drive your car), saving cash to purchase their own car, or saving money to cover the portion of their college expenses that scholarships don't.

THIRTEEN

SAVINGS AND INVESTMENTS:

It's More Than Just Money in the Bank

Many Americans are in serious savings trouble. According to the U.S. Commerce Department, the annual average savings rate has been in steady decline since the mid-1980s. In 1985, as a nation, we were saving about 12 percent of what we earned. As recently as February 2006, according to a Bureau of Economic Analysis report, that rate was -0.5 percent—a negative savings rate! There is no question that spending money stimulates the economy. But a family that consistently overspends and has established no savings for emergencies is in jeopardy of serious financial problems. If you struggle with overspending and have no reserves, it's time to make some tough decisions. These decisions will require some hard work, but we promise that working hard to build an emergency fund and savings in the bank will help you to sleep better and enjoy life more.

BEING PREPARED: HOW TO BUILD AN EMERGENCY FUND

In Chapter 3: Budgeting we covered how we manage our monthly expenses with our spending plan. If you've got those principles down and are saving in advance for all your living expenses, you will most likely have a good chunk of change sitting in your household bank account and probably feel pretty secure.

We don't want to sound pessimistic and tell you that disaster is around the corner, but in today's society, financial catastrophes *are* lurking in the shadows for the unprepared. Like a good Boy Scout, you've got to "be prepared," so let's talk about building an emergency fund that operates independently from your household budget.

Unless you've got a rich uncle who just left you a large inheritance, building an emergency fund is going to take some time. It took us more than five years to complete ours because we were paying off our first house during that same time. But be patient: it is absolutely essential that you keep working on your household budget, living below your means, and avoiding credit to accomplish this task.

Our emergency fund is money that is kept separate from our household budget. It's placed in a money market access bank account. Depending on the amount of money in your emergency fund and your investment knowledge, you could use other investment vehicles. Just remember that this money needs to be readily accessible for emergencies. We have five subaccounts in our emergency fund (these are different from the accounts in our household budget): Emergency Medical, Emergency Home Repair, Emergency Travel, Unemployment, and Car Replacement. We'll explain the value of each one.

Emergency Medical

In our regular household budget, we have two accounts for medical expenses: Medical Insurance, for paying monthly premiums, and Medical Expenses, for the costs related to routine doctor visits, medication, and vitamins. Should there be a real medical emergency, however, and one of us had to be hospitalized for a period of time, we would need additional financial resources, and that's what our emergency medical fund is for.

Because we own a very small business (it's just our family) and more affordable group policies are not available to us, to keep our monthly costs down we opted for a policy with a very high deductible. Based on this policy, we calculated our financial goal for our emergency medical savings. (If you don't have medical insurance, you need to get it. See Chapter 8: Medical for more information.) Most insurance policies will tell you what your maximum annual out-of-pocket expenses will be. In our case our deductible is $2,500 per person, with a maximum of two deductibles for our family. Our maximum out-of-pocket expenses (including deductibles and co-pays) is $10,000 per year. Yes, this is a lot of money, but based on your insurance policy, your emergency medical needs may be less. So your aim should be to start saving something toward your maximum out-of-pocket expenses—realize that it may take several years to achieve this goal.

If your employer provides a Health Savings Account (HSA), you can accumulate your emergency fund money tax-free and build the amount from one year to the next. HSAs are becoming more popular and easier to obtain. There are some banks that provide HSAs in connection with specific insurance companies. Consult with your insurance provider or your employer's benefits department for more details.

Calculating what you need in your emergency medical fund may take you a few hours. If dissecting your insurance policy makes your head spin, you will probably want to sit down with a benefits person at your place of employment or your private insurance agent and ask for help in calculating your maximum out-of-pocket expense for a single year. Just remember, even if your calculation is off a little bit, but you have put aside some money to cover these expenses, you're still ahead of the game if a medical crisis occurs.

Emergency Home Repair

We believe that homeowners need to have at least 1 percent of the value of their home saved for emergencies. This money is a supplement to your homeowner's insurance, and it's used if you need to replace a major appliance—refrigerator, air-conditioning unit, furnace, et cetera—or to repair your roof or some other part of your house.

In recent years we've watched the news as Americans have experienced an unprecedented number of natural disasters: hurricanes, floods, wildfires, and tornadoes. The losses have been staggering. Add to these disasters the thousands of claims for water damage and mold infestations, and you'll understand why homeowner's insurance companies are not only raising rates but also becoming increasingly selective about whom they will insure. Having money saved to take care of minor emergencies allows you to carry a higher deductible and put in fewer claims. The end result for you will be lower insurance premiums and less extreme rate increases.

Don't let the size of the 1 percent figure cause you to do nothing. (On a $200,000 house you'd need $2,000.) Remember, this too is a long-term savings goal and may take several years. Get started with any amount and build on it. Once our minimum amount was accumulated, we kept adding to this account for other home improvement projects such as redoing our kitchen and putting in new flooring.

Emergency Travel

This account is to be used in case of a family emergency. Annette's parents and siblings live locally, so we don't have to set aside money to see them. But Steve's dad and his siblings live in the Midwest, so this money allows us to fly out of town on short notice so we can be there if the need arises. We based the figure on $500 per person times seven of us and came up with $3,500. We picked this amount because these days airlines are less lenient on bereavement fares and buying last-minute tickets can be really expensive.

After years of sitting dormant and gaining interest, this very account was used in January 2006. Steve's mom was dying of lung cancer and we used this money for all of us to travel back to Chicago and help care for her in her last days. Grieving is tough enough without piling financial worries on top of it.

Unemployment

Many conservative financial experts recommend having three to six months' worth of living expenses saved in case of a financial emergency, disability, or unemployment. With the economy so uncertain, having this account funded is a better idea now than ever before.

Building this portion of our emergency fund took the longest time. Because we have kept our overhead low, however, the amount was large but not insurmountable. We calculated our monthly need, excluding some of the "luxury" items on which we currently spend money, and eventually saved six months of living expenses. It was this very account that allowed us to start our own business—publishing the *HomeEconomiser* newsletter—when Steve's job evaporated for the third time in three years. Without this fund in place, the prospect of unemployment could have spelled financial disaster.

Another advantage of having built an emergency unemployment fund is that you are free from employer coercion. At a seminar Steve attended in 1985, a seventy-two-year-old gentleman spoke about his experiences of working for various employers. He had built an emergency fund and referred to it as "Fat Freddie's Go-to-Hell Fund." He let his employers know that he didn't "need" their job. He would work and work hard for them, but if they ever crossed the line ethically and asked him to compromise his standards, he would simply pack up and leave. It provided a hedge against doing anything that would violate his personal convictions.

Car Replacement

If your goal is to eliminate car payments, this is another account you should create. By paying yourself a car payment each month, you'll soon accumulate enough money to begin paying cash for your cars. Even a partially funded Car Replacement account gives you more options than none at all.

We keep our cars for a long time, using our auto repair account in our household budget to maintain and repair them until we have enough money saved to replace them. Our old 1984 Honda Accord was "retired" in 2001 after our son John drove it into a curb and bent part of the frame, but it was ready to go: it had 250,000 miles on it. We repaired the car and then sold it for a couple of hundred dollars more than the repair cost. If we hadn't had the money saved to replace that faithful Honda with a newer model, we would have either kept driving it or used what money we had saved combined with the sale price to buy something a little newer.

A simple calculation to determine how much you should save each month would be to:

1. Determine how soon you will want to replace your vehicle (number of months).

2. Calculate how much you will want to spend.

3. Divide the cost of the car by the number of months and you'll come up with a monthly "payment."

We look at interest gained as a little cushion to our calculations. Fifteen thousand dollars (replacement cost of a fairly nice used car) divided by 48 months (4 years) = $312.50 per month. You can vary this amount by either lengthening the time period or purchasing a less expensive car. Cars aren't cheap, but by paying yourself a car payment each month you'll avoid interest and all the other headaches associated with borrowing money to buy a car.

It's important to realize that we can't shield ourselves from every problem that could possibly arise. Nor should we hoard so much money that we think we are impervious to disaster. Some of our greatest blessings have come when we've had to depend on others because our own resources were exhausted. But if you are able to create an emergency account and keep it all in proper perspective, emergencies will seem to occur less often and will be far less stressful when they do. Additionally, if you have started to build the emergency fund and disaster does strike before your accounts are fully funded, you are still protected; you can shift money from one account to another to cover the current need.

Like us, you may have months when your income drops drastically

WHAT THE KIDS SAY ABOUT SAVINGS

Roy, at age sixteen, said, "I save 20 percent of all that I earn. My parents taught me this in our Payday system. [See Chapter 12: Kids and Money.] But the cool thing is that because I've learned to save money regularly, when I get large amounts of money for my birthday and at Christmas (at least amounts that seem large to me), I can use most of that money for special purchases. I've bought a radio-controlled plane, a K'nex roller-coaster set, and a radio-controlled robot named Robosapien. Sometimes my parents aren't crazy about my purchases, but we always talk about it before I buy and eventually they see my point of view . . . well, almost always."

and you don't meet your savings goals. Don't sweat it. Keep the goal in sight, and if additional money comes in, then catch up. If you can't meet your monthly savings goal, just save what you can.

Remember, a mountain is climbed one step at a time, and the same is true of building an emergency fund. Little by little you'll see the fund grow. By being prepared and diligent, you'll realize an undeniable sense of financial security.

MAKING THE MOST OF WINDFALLS

Have you ever dreamed that you won the lottery or that an extremely rich, twenty-four-times-removed relative died and left you a fortune? Of course, most of us know exactly what we would do with all the money! Despite the unlikelihood of this type of situation, smaller "fortunes" come our way on a regular basis.

Consider these potential sources of unexpected money: tax refunds, cash birthday gifts, overtime pay, bonuses, garage sale proceeds, stock dividends (remember those?), and overcharges in a mortgage impound or escrow account. These additional funds aren't fairy tales or dreams but windfalls, extra money that appears and that can help you reach your financial goals faster. If you take a stroll through last year's checkbook register, you'll find them sitting there, those wonderful little unexpected bonuses. What did you do with them? If you're like most people, they evaporated . . . absorbed into the abyss of everyday living and bill paying.

Years ago, we decided to stop letting our windfalls evaporate. We came up with a plan, a general agreement as to how we would deal with any excess, big or small, that came our way. But before we get into the specifics of the plan we used, we've got to tell you that the only way you'll know if you truly have a windfall is if you have a spending plan or budget in place (see Chapter 3: Budgeting for an in-depth explanation). Without some sort of spending control/financial management, you can't comfortably spend a windfall for fear that the money will be needed somewhere else.

Because we regularly update and consult our budget, we know when we really do have money that can be used for what we call the Windfall Plan.

America's Cheapest Family Windfall Plan

"I want a boat!" This is a standing family joke. Whenever we're out driving around town and see a boat for sale, Steve will usually quip, "Honey, that's the boat I want to buy with our next windfall." He admits, "As a man, I seem to have an incurable ability to find all kinds of toys—most of them costly to maintain—on which to spend our money." Author Larry Burkett observes that most women will overspend a bit on groceries or buy a few too many clothes, while their husbands will come home with a new car or boat.

After having a few extended "discussions" about different wishes or goals for a specific windfall, we knew we needed to do things differently. It always seemed that we just weren't on the same page. So the windfalls actually created a tense situation, instead of a celebration. We decided to each write up a "wish list" of different things we would each like to buy with extra money. Then we discussed the items and came up with agreed-upon priorities. While this system was better than the wrangling of the past, it was still pretty stressful. It's hard to negotiate and be patient while the money is just sitting there in the bank waiting to be spent. We wanted something better so we could really enjoy the benefits of the windfall and avoid clashes over cash.

What we needed was a more proactive approach. So we developed a percentage plan before any more windfalls came into our possession. At the time, we were paying off our first house. So we decided that whenever excess money came in, it would be allocated to three categories: one-third to an extra house payment, one-third to charitable giving, and one-third to special projects (having fun and buying stuff we've wanted). We were debt-free except for the house, and through the application of this percentage plan, we paid it off in nine years. We could have eliminated the special projects and fun portion of the plan and paid the house off faster, but we came to the conclusion that if we allowed ourselves some enjoyment in the midst of working toward a goal that involved some sacrifice, we would be more likely to stay the course and reach the goal. It was truly amazing to see the mortgage principal plummet as we applied the extra payments. We still remember making the last payment: the phone calls to the mortgage holder, setting the final date and payment amount, writing the check and getting the deed in the mail. Wow, what a great feeling!

Windfall Plan Options

So what might your plan for unexpected money look like? Of course, it's different for every family.

Consider the following if you've got debt (other than a mortgage) to pay down:

- 60 percent for debt liquidation
- 20 percent for savings (emergency funds to keep from using credit in the future)
- 10 percent for charitable giving
- 10 percent for you to enjoy

Try this if you're out of debt and paying off your house:

- 30 percent for additional principal
- 30 percent for savings (emergency funds or IRA/retirement savings)
- 20 percent for home improvement projects
- 10 percent for charitable giving
- 10 percent for you to enjoy

If you are mortgage- and debt-free, you have the option of increasing any of the percentages as you see fit.

The Windfall Hall of Fame

Take some time to think about how you can apply a windfall plan to your situation. Come up with percentages that you can live with. Write down the plan and then start applying it. Remember that you can always fine-tune your plan if you're not totally satisfied with it. Just be ready! It seems that whenever someone we've helped came up with a windfall plan, very soon afterward they'd experience a "dump" of unexpected money. If you take these steps, you'll join the many people who we've inducted into our Windfall Hall of Fame. Here is a short list of some windfall-savvy people.

Wedding Bells Windfall. We were helping a pastor and his wife with a very modest income learn to manage their money and make a plan for their windfalls. They found it hard to believe that they would ever have extra money come in. Within a few weeks of putting their windfall plan in writing, they received some unexpected money from a wedding he performed. Because they had made a plan, they were in agreement about where the money should be used, and were really excited about the results.

Christmas Windfall. In another instance, a $500 Christmas gift came at just the perfect time for a couple who had recently started applying their spending plan and debt reduction strategies. This windfall allowed them to reupholster their car, buy a "new" used refrigerator (theirs was leaking), and purchase some dress shoes and a "new" used suit for the husband so he could go out and interview for a new job. The timing was ideal—they had agreed on the priorities and thoroughly enjoyed the money

Huge Windfall. We were coaching a couple with four children and one on the way. Unexpectedly, they received $49,000 from the liquidation of an investment plan at the husband's office—the owner had been putting the money away for years and never told the employee. This windfall had to be handled carefully due to the tax liabilities and penalties, but it came at a time when they especially needed the money to expand their home and buy a larger car.

Grape Windfall. A divorcee we were helping was given $30,000 from the proceeds of a vineyard her ex-husband had sold. It allowed her to pay off the small balance on her mortgage, get completely out of debt, and start an emergency fund.

Windfalls will come your way. Be prepared—then enjoy the bonus of reaching goals and laughing all the way to the bank.

INVESTING FOR THE FUTURE

What about investments? Many people have asked us about 401(k)s, 403(b)s, IRAs, 529s, mutual funds, real estate, and a host of other investment possibilities. We aren't investment professionals and thus can't advise you as to which, what, or how much you need to invest so you can retire comfortably. There are a number of well-written books by experts that will be able to show you a multitude of investment strategies. Our only caution is to avoid the books that advocate a "get rich quick" mentality. In our experience the only people who make the fast buck are the ones selling these programs. Slow and steady saving combined with careful spending, while not a glamorous philosophy, is the way most of us are going to get ahead.

We hope that after reading our priorities for investing you'll be able to establish your own philosophy. If you create a habit of disciplined budgeting (saving in advance of expected expenses), building your emergency fund, and developing a windfall plan, you will have seasoned your money management and research skills, and you will have no problem learning about investments.

Here is our hierarchy for investing.

- **Pay off all consumer debt.** Carrying credit card balances at 18 percent (or more) while investing just doesn't make sense. Sure, you could possibly make somewhere between 5 to 20 percent on your investment elsewhere, but you could also lose the principal. Plus, if you compare the spread between interest earned and interest paid you're still losing money in most cases. Pay off those credit cards first before investing in mutual funds or stocks.

· **Pay off your cars and start saving for replacement.** Since cars, in most cases, are a necessity, this one decision can save you hundreds of thousands of dollars in interest over a lifetime.

· **Build your emergency fund.** Having this money set aside in a fairly liquid account—money market access or short-term CD—is the next level of protection for your family.

· **Evaluate your life insurance needs.** By this point you will have learned to live on less, and as a result your life insurance needs will be less also. We buy level-term life insurance. Our coverage is enough to provide for our family in the event that one of us dies, but no one is going to get rich. Our goal is to be self-insured and drop the life insurance once all the kids have left home.

· **Start paying off your house.** We saved almost $100,000 in mortgage interest by paying off our first home in nine years. If the only thing you owe money on is your house, then consider doing what we did. Divide your investment money into two portions: half for paying off your house, and the other half for 401(k) (especially if your employer matches a portion of your contribution) or IRA contributions.

· **Invest in IRAs or 401(k)s.** We recommend investing only after you have built your emergency fund, established a working budget, and have all your credit card debt, family loans, and cars paid off. Make sure you are paying down on your house at the same time.

Both of us have read several books on various investment strategies. We've concluded that for our retirement nest egg, investing in mutual funds is our best option. Several years back we tried our hand at buying stocks—we won't go into details here, but just be assured we

WHAT THE KIDS SAY ABOUT SAVINGS

Becky, age twenty-one, has always been a saver, and here's what she says: "Mom and Dad have always helped me with my goals. I love seeing my money grow when I'm saving for a specific goal. Going shopping is more fun once I have the money saved. Plus, there is less of a temptation to overspend because I know what my limits are. Over the past few years, I've purchased a model horse barn to house my collectable Breyer horses—I have over a hundred of them. I've also saved for and purchased a great-looking leather coat and a stereo, and paid for trips with my grandparents to Kentucky and Disney World.

"I've just about completed my equine science degree and am saving to buy a couple of miniature horses so I can achieve my dream of owning horses and starting my own horse business."

Finally, here's Becky's bottom line: "I've learned that saving money may take some time, but with patience and focus I can reach any financial goal that I aim for."

won't be paying any capital gains taxes on that investment. We don't have the time or expertise to be confident in buying individual stocks. Our mutual funds are conservative in nature. If you want a reliable evaluation of mutual funds, go to the library and read *Consumer Reports*. They regularly publish an analysis of these investments. It's easy to read and unbiased.

A BALANCING ACT

A balance is required between living, saving, and investing. Spending too much time moving money from one place to the other or plunking too much money in investments can have detrimental effects for you and your family.

Dave and Diane have been married about as long as we have. Dave is a hard worker and has a good job with a large company. He has always been diligent about putting money into his company's matching 401(k) program. He has over $500,000 accumulated so far. Every once in a while he borrows money from his 401(k) to buy a used car, but beyond that, he leaves the money alone. What's the big deal about this story, you ask? It's just that Dave is so concerned with having enough money in his retirement account that there have been many times throughout his marriage to Diane when they were just barely able to get by on his take-home pay. It's caused stress in their relationship and resentment in Diane's heart. Investments and savings are important. But putting money aside out of fear and to the detriment of your relationship with your spouse or friends isn't the right way to go.

Life is more than the money you have in the bank, the cars you drive, and the houses you own. When you come to your last days, your investment portfolio won't matter nearly as much as the relationships into which you've invested your time. Make your emergency plans, set aside your savings, put some of your money into investments, but all the while be sure that you're putting as much, if not more, time and effort into those precious relationships that surround you. If your investments ever fail or emergencies deplete your savings, having strong bonds with friends and family will pull you through. These are the investments that really matter.

WHAT YOU CAN DO NOW ABOUT SAVINGS

TIMID MOUSE:

Write down your plan for windfalls. Make it a priority to save a set amount or percentage of money from every paycheck to be direct-deposited into a savings account.

WISE OWL:

Start building your emergency savings and store it in a liquid account after you've paid off everything but your house.

AMAZING ANT:

Evaluate your retirement plan options—IRA, 401(k), or other tax-deductible plan. Set a portion of your excess to go to retirement and a portion to go to paying off your house. Once your house is paid off, have a great celebration and increase the amount of money that you put into investments.

FOURTEEN

ATTITUDES:

Thinking Differently
Can Change Everything

We've placed this chapter near the back of the book because we first wanted to give you lots of practical advice so that you could start to take steps that would better your financial situation. Once you start applying the practical tips, you will want to think about the role that attitudes might be playing in your finances. Attitudes about money can come from your childhood, your marriage, the people you hang out with, or any number of other sources. Regardless of where they came from, it's time to evaluate whether they are helping or hurting how you handle your money.

What does attitude have to do with getting you right on the money? Just about everything. Our attitude toward living below our means and avoiding debt affects everything we do. If we look at our financial situation as a challenge and an opportunity to discover new and exciting solutions, everything becomes a game. But developing a frugal attitude and mind-set takes time. It's not a one-time decision: "Okay, that's it, I need to stop spending money, I'm going to be frugal if it's the last thing I do!" And then instantly you become a coupon-clipping, thrift-store-shopping, super-saving diva.

We've discovered in our own lives that lasting habits are slow to develop. They usually start with a realization that there is a better way to do something. Then comes the decision to try to do it in a new way. Then, finally, we repeat the new method enough until at last it becomes second nature. The point is that it takes time and reinforcement to ingrain new habits and new attitudes to the point that they become a part of our fiber, our very being. Never for a minute do we expect that anyone will read this book and suddenly adopt our lifestyle lock, stock, and barrel. It's just unrealistic. But as you dip your toes into the sea of frugality, with each passing moment the water will feel more comfortable and you won't be afraid to wade in deeper.

It is our attitude at the beginning of a difficult task which, more than anything else, will affect its successful outcome.

—WILLIAM JAMES

FRUGAL QUALITIES

While there is no one right way to live out the frugal lifestyle, beneath the surface of every super-saver you can often find some similar traits. Here are five of the most common. As you read through these qualities, see if you have developed any of them. Put an X next to the ones that describe you.

> *1. Lifestyle Trait.* Frugality isn't belt-tightening during a crisis; it's not a fad or temporary thing. It's a lifestyle, usually born out of necessity, but continued because it is fulfilling and because we just couldn't imagine living any other way.

> ❏ I love living the frugal lifestyle.

2. Brand-Disloyalty Trait. To economizers, in most cases brands don't matter. Our bottom line is to be fashionable and well-fed while still being frugal.

❐ I'm not loyal to any one brand.

3. No-Fad Trait. Most economizers avoid trendy toys, décor, or fashion for two reasons. One is cost. The newest stuff is usually the most expensive. If you wait awhile, the price will go down or you'll find it in the thrift store for pennies on the dollar. The second is that we tend to be independent sorts, not caring much what others think. We wear what we like and usually buy standard or classic fashions. If we need something dressy, we'll hit the consignment store or thrift shop.

❐ I laugh at fads.

4. Wear It Out Trait. We wear things out. Clothes are handed down from one kid to the next. Toys face the same fate. We'll sew, tape, glue, or screw things together to keep them serviceable. As a last resort, we'll replace a broken what-cha-ma-call-it with a used one, if possible. When we get rid of something, you can be assured it has lived a long, useful life and probably won't be accepted by any self-respecting thrift store or dumpster diver.

❐ I regularly repair things rather than replace them.

5. Nonmaterialistic Trait. Less is more. Most frugal-minded people realize that stuff costs money to buy, then money to maintain, and then money to replace. When we have a need, we'll try to either make do with what we have, substitute with something that will work, or borrow from a friend before plunking down our hard-earned cash.

For example, our property originally had seventy trees on it. When we wanted to lower that number, we borrowed a chain saw from a friend (thanks, Bart!). After doing so a few times, we realized cutting down trees would be an ongoing chore, and we needed to purchase our own tool. Most consumers would have run out and purchased something to meet their immediate need before determining if it was really a necessity. Not so with economizers.

❏ I regularly evaluate all of my options before I spend money.

So, how did you do? Do you have any of these traits? If none of these characteristics is evident in your life, don't despair. It may take some time, but by applying a few of the tips in this book, you'll start to see your frugal qualities and your finances multiply.

Benjamin Franklin once said, "A penny saved is a penny earned." In today's high-pressure, fast-spending society, his motto has a hollow ring to it. But as you'll see in the next section, little things, like pennies, really do add up.

IT'S THE LITTLE THINGS THAT MATTER

Recently an interviewer said to us, "No one's going to get rich by slicing open the toothpaste tube to get out the last little bit. But one of the things you said was, 'It's an attitude, and it's an attitude that says little things add up.' What do you mean by that?"

Some people put loose change in a jar to reach a goal; others reuse aluminum foil, clip coupons, or wash and reuse plastic zip bags to save money. None of these is a revolutionary new idea that will save you millions of dollars and make you rich overnight. These are little things. But we've come to realize that if we pay attention to the little things—turning off lights, watching gas mileage, being careful at the grocery store—all those little bits of money over time do add up. More important, the attitudes of conserving, planning, researching, and saving are being learned, reinforced, and improved upon. If we have established a habit of paying attention to saving with little things, what will we do when we are faced with a large expense? We will practice the same habits. The biblical adage "If you are faithful in little things, you will be faithful in much" is really true!

Conversely, people who think that loose change doesn't matter, who stop at the convenience store and drop a few bucks on a drink every day, will probably be just as spontaneous in their spending on more expensive items. Later, many of those items will turn up at garage sales. We call it the "it's no big deal" attitude. This attitude results in wasting money and wasting a lot of it.

Here are a few other excuses we've heard and examples we've seen.

- **Convenience stores, coffee shops, and smoothies.** "It's just a few bucks—no big deal." A soda, double decaf, skim latte, or a strawberry banana smoothie. But do it enough times and the dollars start to add up. With a little planning you can get the same jolt for much less by making your drink at home and bringing it with you.

- **Change machines.** One day we saw a guy enter the grocery store with a five-gallon water bottle full of change. He lugged it through the store and over to the change machine. We heard the rattle of coins as the bottle was slowly emptied. Did you know that he spent almost 8 percent of his savings just to pay for the convenience of not having to roll the change? "Hey, it's just small change—no big deal!" Most banks will give out coin rolls as a courtesy to customers—and then allow you to keep all your savings.

- **Movies.** Renting movies because "it's the only thing we spend recreation money on" may be a justification, but what is it costing you? Go back over the past few months and add up what you've spent. If it's more than the cost of a tank of gas, it's time to reevaluate. If you need a movie fix, check out your local library or borrow from a friend's collection. That's how we've introduced our kids to some wonderful old movies that support our values.

- **Vending machines.** *Cha-ching!* Great for the vendor, bad news for us. The items sold in most vending machines are double or triple the price you would pay for the exact same item from the grocery store. If you have a snacking need, plan ahead—buy a supply from the store to have at home and bring it with you to work or wherever the temptation lies.

· **Lottery tickets.** "Hey, they're only a buck or two, right? No big deal, and if I hit it big, there's so much I could do with that money!" Why not set aside that same money in a savings account and have a sure thing when you reach retirement age? And if you are retirement age and really don't need the extra money, why not set it aside in savings bonds for your grandkids? We've heard it said that "the lottery is a tax on those who are bad at math."

· **The ATM.** "Hey, twenty bucks here, twenty bucks there, it's really not much," and "It's too much hassle to write it down in my checkbook, 'cause I'm in a hurry!" Add in a few fees because you didn't use your own bank's ATM, and before you know it, *boinggggg* . . . things in your bank account will really be bouncing.

· **Balancing your checkbook.** A couple of times each year we find errors, overcharges, or other discrepancies when comparing our records and receipts with our monthly checkbook statement. At least once each year we discover we've been double-charged for an item. Most banks won't argue over a few cents, and most mistakes can be corrected with one phone call. But if you never balance your checkbook these mistakes will just keep coming out of your bank account—and you'll never even know it. Even though this can seem like a hassle each month, it's well worth the effort.

Little things do add up, and they add up quickly. You can achieve huge savings by paying attention to these and other small expenses. We aren't talking deprivation but planning. There is nothing inherently wrong with any of the little *indulgences* we've mentioned above. The problem lies in thinking that spontaneity is a much-needed and deserved reward. If your financial goals are a big deal to you, then you'll enjoy making the changes necessary to save all the change you've been exchanging.

We hope you're convinced that paying attention to the little things is an important and beneficial attitude, but brace yourself—because the next attitude we're going to tackle may not be as easy to measure or conquer.

CONTENTMENT: LEARNING TO LOVE YOUR LIFE

Contentment—easy to say, but difficult to live out. Especially when we're stuck in a dead-end job or staring a mountain of debt in the eye. How can we get past our debilitating feelings and turn "lemons into lemonade?"

First, we need to acknowledge our discontentment and identify its source. We've found four things you can do to foster contentment in your financial life:

Don't Look in My Bag!

Many of us are stretching our necks or turning our heads to see what other people have in their "bag of life." They may have a larger house, a fancier car, or more toys than us. But focusing on what they have and what we don't is a fast track to all kinds of financial and emotional problems. When we focus on what we don't have, what we do have seems blasé, worthless, and undesirable. Cultivating an attitude of gratefulness for what we do have brings life into perspective.

Another thing to remember is this: what we think we see in other people's bags may not be reality. We know it's true that nice-looking couples with nice-looking cars may be extremely stressed and unhappy. We don't often see the monthly struggle to make the payments on the "nice stuff"—the fights, disagreements, and anxiety that go along with maintaining possessions that stretch the bounds of the household income. It just ain't all it appears to be.

What Do I Really Need?

If you often find yourself discontented, limit the amount of time you do the following things: watch TV, surf the Internet, browse through catalogs, or walk through the mall. All of these stimuli play on our desire to possess and buy more things. Just watch a beer commercial or two. Do they depict reality? Everyone is twenty-two years old with perfect teeth and a perfect body. And they drink as much beer as they want and never gain an ounce. *Get real.*

We've got to realize that what we *need* and what we *want* are usually two very different things. All of us *need* transportation, but in what form can that need be met? Early in our marriage, Steve rode a bicycle to work. It was one mile each way, and the bicycle met his need perfectly. His second job was farther from home, and the bus met that need most of the time—it provided time to read some fantastic books. Is a brand-new Mercedes a need, or will a used Chevy get you where you need to go? Once we understand the difference between needs and wants, contentment is just a step away.

Real Needs Bring on Real Creativity

There are appropriate times to be discontent—times when real needs require real action. Contentment is not laziness or a fatalistic attitude. If we have a need and don't have the money to meet it, we have the opportunity to exercise real creativity. This opportunity is often lost as we whip out a credit card to "solve" the problem. There are always creative options if we'll just pause and look around. We've found that asking others for help, borrowing an item, buying used merchandise, or waiting for a little miracle are all ways that our real needs have been met when the money wasn't there.

The Maximum Lifestyle

Establishing a limit on the size of our house, the amount we'll spend on a car, our monthly budget, the brands of clothes we'll wear—basically a maximum lifestyle—has gone a long way in minimizing our times of discontentment. When we look back on how far we've come, we can't help but be grateful and content.

Whew, and if we look at the rest of the world, how can we in any Western, industrialized nation think we are lacking?

In a letter that public relations expert Robert L. Dilenschneider sent out to his clients, he encouraged them to have a more accepting and understanding view of people with different perspectives. His numbers illustrate that we continue to have an abundance of the world's resources at our beck and call.

If we could shrink the whole earth's population to a village of pre-cisely 100 people, with all the existing human ratios remaining the same, it would look like this:

- 59% of the wealth would be in the hands of only 6 people and all 6 would be citizens of the United States
- 80 would live in substandard housing
- 70 would be unable to read
- 50 would suffer from malnutrition
- 1 would be near death
- 1 would be near birth
- 1 would have a college education
- 1 would own a computer

Just to clarify, we aren't saying that having things is bad and that living in poverty is good. What we are saying is that contentment is im-portant and that knowing when enough is enough not only is going to allow us to enjoy our lives but most likely will allow us to share our ex-cess with others in need.

THE FREEDOM OF IDEALISM: STAND FOR WHAT YOU BELIEVE IN!

Idealism is just as important as contentment in helping us stick to our vision in the face of opposition.

In the summer of 2005 we took an inspirational two-week trek though the annals of American history. We visited monuments, memo-rials, buildings, and battlefields all preserved to honor the memory of great men and women who risked everything they possessed so we could possess everything we now enjoy. It occurred to us that the ideals of great patriots, in any country and during any time period, can teach us much about how we should live, save, and spend our money and time. We are fighting a battle for financial independence, and because of our ideals, we will encounter opposition, much as our founders did. We can draw many parallels from the characteristics of these idealistic leaders.

Idealism Takes Courage

Our founding fathers were oppressed by *external* forces: England imposed numerous taxes through the Stamp Act and the Townshend Act while instituting restrictions on the use of raw materials. The colonists were not represented in England's Parliament and had no say regarding the taxes that were levied on them.

Often our financial oppression comes from *internal* forces—our own choices, such as regularly overspending, the overuse of credit, or a lack of planning. Other times financial distress is the result of a calamity—a major medical condition or business failure.

The colonists came to a point in their lives when they stood up and said, "Enough is enough!" Thomas Paine published his pamphlet *Common Sense,* which inspired the nation to move toward independence. Patrick Henry was vociferous against King George III's domination of the colonies. Both of these men (and many others) realized that continuing to subjugate themselves to a nonrepresentative form of government was unacceptable. It was time for a major change in the way life was lived.

We've seen many families, finally fed up with living in financial anguish, stand up and say, "This is it; I'm tired of living this way." It takes courage to cut up the credit cards, to pull the plug on cable TV, to cancel the newspaper, or to say no to the kids when they want you to pay for yet another recreational expense. These aren't easy decisions, but they may be necessary—even if only temporary. A courageous stand will be costly in the short run but will provide freedom for years to come.

Idealism Is Costly

Our founders, in many cases, exchanged a lifestyle of luxury and privilege to pursue their dreams. Not all who lived in America's revolutionary times agreed with their stand for independence from England. Many of our forefathers were despised, ridiculed, and cut off from the society to which they belonged. And in later years, the idealism of freedom for all men cost Abraham Lincoln his life.

We might not be facing death as economizers, but when we make it our priority to live within our means and shun debt to achieve financial freedom, we may experience a great social cost. We may miss some of what our society says is necessary to a fulfilling existence—plasma TVs, gigantic SUVs, exotic vacations, private education for our children, or the latest fashions. When we take a stand to spend only what we truly can afford, some friends or co-workers may ostracize us, finding our choices peculiar, restrictive, or even idiotic. Are we willing to stand firm on our convictions? If we are, we will prevail.

Idealism Involves Others

The American colonists received financial and military aid from many sources—farmers, plantation owners, American Indians, and other countries. Without the support they received, the American experiment would have been short-lived. Whether help was offered in response to the ideals of the founding fathers or because England was disliked is unknown, but the point is that we accomplish much more when we have the support of others.

Our family never could have accomplished what we have without the support of friends and relatives. Whether it's through hand-me-downs, babysitting, emotional support, or help with painting or home repairs, having an established network of support is critical. We're not saying that we should look at friends and family as a resource to be used for our convenience. This is a network of reciprocity. Helping and being helped makes us all better and stronger.

Idealism Takes Time

The American Revolution was brewing for years prior to its start in 1776. It really wasn't complete until the War of 1812 ended in late 1814. Beginning with the Jamestown settlement in 1607, the colonies spent 170 years under the Union Jack. Ultimately, it took thirty-eight long years to achieve total independence. With each military victory, our nation's determination and desire for absolute freedom and autonomy grew.

Maintaining a lifestyle with strict financial ideals isn't like winning the lottery. Significant changes in your spending habits take time to grow strong enough to weather emergencies. These new habits settle in deeper with each test you pass as you withstand the urge to impulse-buy an item. It may seem tediously slow going when you're staring at a list of debts. But with the goal of financial freedom in your sights and strong determination, most people can fight their way through a pile of debt in eighteen months. Even massive goals that may seem unachievable, such as paying off a home mortgage, can be completed.

As we've mentioned, we started by applying $2 extra principal each month to our mortgage payment. As our income increased and we learned more and better ways to save money, we were able to pay more excess to the remaining mortgage balance. It was exhilarating to watch the amount we owed decrease. Yes, it took nine years to pay off, but after conquering a goal of that magnitude, we were convinced that with time, patience, and perseverance, no goal was out of reach.

Idealism Finds Deals

While touring the ornately decorated Library of Congress in Washington, D.C., our tour guide pointed out many of the beautiful sculptures, paintings, and the marble construction. He said that when Congress allocated $6.1 million for construction of the building in the 1880s, no one thought it would be enough. But Edward Pearce Casey, the new architect assigned to finish the building, saw the monetary limit as a blessing. The country was in the midst of a depression, so he negotiated bargain prices with marble quarries, stone workers, and artists, who were happy just to have work to do. As a result of his budgetary goal, he was able not only to complete the entire project under budget but to create one of the most beautiful buildings in the history of the United States.

Financial limits are a blessing. They encourage creativity and allow for bragging rights. Have you ever heard someone brag about paying retail? Nope. There is no glory in paying what everyone else pays. But use a coupon, negotiate a lower price, or stumble upon a deal, and you can tell everyone about it. And if it's a good enough deal, like Edward Casey, people will still be talking about your bargaining ability 120 years from now.

Idealism Requires Faith

In spite of recent Supreme Court rulings regarding the future role of religion in our country, you would be hard-pressed to read any of our founding fathers' accounts of the events that formed our country without hearing their references to Providence or the Creator. They believed in a Power and Person greater than themselves. It is well documented that George Washington embarked on each day's duties by spending time in prayer. From winds that blew British ships away from the Battle of Boston in March 1776 to the final battle in Yorktown, faith in God played a huge role in the founding of America.

We don't want to preach or pressure you, but we have found that for our family, our greatest joys come when we lean fully on God to provide for us. We aren't saying that we lounge around and do nothing, waiting for the things we need to fall from heaven. We rely on Him to provide wisdom and the right timing for our needs rather than using our own planning and methods to get what we think we need. Was it just "luck" that we found a perfect vehicle for our family in just three days' time when our other van was wrecked? Was it our great PR ability that caused an assistant producer from *Good Morning America* to actually answer the phone one day in April 2004? We could say it was luck or chance, but these types of things happen all too often for us to believe anything other than Divine Providence.

Idealism Endures

Because of the idealism of several focused, brave men and women, the cause of liberty has spread through their descendents across this country and around the world. Idealism has far-reaching effects.

Our financial ideals have already shaped the future of our kids, affected friends and relatives, and now encourage people around the world. Making the decision to improve your financial management will have profound effects on your future and those you love.

A revolution founded on frugal financial ideals isn't restrictive. Instead, it's the road to real freedom. Our ideals are:

· To always live within our means
· To avoid debt . . . with a smile
· To never pay retail *if at all possible*
· To plan and save in advance of all purchases
· To realize that there is always someone who wants to get rid of the very thing that we need—find the person and we will find a deal

So what are your financial ideals?

Freedom! Ah, the sound just brings relief to the soul. Financial freedom can be had without millions of dollars in the bank. It's based on your attitude. If you're content with your lot in life, are willing to learn new frugal habits, pay attention to the little things, and stand up for your ideals, you'll experience abundance in every area of your life. So what do you think? Are your attitudes right on the money?

WHAT YOU CAN DO NOW ABOUT ATTITUDES

TIMID MOUSE:

The next time you think you need to buy something, step back and think about whether you really need to own it or not. Consider borrowing or renting. If it is something you'll use regularly, research the possibility of buying it used for a fraction of the cost.

WISE OWL:

Think of something that may need mending or repairing at your house. Instead of tossing or donating it, fix it. It will not only save time by eliminating the need to shop for a replacement but save you money as well.

AMAZING ANT:

What do we really need to possess to be happy? Evaluate your life and determine if you're using too much of your energy to make money or to buy stuff. Evaluate if you are investing enough time and mental energy in the important relationships in your life. If not, make a change.

FIFTEEN

THE FINAL PAYOFF

This is it, the final chapter. A final encouragement that no matter what effort you can muster toward learning and practicing new habits, it will produce great benefit in your life. Just in case you're still wondering if living a frugal lifestyle is worth the energy, read on.

IT'S BETTER TO BE THRIFTY

Is thrifty living only for those people who can't afford to pay retail? Nope. Is a frugal lifestyle only to be employed during times of financial distress? Of course not. Is living cheap just for those who are retired and on a fixed income? Sorry, the answer is no to this one too. There are so many benefits to living below our means that we wanted to make a list of our top six reasons. No matter what our neighbors, friends, family, or even kids say, we're proud to be economizers and we hope you are too.

1. Living Thrifty Saves Time

Skeptics will say that being thrifty takes more time, but we disagree.
Sure, we spend time cooking from scratch rather than buying pre-

pared foods, but meal preparation doesn't need to be a huge time consumer. By planning a menu in advance and stocking a pantry and freezer with favorite ingredients, throwing together a meal takes minutes, not hours. And the flip side is the person who is in the grocery store every other day—those quick trips to the store eat up a lot of time. And what about eating in restaurants several times each week? You've got drive time, waiting to be seated, waiting to order, eating, waiting for the check, and finally driving home. Plus eating out reduces the quality of your family time. Sure, the drive-through may be faster, but what are the health ramifications? Even picking up a carry-out meal can take longer than making a simple meal of tacos, hot dogs and beans with applesauce, or spaghetti and meat sauce with a salad— mmm, we're getting hungry just talking about it.

Another time thief is an unmaintained car. How many hours does an emergency car repair steal from your life? In our years of marriage, we've only had three times where we had to have the car towed due to a mechanical problem. We set aside car maintenance money and keep ours running . . . and running. Sure, it takes some planning and time to maintain them properly, but the prospect of being stranded with the kids in the car just isn't a possibility we want to think about. Time is a precious commodity, too often taken for granted. We want to manage not only our money to make it go further but also our time to do more of the things that we value most.

2. Living Thrifty Puts You in a More Secure Financial Position

When we choose a thrifty lifestyle, life tends to grow less complicated. Contentment is easier to achieve. Patience and planning ahead become a way of life. The impulse to possess everything that advertisers hawk pales, and keeping up with the "Joneses" becomes unnecessary.

If we keep our overhead low, when hard times come—such as sickness or unemployment—these storms can be more easily weathered. Keeping your monthly expenses low also allows you the freedom to step out and try something new. This is what we did when we started the *HomeEconomiser* newsletter. We could take the risk, knowing that our savings could carry us through the first year or two.

3. Living Thrifty Is Better for Relationships

Because we focus on keeping life streamlined and simpler, there is more time to spend with the people we love. Like a growing number of other families today, we've made a decision to live on one income. We have never regretted that decision. We firmly believe that our children need quality *and* quantity time with us to develop to their fullest potential. Sure, our household income has been lower, and as a result, we've climbed the household possessions ladder more slowly than some of our peers. But over time, we've accumulated all that we really want and need. Many times we've found the solution to a need using creativity rather than spending money. Talking about a need as a family and working on the solution together allows us all to share in the victory.

In our city, there are many Romanian families who have found a creative way to own a home, raise a family, and earn a living. They have purchased luxury homes and converted them into assisted-living residences. The husbands and wives work together providing excellent care to the few elderly residents who share their home. Their children learn to be well behaved and enjoy spending lots of time with their parents rather than long hours in day care. This option is not for everyone, but the point is that when we work together there will always be a good solution.

Many families are questioning the norms of society. In the 1950s a one-income family was the norm. Now that there are "so many more things we need," most people say, "we've got to have two incomes to survive." This has now become the norm. Where does the line get drawn so that relationships are given the time they need to develop, bond, and grow strong? We're talking about relationships not just with our kids but also with spouses. It's almost a parable—the young couple, so in love that they can survive on pork and beans and be happy. And then they grow older, earn more, and buy a larger car and a bigger house, but instead of bringing happiness and peace, it brings stress and they end up divorced. They sacrifice their relationship on the altar of earning and possessing more. Let's not go there—this "norm" must be avoided. Learning to live with less brings more to relationships.

4. Living Thrifty Is Better for Kids

Kids who are taught to be content with little can always adjust to having more. They can also be happy when they strike out on their own—single or married—with very little. Our Payday system, described in Chapter 12: Kids and Money, doesn't make our kids rich financially, but it does enrich their ability to handle, manage, and calculate money. It works so well that as our older kids have entered the workplace, they have been commended on their money-handling ability and frugal habits. Roy worked his first "real job" during the 2004 Christmas season as a cashier at Barnes and Noble. To his employer, Roy was a real gem, his cash drawer balanced to the penny almost every day. To Roy, his earnings seemed like a gold mine, not just pocket change.

We all know that an indulged child is an unappreciative child. Teaching our kids that there are limits in life and that those limits can stimulate creativity is a good thing. When we live frugally, it teaches our kids that looking for creative ways to meet our needs can be fun and exciting. Letting them experience the joys of finding a deal at a young age will benefit them for a lifetime.

5. Living Thrifty Is Better for the Economy

In 2004, over 1.6 million people declared bankruptcy. That's an average of 30,769 filings per week. Right before the tougher restrictions on bankruptcy filings began on October 17, 2005, the numbers spiked. In the first week of October, there were over 102,000 filings. In 2005, the total number leaped to over 2 million. What's the big deal? Well, if those 2 million people declared bankruptcy and didn't pay back just $10,000 each (a small and unrealistic amount), the total amount of money siphoned out of our economy would be $20,000,000,000—that's $20 billion for those of us who aren't used to so many zeroes.

And that's with conservative numbers—in reality it's probably five to ten times that amount. What does this mean for the rest of us? Higher interest rates, higher prices in stores, more repossessed homes in our neighborhoods, and higher fees for mortgage insurance protection, just to name a few.

Disregarding these dire statistics—and the examples of our parents and grandparents—many people just keep on spending every penny they earn, never setting aside anything for a rainy day.

But thrift-minded savers can do wonders for the economy. Our bank accounts will be stouter. We'll own more of our houses. Our cars will be purchased with large down payments or cash. Sure, an economy filled with thrifty folks would be completely different from the current economy, but it would be more stable and there would be plenty of money for investing, starting new businesses, lending, and helping those in need.

6. Living Thrifty Is Better for the Environment

The Center for a New American Dream stated in one of their past annual reports that "Americans make up less than 5 percent of the world's population, but consume nearly 30 percent of its material resources. We consume 40 percent of the world's gasoline, 25 percent of the oil and 23 percent of the coal. Since 1940, Americans alone have used up as large a share of the earth's mineral resources as all previous humans put together. Americans also generate a disproportionate amount of waste. The average American generates over twice as much garbage as the average European—over 1,600 pounds of trash per year."

It should come as no surprise that we create so much trash. The prepared-food aisles of the grocery store are the fastest-growing section. Consider the packaging involved compared to what is consumed. This overpackaging extends far beyond the grocery industry. We've also seen some gross examples of overpackaging in software, perfume products, and home repair items. We once heard a story about a visiting Chinese minister who was asked what impressed him most about America. He replied, "Your garbage. I could provide for an entire village with the things that you Americans throw away."

Cooking from scratch reduces our trash output considerably. All vegetable scraps go in our compost pile. Paper and plastic are put in our recycling bin. All the rest goes in our regular trash. Compared to many other families in our neighborhood, our trash output for our larger family is much less than theirs. We often see this specifically on the day when the blue recycling containers are put out at the curb.

Gas consumption is also less. We always plan efficient routes and combine errands with planned trips. Several years ago, Steve realized that his twenty-mile commute to the office was a supreme waste of time, gas, and money. He decided to look for a job closer to home and eventually found one just two miles away. Then he rode a bike or was dropped off at work so Annette or one of the kids could drive the smaller, more gas-efficient car. When our kids get jobs, we encourage them to look for work near home. This way they can bike or Rollerblade (though never in the dark) to and from their jobs.

Used clothing is a huge issue. As we mentioned in Chapter 9: Clothing, researchers in the state of Washington determined that 45 percent of all clothing purchased was ending up in landfills. To combat this waste, they encouraged donations to thrift stores. And a new industry has developed that recycles clothing. Some is sorted and sold overseas. Other items in worse condition are shredded and incorporated into home insulating materials.

Buying used clothing and other household items from thrift and consignment stores not only diminishes landfill bulk but also reduces the amount of fossil fuel needed for the manufacture, transport, and merchandising of these products. As economizers, we take care each year to keep, repair, or reuse old clothing and other household items, rather than assigning them to a landfill.

While we don't advocate keeping every last thing that we ever owned, the frugal-minded will extend the life of almost everything they do own, or they will find someone else who could benefit from having the item.

Livin' thrifty isn't just a passing fad. It is done for the benefit of family, friends, and the environment as a whole. Let's keep the frugal lifestyle alive. *Use it up, wear it out, fix it up, or do without!*

LIVING BETTER STARTS NOW!

Choosing a frugal lifestyle has many benefits, several of which you've just read about. The thing that is most rewarding to us about our budgeting habits and thrifty lifestyle is the peace of mind we experience. Please don't misunderstand us—there are many areas in our marriage (or in any marriage, for that matter) where conflict and distress can occur, such as in choosing priorities, disciplining the children, basic differences between men and women, time management, organizational skills, in-law relationships, and financial decisions, just to name a few. Families today are operating with such high levels of stress that it just has to affect marriages, parenting, and relationships as a whole. Isn't it great when one whole area of conflict or stress—such as finances—can be totally eliminated, or at least significantly minimized?

Not only have *we* reaped the benefits of the economizer lifestyle, but our children have too. They are free to evaluate material possessions based on their needs and product quality, rather than status and peer pressure. Having more material possessions doesn't guarantee happiness—but it does guarantee that there are more things to be maintained! We believe that our children will live a fulfilling life, full of joy and devoid of financial stress. And it won't be because they earn a "boatload" of money. Rather, it will come about because they have learned to manage what they have earned and, more important, they have learned the secret of contentment. Armed with this knowledge, they will be able to possess everything they need.

Your History

We don't know who you are or how you were raised. Perhaps you were raised in a thrifty home and the sharpening of your skills is a lifelong and very fulfilling journey. There is also the possibility that you weren't raised in a frugal home but somewhere along the way you saw real value in being penny-wise and have begun to embrace these new habits, discovering great joy in this lifestyle. Then there are those of you who were never taught to evaluate your purchases or distinguish quality. Perhaps you were raised by parents who indulged you, substituting money and possessions for real love. And finally there are those of you who were raised in real poverty, where there was never enough of anything. Maybe your financial history is a mixture of these four lifestyles, or something totally different. Regardless of your past, and no matter where you are currently in life, thrifty living can improve it!

Forge Ahead

There is no place where household money management skills are taught. The school system just doesn't cover it. Colleges may have economics courses, but they aren't going to teach you to save on groceries. Even consumer credit counseling firms don't teach detailed budgeting. So if you didn't learn this in the home you grew up in, don't condemn yourself or feel stupid. Just pick yourself up and get busy. Choose one or two things to work on this very week. As you do, the stress will evaporate from your life.

Life can hand out some pretty devastating blows—chronic or emergency medical conditions, divorce, lawsuits, and a handicapped child are just a few examples. No matter how desperate it gets, don't give up. Don't ever give up! There is always a way up and out of the pit you are in, and today is the day to start! You are learning a disciplined approach to life, a new habit. Your first steps as a child were wobbly, and so was your first bicycle ride. Even brushing your teeth started out as a task that required full concentration. Now all of these things have become second nature—so ingrained in your fiber that you don't give them a second thought. The same thing will happen to your skills as you grow to become an experienced economizer.

Don't be too hard on yourself either. You'll take two steps forward and inevitably one step backward. Don't get discouraged; you will conquer it all. For a time, you may need to minimize your exposure to the advertising in your life. The few times we watch TV, we mute the commercials. It helps, it really does. Our culture is constantly delivering the message that we never have enough. There is always something else we need to make our life complete. *Bull.* There is something we need, but it's not for sale—it's a new mind-set.

Your Choice

You have at your disposal one of the most powerful tools available to mankind: the power of choice. You can choose to be defeated and give up, or you can choose to become a victor, making healthy financial choices and each day seeing positive results. The people we've seen who chose to deal with their finances often went from a negative balance in their checking accounts to having several thousand dollars saved within two years. Without exception, they've all emphatically said, "I can't believe I was living that way. I'll never go back to that type of lifestyle!"

So what's stopping you? Even if you have a spouse who doesn't want to change, there's still plenty you can do. You can start making choices and changes. Anything—and we do mean any single thing that you choose to start doing right now—is going to improve your situation. You can live much, much better while spending less!

Your Story

Nothing encourages us more than hearing about you taking control of your finances. We'd love to hear your story of financial victory. Send us an e-mail through our Web site, www.AmericasCheapestFamily.com, or mail to: Annette and Steve Economides, PO Box 12603, Scottsdale, AZ 85267-2603.

Economizing Together,

Annette & Steve

Annette & Steve Economides

ACKNOWLEDGMENTS

We couldn't have completed this book on our own. There were so many "angels" who helped us along the way, we just wanted to say thank you.

Talia Cohen, our literary agent, who believed we had a story to write even before we did.

Shana Drehs, our editor, and all the folks at Crown Publishers, your fresh set of eyes and many questions made our book a better read for everyone.

To our friends in Arizona who encouraged us to start the *Home-Economiser* newsletter and walked with us and supported us on this unknown trail.

Subscribers to *HomeEconomiser*, your faithful encouragement and great money-saving tips keep our writing fresh and full of new ideas.

Pauly Heller, an awesome friend who has encouraged us and edited our writing since we started the newsletter.

Jody Humber for training us and believing that we could manage the church financial coaching ministry.

Tim Kimmel and John Trent for all your savvy book advice. You've been great friends.

Sam Mittlestadt for writing our first full-length newspaper feature story in the *East Valley Tribune*! Whew, it was the start of a wild ride!

Brahm Resnik for exposing us to all of Arizona through the *Arizona Republic* newspaper and believing in us enough to introduce us to the wonders of early-morning live TV.

Claire Alpert for thinking our story was interesting enough to get us on the set of *Good Morning America*! That was a great experience for our whole family!

To all of the other media people who have shared our story and promoted our frugal lifestyle in a positive light.

To our five kids: Thanks for pulling up the slack while we were writing, editing, or on the phone to New York. You guys are awesome and make life worth living—*you're pretty good with money too!*

ABOUT THE AUTHORS

ANNETTE ECONOMIDES spent twenty-one years as a stay-at-home mom until she joined Steve writing and publishing the *HomeEconomiser* newsletter in 2003.

At ten years old, driven by an innate desire to earn money, she found several of her siblings' unused toys lying around the house. Seizing the opportunity, she promptly set up a trading post in the front yard. Neighbors from blocks around picked up many bargains that day and Annette pocketed most of the money. That was until her older brother came to see if he could purchase a bargain-priced item only to find one of his toys there for sale. He sounded the alarm and the trading post was promptly closed.

As a teenager Annette shunned anything having to do with cooking or housework. Her favorite hangout was the mall and her favorite pastime was shopping for clothes. The full extent of her domestic aptitude was the ability to boil water and scramble eggs. Little did she know that her latent frugal abilities and aptitude for culinary excellence would later come to her aid as a "domestic goddess."

STEVE ECONOMIDES spent twenty-three years in the graphics and advertising industry in Phoenix, Arizona. He's enjoying spending time being a dad while writing and working from home.

Steve wasn't always financially disciplined, but is a living testament that right-brained creative types can learn to manage money. In 1981, the week before he was to leave on a motorcycle trip, he received an unanticipated motorcycle insurance bill. He drained his bank account to pay the bill and had just enough money left for gas and food for his trip. A few days later, while driving through the Colorado mountains during a stormy downpour he slid off a rain-slickened road. The motorcycle was laid down and flipped, while he and his backpack were thrown clear. Miraculously, he sailed off the motorcycle, did a diving somersault between several trees, and rolled down a soft embankment. Though a little bent up, the motorcycle was still drivable, so he completed his vacation. Of course when he returned home, he did what any man would do after surviving a near-death experience—he proposed marriage to Annette.

Steve and Annette live in Scottsdale, Arizona, with four kids at home—one lives on his own. They publish the *HomeEconomiser* newsletter and have been profiled on TV and radio and in newspapers and magazines worldwide. They are seasoned seminar speakers and travel with their kids, as America's Cheapest Family, working to convince the world that a frugal lifestyle can not only get you right on the money but also help you cash in on your dreams!

You can contact the Economides Family at:
PO Box 12603, Scottsdale, AZ 85267-2603
or by visiting www.AmericasCheapestFamily.com